Peak Learning

with

Keys to Success: A Supplementary Reader

OTHER BOOKS BY RONALD GROSS

The Lifelong Learner

Individualism

The New Professionals

The Independent Scholar's Handbook

*Independent Scholarship:
Promise, Problems, and Prospects*

The Great School Debate

Radical School Reform

Pop Poems

The New Old

Peak LEARNING

How to Create Your Lifelong Education Program for Personal Enlightenment and Professional Success

Ronald Gross

Featuring material from *Keys to Success:* A Supplementary Reader

REVISED EDITION

Custom Edition for University of Phoenix

Jeremy P. Tarcher/Putnam

a member of Penguin Group (USA) Inc.

New York

Pearson
Custom
Publishing

Professional Speaking, Workshops, Seminars, Consulting

For information on Ronald Gross's services please contact:

Gross and Gross Associates
17 Myrtle Drive
Great Neck, New York 11021
Phone: (516) 487-0235
Fax: (516) 829-8462
E-mail: GrossAssoc@AOL.com

Jeremy P. Tarcher/Putnam
a member of
Penguin Group (USA) Inc.
375 Hudson Street
New York, NY 10014
www.penguin.com

ISBN 1-58542-243-6

Excerpts taken from:

Keys to Success: How to Achieve Your Goals, Second Edition,
by Carol Carter, Joyce Bishop, and Sarah Lyman Kravits
Copyright © 1998 by Prentice-Hall, Inc.
A Pearson Education Company
Upper Saddle River, New Jersey 07458

Keys to Success Reader,
by Joyce Bishop, Mary Jane Bradbury, and Julie Wheeler
Copyright © 1999 by Prentice-Hall, Inc.

Printed in the United States of America
10   9   8   7   6   5   4   3   2   1

BA 996781

In a world that is constantly changing, there is no one subject or set of subjects that will serve you for the foreseeable future, let alone for the rest of your life. The most important skill to acquire now is learning how to learn.

JOHN NAISBITT

Mind Map for *Peak Learning*

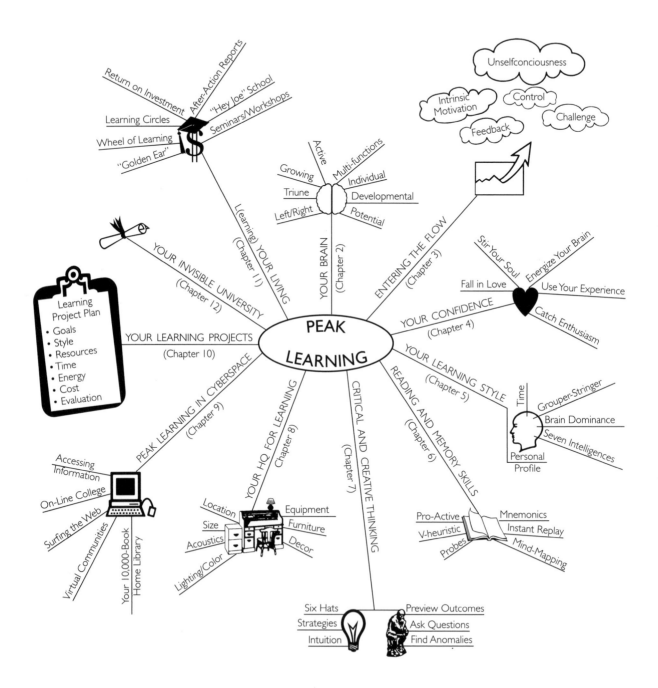

Contents

Acknowledgments

For this 1999 revised edition I am deeply grateful for the inspiration and advice of a "virtual committee" of friends and colleagues:

Linda Meyer, founder-director of the Meyer Learning Center, Denver, Colorado, and convenor of The Rocky Mountain Learning Coalition which provided invaluable input to the work; Jane Beckhard, Beckhard Associates, Glen Cove, Long Island, New York; Ralph Suozzi, Glen Cove, Long Island, New York; Elizabeth Cohn, North Shore Hospital/Cornell Medical Center; Peter Gross, Magic and Other Suspect Activities, Brookline, Massachusetts; David Baron, Los Angeles, California; Susan Denson-Guy, Manhattan, Kansas; Dorothy Puryear, Nassau Library System, Long Island, New York; Emiliano de Laurentiis, Lifelong Software, North Adams, Massachusetts; Corene Hansen, Denver, Colorado.

Friends and colleagues have contributed enormously to this book, personally or through their published works, and it is a pleasure to acknowledge them:

Carol Aslanian, Richard Bolles, Edward de Bono, James Botkin, Tony Buzan, Dee Dickinson, Ruth van Doren, William Draves, Kenneth C. Fischer, Howard Gardner, Michael Gelb, Maurice Gibbons, Beatrice Gross, Elizabeth Gross, Peter Gross, Tom Hebert, Cyril Houle, Jean Houston, Michael Hutchison, Ivan Illich, Malcolm Knowles, Herbert Kohl, Kenneth McCarthy, Patricia McLagan, Roger von Oech, Anne Durrum Robinson, Elisabeth Ruedy, Robert Smith, Alvin Toffler, Allen Tough, Win Wenger, and Andre de Zanger. Special thanks to David Eggleton, creator of the Learning Support System, for his contribution to the treatment of learning technologies.

Four departed friends deeply influenced the ideas in this book: Michael Gross, Alvin Eurich, John Holt, and Buckminster Fuller.

For intellectual support I thank my colleagues in the University Seminar on Innovation in Education, Columbia University. For financial support for some of the research and experimentation that underlies the book, my gratitude to the Fund for the Improvement of Postsecondary Education. For the opportunity to test the ideas in practice, my appreciation to Dorothy Puryear of the Nassau Library System and to my fellow *Roundtablers,* and to the students in my Peak Learning workshops.

Lastly, I express my grateful thanks to my publisher, Jeremy Tarcher, for his inspiration and patience; my editor, Rick Benzel, for his valuable and insightful advice in organizing and developing the manuscript; production editor Paul Murphy, for his classic design and production talent; and to Allyn Brodsky for his research and revising efforts that brought this book to completion. I also owe a great debt to Mitch Horowitz, who inspired this revision, then contributed significantly to whatever wisdom and insight it contains.

Preface

Our world is changing faster than ever before, and the importance of learning is growing even faster. Any significant improvement in life—from a more rewarding job to more enjoyable leisure time—is based on learning.

This book has a simple goal: I want to change your idea of learning. I want to show you how you can create a kind of learning style that is fast, efficient, thorough, productive, and more downright enjoyable than you could have believed. I want to show you how you can keep learning throughout life.

You are already something of a lifelong learner or you wouldn't have started reading this book. In your own way, you may well have done many of the things I will propose. But you may also have felt from time to time that you could learn even more, do it better, and have more fun at it. If so, you are just the kind of reader I am looking for.

The Peak Learning system described here is a set of techniques that you can use to achieve broader, deeper, and more personal learning skills than anything you experienced in your previous schooling. Every day can become a rich adventure in discovery, with opportunities to add to your experience and knowledge, to make new connections and see new patterns in yourself and in the world around you. Rather than struggling to merely persist through the usual ruts and routines, you can turn each passing month into a milestone marking your continuing exploration, inquiry, and development.

Peak Learning is a new kind of learning, one that professional educators increasingly recognize as necessary for every individual. It is a program of self-directed growth. It means acquiring new skills to understand yourself and the world—true wealth you can never lose. It is an investment in yourself, a way to take better advantage of the chance to fulfill your potential.

Many people have trouble at first with the idea of self-directed learning, because they have been trained by society to equate learning only with what is taught in educational institutions. They assume that the *right* way to learn is in a classroom, from a teacher and textbooks, by listening to expert authorities, doing assigned readings, memorizing stale information for tests, and getting grades.

But Peak Learning does not involve consciously studying, or having to memorize something someone tells you to, or pursuing a certain set of subjects considered important by some school. Instead, independent, unconstrained, noninstitutionalized learning is the *realest* education there is. From the attitudes and techniques described in the following chapters you will acquire:

Fresh confidence about yourself as a learner. You will discard negative attitudes and self-blocking learning strategies carried over from school days. You'll experience learning as exhilarating, as an open road direct to the person you want to become.

Powerful learning skills based on new discoveries about how the brain works, and ways to apply those discoveries to your own personal learning style. In developing your personal learning style, you will find how *you* learn best and how to arrange your learning for maximum productivity, ease, and enjoyment.

Ways to find learning resources from all over the world, which are ready for you to call on when you need them. You will discover how to tap into the *invisible university*, the multitude of sources of information, advice, and help that can assist your learning.

Step-by-step guidance that will allow you to apply these learning techniques in your own life. As you read this course book, you will find exercises that will help you make these learning skills a part of your daily activities. Applying them yourself will do more for your understanding and enjoyment than any number of abstract, theoretical descriptions.

This book was inspired by a series of Peak Learning experiences in my own life. These were moments when I gained knowledge, understanding, or insight that changed me dramatically.

The first was with my father, Michael Gross, a self-styled *auto-didact* who gave himself a first-class do-it-yourself university education (after dropping out of school in the sixth grade). Mike showed me how much you could learn traveling to and from work on the subway, or at the reading room at the glorious public library on Fifth Avenue and Forty-Second Street.

The second Peak Learning experience occurred while I was working at the Ford Foundation in its Education Division, and writing books about school reform in the evenings. It was there that I came to the conviction that improving schools and colleges, even with handsome grants, was not the answer to the education problem. Rather, education had to become a lifelong activity throughout society. People of every age and in every kind of life circumstance needed to be empowered to learn, change, and grow.

I set up an Experiment in Learning program at New York University—the first university course with no syllabus, no textbooks, no preset lectures, no tests, and no grades. Instead of offering students what some teacher wanted to teach, we offered them help in learning what *they* wanted to learn. Experiment in Learning was a course for people who had, in a sense, graduated from taking courses. We were looking for people who knew what they wanted to learn but felt they could learn it more effectively with better techniques, friendly companionship, more resources, and improved planning. In short, it was the first attempt to teach what this book teaches.

That first year I worked with about two dozen students who ranged from Ph.D.s to high-school dropouts, several of whom number among the best friends I've ever had. This experience taught me that whatever our fields of interest, the same basic principles and strategies apply to all—we need to set goals, plan for our learning, adapt to our individual learning styles, marshal and access resources, and monitor how we are doing. I also learned that lifelong learning is possible and immensely gratifying but that it requires new skills and resources. Peak learners need special skills to take command of their own lifelong self-development, skills that are seldom taught explicitly in classrooms. Furthermore, the resources for self-education need to be made more visible and accessible to those who need to find them.

I eventually became editor-at-large for the journal *Adult and Continuing Education Today.* I had the chance to meet, help, and learn from the best learners throughout the United States and abroad. Always and everywhere, I found men and women who were using learning to lead richer, healthier, more successful, and more useful lives. Some of my insights were collected in a book I wrote in 1977 called *The Lifelong Learner,* which introduced this term and helped spread its usage.

Encouraged by these discoveries, I began to give workshops, seminars, and *train-the-trainer* sessions. In 1980, I received the first of two federal grants to investigate outstanding learners and identify the skills and aptitudes that made them so good at learning. More than two hundred interviews produced an answer.

These exceptional learners did indeed share a definite set of skills and attitudes that accounted for their success. Moreover, these techniques were not natural talents—almost all were things these people had *learned* to do for themselves on their own, and they had no doubt that others could learn them as well. My most recent and current experience demonstrates just how true this is. The power of these learning techniques is indicated by the fact that they work equally well with every kind of learner—from genius or near-genius independent scholars to individuals with mental disabilities.

During the past ten years I have successfully taught these methods to highly diverse people, ranging from top corporate, association, and public-sector executives, to persons with severe mental and physical disabilities. During a typical week of seminars and workshops, I often find myself dealing on Monday and Tuesday with, say, senior managers at the McDonnell-Douglas Corporation or United Way of Greater New York, and Thursday and Friday with eighty- to ninety-year-old retirees, some of whom have ailments such as Parkinson's syndrome. They *all* enjoy, learn, and use the same basic techniques to take charge of their growth and development.

A final testimonial to the power of these techniques is that, as this book goes to press, the audiotape of some of its major techniques is a national best-seller. Thousands are discovering these methods every day and using them to learn what they want and need to know.

Everyone can learn how to learn. Easy, enjoyable learning is accomplished by using a set of skills and techniques that can be acquired. You will learn these techniques and attitudes in this book.

In addition, I have included some of the best new learning methods developed over the last decade in such areas as human development, corporate and business training, government agencies, the military, and associations.

By this point you may be wondering what is so new and different about the Peak Learning approach I'm presenting here from other learning systems and theories. From my experience in developing and using it, there are four reasons why Peak Learning has proved to be the most powerful and enjoyable system for my students.

First, this system is tailored to *your* adult learning needs. You will select those techniques and materials that suit the sort of learning you want to do. Most other learning systems propose one method as the key to success. The well-known educator Mortimer Adler, for example, will tell you that there is one kind of subject that is worth learning above all (the liberal-arts classics) and one way to learn them (through reading and discussion). I believe that it is *you* who can and must decide for yourself what is most worth learning. My method enables you to determine that and plan your learning strategy, both methods and materials, accordingly. Peak Learning offers you a set of tools; you decide which ones fit your personal style and the subject you want to study.

Second, unlike other systems, Peak Learning deals with both the psychological techniques for improving learning and the wondrous array of resources now available to stimulate and enrich your mind. Successful learning depends as much on being clever about finding the best learning materials as it does on psychological techniques. My system shows how to use the entire world as a storehouse of learning resources.

Third, Peak Learning helps you to discover your individual learning style. Few of the systems mentioned above take into account this factor. For me, "Know thyself" is a basic commandment. Since each of us is different, there is no universally optimal method of learning. Effective, productive, and gratifying learning comes directly from choosing methods that are right for *you* as well as for the subject you wish to learn.

Finally, some learning methods depend strongly on a powerful *guru* as teacher or on using cumbersome or expensive equipment, or sometimes both. Often an innovator includes some elements in his or her system that derive from their own personal tastes and styles rather than from empirical evidence or sound theory. These elements may not work, or they may work only when the guru presents them.

In either case, learners often are left with the feeling that they need to buy the whole farm in order to take a ride on the horse. By incorporating the best of many sources, Peak Learning separates techniques from their creators. While I will describe many kinds of resource materials you may choose to use, the essentials of Peak Learning require no specialized equipment. Whatever tools you need are easily available anywhere.

RONALD GROSS

1

Peak Learning—Skills for Today and Tomorrow

What is a peak learner? It is someone who has learned how to learn, in the fullest sense of the word. Although this label may be unfamiliar, chances are you already know peak learners. In fact, you've probably been one yourself from time to time. For example, think about those occasions when your mind has quickly soaked up information about a new subject that fascinated you—whether new recipes or batting averages—seemingly without effort. Or when you got a sudden flash of insight about how to solve a difficult problem that had been stumping you. These were moments of Peak Learning.

Perhaps you can also think of people you know who constantly are getting excited and involved in some new interest and running to tell you the latest new information they've found out about it. While they are in that first flush of enthusiasm, the excitement and delight they find in their new discoveries seems contagious. They too are peak learners.

At work, you probably know colleagues—or competitors—who miraculously seem to stay on top of new developments. They can sift through stacks of memos, newsletters, advertisements, correspondence, magazines, and books to find just the

O! this learning, what a thing it is.

WILLIAM SHAKESPEARE

1

Learning can be defined as the process of remembering what you are interested in.

RICHARD SAUL WURMAN

nuggets of fact they need. Their capacity to handle that flood of information and ideas gives them a decided edge. They too are peak learners.

Learning has a different *feel* for these people. It isn't just a matter of going back to school to sit in a classroom and listen to a teacher. It has little to do with tests or grades. Instead, this type of learning springs from within them: it is self-education. Whether sparked by joy or driven by need, it expresses who they want to become, what they want to be able to do or to know about.

Peak learners have a number of distinctive characteristics. First, they feel best about themselves when they are learning something new. They are unusually open to and interested in new experiences, ideas, and information, whether they be sampling a new cuisine, listening to a scientist describe her work, or reading an article on corporate mergers. Typically, they do not think of learning as some special activity; for them, learning is just part of the way in which they habitually live. They take pride in meeting their daily challenges, from a newspaper's crossword puzzle to mastering a new computer program.

Another characteristic of peak learners is that they are keenly aware of how much they don't know, but that doesn't bother them! As they wander along the shoreline of wonder— the boundary between what they know and the vast sea of things they *could* know—they feel exhilarated by the prospect of constantly learning new things. They know that there are always things to know more about, to appreciate more deeply, or to learn to do. Because they are not afraid of their own ignorance, such learners aren't afraid to ask *dumb* questions or admit they don't understand something the first time it's explained. Instead of pretending to understand, they keep asking until they do. They then take action to use their new information quickly, to draw connections between what they already knew and what they have just learned. Peak learners look for similarities and differences, make analogies, and try to find out what something is *like* in order to understand it.

Peak learners have learned enormously from important life experiences and in other ways outside the usual channels of study. They seek a wide range of helpful resources for learning, rather than giving up if their usual sources of information run dry on a particular topic.

Confidence in one's ability to learn and to understand is another key characteristic of peak learners. They know that anything that *one* human being truly understands can be understood equally well by others willing to follow the right steps. They know how to judge sources of information shrewdly and how to narrow down any gap in an explanation. These learners have a repertoire of simple but powerful tools for processing information, tools that help to select the information they need, to store it in memory, and to use it.

Finally, peak learners believe that investing time in their own personal growth is the best investment they can make in the future, occupational or personal. They begin to learn new things *now* in order to prepare for the life they want to be leading in five years.

These and other characteristics are what define a peak learner—someone who has made learning a part of his or her lifestyle.

Our lives today call on each of us to become a peak learner. When you think of the people you most admire, or of yourself at your best, it is easy to recognize that this sort of learning is a major part of the *good life.* At work or in our personal lives, practically anything we want will involve some kind of learning above and beyond the knowledge and skills we got in school.

Anyone who stops learning is old, whether at twenty or eighty. Anyone who keeps learning stays young. The greatest thing in life is to keep your mind young.

HENRY FORD

WHY BE A PEAK LEARNER?

We are the first generation of human beings born into a world that will change *drastically* during the course of our lives. As the noted anthropologist Margaret Mead pointed out, only two hundred years ago people knew that the world they grew up in would be about the same when they died. A few things might change, but the basic texture and quality of their lives would remain constant throughout their life span. Things simply changed more slowly. When she pointed this out some thirty years ago, Mead could already see that modern men and women no longer had that assurance.

The illiterate of the year 2000 will not be the individual who cannot read and write, but the one who cannot learn, unlearn, and relearn.

ALVIN TOFFLER

In 1970, in fact, Alvin Toffler introduced the term *future shock* to describe a pervasive reaction he saw developing: People seemed to be overwhelmed by accelerating change. In every field, knowledge was doubling every decade or so. Doctors and engineers found that the information they had struggled to master in their professional training had a *half-life* of about fifteen years—after that, half of it was no longer true or relevant. New discoveries seemed to be made every week, and they resulted in newer ways of doing things or new kinds of gadgets almost every day.

Today, the pace has not let up. At this very moment, it is already trite to talk about an information explosion. As computers have become ever more capable of generating quantities of new information, we human beings have been increasingly challenged to keep learning and to remain up-to-date. Continual growth has become a requirement of contemporary living. We must be able to master new facts, new skills, and even new attitudes and beliefs.

At work, for example, most Americans will change fields three or four times in their careers—to say nothing of even more frequent changes of *jobs*. All of these changes require substantial learning. Indeed, in today's world, *learning a living* is an integral part of earning a living for most people in professional, managerial, and other high-level jobs. Change is so rapid in the business world that virtually every day presents new challenges and opportunities to learn.

In our personal affairs as well, the mobility and fluidity of social life means we have to be more adaptable, better able to learn quickly. Just consider how many of these areas you needed to learn about in the last year, in response to needs of your own, your family, friends, or your company:

- Health and medical developments, including new knowledge about diet, exercise, and stress or new treatments for specific illnesses.
- Economic developments affecting your business or profession, such as new tax regulations, investment opportunities, or dangers, or financial innovations in your field.

- Technological developments that have an impact on your career and personal life, including new machines, appliances, materials, and methods of information transfer.
- Social developments around the country and in your own community that have an effect on your lifestyle or that concern you as a citizen, such as housing trends, employment policies, or legislative proposals.
- Changes in your personal or business relationships that require you to learn more about the causes and consequences of your own behavior or that of others.

In short, learning in our time has become a stern necessity. "Under the conditions of modern life," warned the philosopher Alfred North Whitehead fifty years ago, "the rule is absolute: The race that neglects trained intelligence is doomed." Today we must update Whitehead's warning. Under today's conditions of future shock, *this* rule is absolute: The individual who neglects self-development is doomed.

Leading experts in our emerging world of ever more rapid change agree that *learning throughout life* is now a key to personal success. "In the new information society where the only constant is change," says John Naisbitt, author of *Megatrends*, "we can no longer expect to get an education and be done with it. There is no one education, no one skill, that lasts a lifetime now. Like it or not, the information society has turned all of us into lifelong learners." And Alvin Toffler agrees that "in the world of the future, the new illiterate will be the person who has not learned how to learn."

All human beings, by nature, desire to know.

ARISTOTLE

THE LEARNING TRADITION

It is surprising to realize that school-learning is a relatively recent invention. One of the earliest roots of Western culture was the Greek city-state of Athens, home to Plato and Socrates and to a vital kind of learning that went far beyond classrooms or grades. Instead, citizens discussed important questions in their open-air market, or *agora*, at the baths or the gym, or over a late, post-theater dinner. Learning was inextricably a part of life, work, and leisure; it drew on every resource of the community: its arts, crafts, professions, history, and laws. "Not I, but the city teaches," declared Socrates.

Belief in a similar kind of learning was a key part of the thinking of the founding fathers of the United States. Their republic could work only if the people could make their own appraisals of their needs and wants. The national ideal was intellectual self-reliance and personal responsibility for self-development.

Our country's political system is based on the belief that each of us can function, in however modest a degree, as free-thinking, independent centers of understanding, judgment, and action. We have encouraged free speech and a free press because we think the best way to find the truth is for the full range of ideas and information to be debated openly by citizens.

"Jefferson was a great believer in schooling," points out educational historian Lawrence Cremin, "but it never occurred to him that schooling would be the chief educational influence on the young. Schooling might provide technical skills and basic knowledge, but it was the press and participation in politics that really educated the citizenry." Thus, the early leaders of the United States did not, as we so often do, make the mistake of confusing schooling with education, nor the still worse mistake of judging people by their diplomas.

We can find many exemplars of this potent tradition of self-education from Ben Franklin and Abraham Lincoln through Thomas Edison and Henry Ford to Malcolm X and Eric Hoffer in our own day.

Now that tradition is under siege. While the sheer mass of information grows beyond the capacity of many, we also find our beliefs in independent thinking and self-education threatened by the conformist pressures of our ever-present, ever-distracting media—what cogent critic of television Neil Postman calls the "and now . . . this" mentality. Our consideration of vital public issues is reduced to the two-minute TV news story and the fifteen-second sound bite.

Another serious threat grows from our mistaken belief that credentials are trustworthy guides to competence. More and more professions try to protect the reputation of their practitioners by creating licensing requirements. And, inevitably, they produce more and more professionals whose major qualification is that they could pass the licensing examination.

As critic and novelist Philip Wylie put it, shortly before he died, "If there are any Americans with an education sufficient for useful criticism and constructive proposals, one fact about them will be sure: They will be self-educated. . . . They will be people who learned how to learn and to want to learn—people who did not stop learning when they received their degree or degrees—people who developed a means of evaluation of all knowledge in order to determine what they had to understand for useful thought—people who, then, knew what they did not know and learned what was necessary."

Peak learners are those people. They are increasing in numbers and becoming recognized in the very nick of time. Their abilities to make learning a continuing part of their living may offer our best chance of survival as a culture, a species, a planet.

LACHES: Did you never observe that some persons, who have had no teachers, are more skillful than those who have, in some things?

SOCRATES: Yes . . . but you would not be very willing to trust them if they only professed to be masters of their art, unless they could show some proof of their skill or excellence in one or more works.

PLATO

BREAKING THROUGH TO PEAK LEARNING

By now, I hope I've given you a good idea of what Peak Learning is about, why it is important, and how it restores a part of the Western cultural tradition we've neglected. My guess is that at this point you're intrigued by the idea of becoming more of a peak learner—but that you have some reservations about the process.

That's entirely natural. In the workshops I give, about 85 percent of the participants feel the same way. That's why we always start off with some ghost busting. We puncture the major fears and anxieties about learning that still haunt most of us from our days in school. We'll deal with these in detail later, but let me just tick them off here to assure you that they will not interfere with your learning when you use Peak Learning methods.

Anxiety about learning. Throughout school and college days, we were constantly being told to learn things—but never told *how.* "Learn the vocabulary words in this chapter for a quiz on Friday" was a typical assignment. And then? Either we sat down and tried to stare at the list of words until, somehow, we found a way to store them in our heads until the quiz, or we didn't find a way and so became fearful and frustrated, because we didn't know what to do when we sat down to learn. But once you really learn *how* to learn, that anxiety will disappear. Peak Learning is relaxing and enjoyable, because you have specific strategies you can select to master facts, concepts, and principles.

Anxiety about time. Typically, the people who come to my workshops have fully packed schedules, both personal and professional. They can't really afford to *take time out* to study. But Peak Learning methods are concurrent with your other activities. Your learning is part of your personal planning and decision-making, part of your professional and personal reading, part of your social contacts and leisure, part of your work and your family time.

Negative myths about learning. School experience has left many of us with a negative attitude toward learning, a nagging sense that learning is boring, tedious, lonely, or unrelated to our real interests. It has been easy to think that learning must be passive, involving sitting and listening to a teacher or struggling to absorb material from a book. None of this is true with Peak Learning, which is first and foremost learning what *you* are most interested in and excited by. Furthermore, Peak Learning is fundamentally *active.* Not only do you choose what to learn, you also choose how you learn it, from a range of techniques most appropriate to your personal learning style.

I'll come back to each of these difficulties, and others, later.

Cultivate your faith in yourself as a learner. Research shows that adults are better *learners than children, if they have the patience to be beginners.*

MARILYN FERGUSON

For now, rest assured that Peak Learning is not only something desirable, a way to develop a greater appreciation of life, but also something *possible* for anyone who wants to try it.

THE PRINCIPLES OF PEAK LEARNING

The principles of Peak Learning are based on some fundamental truths about learning and growth—many still considered heretical by educators—that can liberate you from over-reliance on schooling and strengthen you for the adventure of self-development. Some of these truths are:

- Adults who take command of their own learning often master more things, and master them better, than those who rely on being taught. They tend to have greater zest in the learning process, retain more of what they have learned, and make better use of it in their lives.
- Adults learn in different ways than children. We have a different sense of ourselves, of our time, and of what's worth learning and why.
- No one can learn *for* you, any more than someone can eat for you. *To learn* is an active verb; your education is something you must tailor to yourself, not something you can get ready-made.
- No particular way of learning is in itself superior to another. How you learn depends on your temperament, circumstances, needs, tastes, or ambition. Success in learning depends not on the subject itself or the conditions (how, where, and when) of learning, but basically on the learner's engagement—her or his fascination with the subject.

There are six fundamental principles that define the Peak Learning system. All of the specific techniques and strategies you will learn in this book are derived from them.

1. You can learn how to learn. As you will see in Chapter Two, Peak Learning is not based on wishful thinking or pious hopes but on sound scientific discoveries. Twin revolutions in the study of the human brain and the psychology of learning have overturned the long-held myths that learning is an inborn talent and that people become too old to learn. We now know that the brain is organized in many complex ways, that it is an active, processing organ influenced by our bodies and emotions, and that, with the right stimulation, it continues to grow throughout our lives! We have learned that traditional theories of learning, derived from inaccurate early models of the brain, can be replaced with more effective approaches that enlist our total human capacity in the cause of our learning.

2. You are already a superb learner on occasion, and you can build on that natural skill to make the rest of your learning easy, enjoyable, and productive. Chapter Three discusses many of the blocks to learning we've inherited from school days and shows how they can be removed. You'll see that some of our earliest and most enjoyable learning came before our potential was blocked, a state that is called Flow Learning. I'll explain the nature of this state and provide several different methods for getting back into that state of easy, effortless, enraptured learning. Chapter Four will build upon these techniques, offering two other strategies to enhance your learning confidence.

3. You have your own personal learning style, which you can identify, take advantage of, and strengthen to become an even more accomplished learner. While most of our previous education relied on a single style of learning for everyone, we now know that everyone has his or her own unique combination of skills, talents, and preferences for getting and using information. Chapter Five covers several ways to help you identify your own best approach. You'll learn how to discover the right mixture of facts, feelings, guidance, independence, and resources to help you learn in the way that is most natural for you.

4. You learn best when you are most active mentally (and sometimes physically), making your own decisions about what, how, where, and when to learn and using strategies that activate your mind. Chapters Six and Seven cover the best of the current strategies and techniques for active learning. These specific, practical approaches help you learn by putting you in control, giving you a full range of resources to steer your learning in the most rewarding directions and speed you on your way.

5. You can design your optimal learning environment, one that makes your learning more comfortable and hence more effective. It's easy to be brainwashed into believing that learning happens only if you're squirming uncomfortably in a classroom, lecture hall, or library. In fact, the opposite is true. The more you can create a room or area where you can be alert, comfortable, and productive, the better your learning will be. Chapter Eight demonstrates how you can create your ideal study environment and the positive effects it can have. Chapter Nine then surveys

the extraordinary opportunities for learning on-line. You can
continue your formal education, explore any subject in the
world in cyberspace, and meet fellow-learners around the world.

6. *You learn most enjoyably by choosing from a rich array of media, methods, and experiences.* Chapter Ten invites you to establish
your own Research and Development department, which
works on several learning projects at a time. This is especially
easy today, as the treasures of the human mind and spirit are
available to all of us in unprecedented measure. Inexpensive
paperbacks enable each of us to build a finer library than em-
perors could command two hundred years ago. Fine repro-
duction and printing provides an entree into what André
Malraux calls "the museum without walls," so that you can see
more magnificent art in one afternoon in the library than
Goethe could view on the grand tour of European cities in the
nineteenth century. Crafts, skills, and technologies that once
were accessible only through lengthy apprenticeships are now
available through self-study or expert instruction. The greatest teachers, scholars, and scientists of the age can be brought
into our living rooms via video and audio cassettes.

In short, modern technology has made new means of
learning available to everyone, everywhere, at every point in
one's life. This invisible university of resources for learning is
revealed in Chapter Twelve. It puts at your disposal just what
you want, just when you need it. You can bring the most inspiring authorities in any field into your home, your car, or your
vacation retreat or communicate with them via phone, computer, or mail. You can suit your own style by learning not just via
books and teachers, but through simulations, games, and action projects.

7. *You can accelerate your career by L(earning) Your Living—
mastering new skills and knowledge virtually every day at your work.*
Chapter Eleven will introduce you to powerful and enjoyable
ways to start "The Wheel of Learning" spinning in your occupation or profession. You can build opportunities for growth and
mastery into your tasks, and receive recognition and reward,
whether you're in an organization or self-employed.

MAKING PEAK LEARNING
WORK FOR YOU

The key to becoming a peak learner is to develop your own *program*—a clear, systematic set of learning techniques. Most of us have no such program. We've managed to pick up a more or less random collection of learning tricks over the years: some principles of speed reading, some tricks to improve memorization, and perhaps a few pointers on taking good notes.

These separate skills have only limited usefulness. What good does it do, for example, to take great notes on the wrong book or spend four hours studying when you could derive much more information in only two hours? If we don't have the skills to use what we learn effectively, the greatest training program in the world won't provide much lasting value.

That's what this book will enable you to do. In learning techniques, as in so much of life, the whole is greater than the sum of its parts. Peak learning is most successful when you harness the best skills you already have, complement them with the new techniques you'll learn here, and use them together to become all you are capable of being.

Anyone who can read and write can keep some form of New Diary—a personal book in which creativity, play, and self-therapy interweave, foster, and complement each other.

TRISTINE RAINER

YOUR LEARNING LOG

As you embark on your personal adventure of learning how to learn, the first strategy is to keep track of your progress, right from the start, in a learning log. Beginning such a log now is taking a major step in getting the most out of this book.

First, your log will be the place to do the exercises that appear throughout these pages. For example, you will be creating *mind maps*, conducting *instant replays* of significant experiences, *idea breeding* to create your own new concepts, posing penetrating questions that will guide your inquiry in new fields, and using dozens of other new techniques. By completing these activities in a learning log, you will multiply the benefits from each one.

Second, there is a tremendous benefit to your learning that arises out of writing. A learning log is vital because writing is itself one of the most powerful learning processes. "Writing is how we think our way into a subject and make it our own," says William Zinser in his inspiring book *Writing to Learn*. "Writing enables us to find out what we know—and what we don't know—about whatever we're trying to learn . . . writing and learning [are] the same process."

The most important benefit of your log will be the picture you will be building of *yourself* as a learner. The log will display, visually, the methods and techniques that you find most congenial. It will reveal, especially in review, the kinds of learning activities you enjoy and can use to greatest advantage in your personal learning goals.

In short, your learning log becomes a visual record of your mind's activity in learning. Its special *benefits* (different from the benefits of the typical diary or personal journal) are:

- You will create your own vivid portrayal of the ideas in the fields that are meaningful to you.
- You will develop a flexible playground for indulging your personal learning style by translating and transforming your subject into the medium and mode you prefer. You can write, draw, or doodle in your log to help yourself remember and explore new ideas.
- You will build creatively on what you are learning with your own insights and discover connections among the things you are learning that would not have emerged in any other way.
- You will be able to easily access the most important materials you have collected for subsequent reflection or further development.
- You will have a gratifying record of how much you've done and how your skills of learning are developing, which may prove useful at some point in showing others what and how you've learned.
- You will have a record for review that will be pleasurable and powerful, because it is formed by your own interests.

Learning logs of this kind are behind most great learners. History brims with examples: Leonardo da Vinci's notebooks are coveted by collectors worldwide; Benjamin Franklin's journals have inspired generations of autodidacts; Thomas Edison's logs are so numerous that they fill a warehouse in New Jersey; Buckminster Fuller created miles of notebooks.

Yet most of us are unaware of the essential role of logs in the learning process. When we see the finished products of accomplished learners, whether they are artists, entrepreneurs, or politicians, it's easy to forget the years of previous learning. The finished product, whether a symphony or a treaty, seems to our uneducated eyes to appear full blown, the result of a single clear, complete inspiration.

Every man is his own Pygmalion, and spends his life fashioning himself. And, in fashioning himself, for good or ill, he fashions the human race and its future.

I. F. STONE

Creativity is often portrayed as a lightning flash, exploding mysteriously out of nowhere. However, a less dramatic but more useful model is the beehive. Honeybees tirelessly buzz about, visiting this flower and that, tasting each one. These thousands of intimate visits ultimately result in a mass of sweet honey, a concentration of the nectar of countless flowers. The products of human genius, likewise, are the result of the dedicated pursuit of small gains.

As consumers of ideas, we generally see only Edison's "one percent of inspiration," the tiniest tip of the iceberg. The remaining 99 percent, the trial and error, the blind alleys, disjointed observations, and dreamy musings, lie hidden from view. As a peak learner, you work on that invisible 99 percent in your journal.

CREATING YOUR LEARNING LOG

Use a three-ring binder. This allows you to add items, remove them, and change the order of the pages. It gives you total creative control.

Buy some kind of note pad you can carry everywhere. You must develop the habit of jotting down thoughts as they occur to you. Forget about "making a mental note"—write it down. Our memories simply aren't built to move spontaneous thoughts into long-term memory. You'll lose 90 percent of your best ideas if you don't make some note of them the moment they occur. If you want to start out simply, you can carry a piece of 8½″ × 11″ paper folded to quarter-size, which provides enough space for the spontaneous thoughts you're likely to

You learn as much by writing as you do by reading.

ERIC HOFFER

have during one day. A 5½″ × 3¼″ leather slip-holder holds five or six slips that size.

Whenever you make a notepad entry, transfer the thought to your journal that same day or shortly thereafter. This gives you a chance to permanently record your thoughts in your journal and to reexamine your initial ideas.

We all note such items continually. However, they have little impact, because we don't record them, review them, reflect on them, and respond to them. Your journal provides the medium. It is a culture-bed for these seeds of interest that would otherwise be swept away by the breezes of onrushing circumstances.

Recording your thoughts on paper is essential if you wish to be able to work with them in the future. Newly forming ideas, no matter how vivid they may seem at the moment, are extremely vulnerable to being forgotten. Other activities demand your attention and pull you away from your work for a minute, an hour, a day, or a week. That shimmering idea is like a seed: If it is not tended, it will turn to dust and blow away.

Use a double entry system. Paste into your log passages from your reading (or visual images, musical notation, incidents recalled, and so on) on the left side of your log's double spread, and formulate your own response (even if it's only one word or image) on the facing page.

Start your log *now* even though you may not yet be engaged in a specific learning project. You can even use the log to discover some things you'd like to learn right away. Dr. Ari Kiev, author of *A Strategy for Daily Living,* suggests a method: "Start by clipping and pasting newspaper articles that interest you for the next thirty days. At the end of that time, see if there is a trend suggestive of a deep-seated interest or natural inclination. Keep alert each day to the slightest indications of special skills or talents, even when they seem silly or unimportant to you. Take note of the remarks of friends and relatives when they say that something is 'typical of you.'" In time, your learning logs will become valuable and treasured items marking your journey to Peak Learning.

II

Science Confirms It—You Are a Superb Learner!

There have been many theories of learning, but within the last few decades something revolutionary has started to happen. Thanks mainly to startling new information in two areas of research—how our brains work and the psychology of thinking—our theories about what learning is and how it works have profoundly changed. New answers are emerging to questions like:

- Can we keep learning throughout our lives?
- Are there different learning styles for different people?
- How do we learn anything?

Why is brain research so important? Over the last fifty years, several new tools and research techniques have given us a window into the brain that's beyond anything we've ever dreamed. Brain studies now engage brilliant theorists and researchers from a broad range of fields, such as anthropology, artificial intelligence, linguistics, neurophysiology, and psychology. Today's high-tech instruments and computer-processed

I thank the Lord for the brain He put in my head. Occasionally, I love to just stand to one side and watch how it works.

RICHARD BOLLES

*"Can't you give me brains?"
asked the Scarecrow.*

*"You don't need them,"
answered the Wizard. "You
are learning something every
day."*

*"That may be true," said
the Scarecrow, "but I shall be
very unhappy unless you give
me brains."*

*The false Wizard looked
at him carefully. "Well," he
said, with a sigh, "I'm not
much of a magician, as I
said; but if you will come to
me tomorrow morning, I will
stuff your head with brains. I
cannot tell you how to use
them, however; you must find
that out for yourself."*

*"Oh, thank you—thank
you!" cried the Scarecrow.
"I'll find a way to use them,
never fear!"*

L. FRANK BAUM

experimental data offer scientists an unprecedented view of the brain at work.

This chapter will explode some physiological myths about learning, outmoded theories that have told us that our learning was more limited than it really is. It will briefly survey some of the surprisingly complex ways in which our brain is organized. Simply and directly, you will start to see how this new information leads to new conclusions about how we think and learn from experience.

The chapter will then turn to the realms of psychology to examine how older kinds of learning theories have changed. In recent years, new theories of learning have been created that give us a solid foundation for the learning techniques you will practice in later chapters.

THE NEW BRAIN

Make both your hands into fists, and put them together with your thumbs on top. This will give you a good rough model of the size and shape of your brain. Your forearms represent the spinal cord, the nerve highway that continues down the back and carries information between the brain and the body.

The brain is a double lump of pinkish-gray jelly weighing about three pounds. It is made up of billions of *neurons,* specialized brain cells that function like electrochemical circuits and connect with other neurons in all directions. The place where extensions of two neurons, called *dendrites,* almost meet is called a *synapse.* That's where a tiny electrical signal, generated in one brain cell, releases special chemicals that cross the gap to another neuron.

Don't let these terms throw you. The key point is simply that the never-ending dance of signals from neuron to neuron is the essential feature of the living brain. Moreover, the neurons in our brains are intricately connected in vast networks, suggesting that learning and memory are incredibly complex.

Our exciting tour of brain-research results begins by looking at the most visible feature of the brain—its two halves.

THE TWO-SIDED BRAIN

A breakthrough in our understanding of the brain occurred in the late 1960s and early 1970s, when Professor Roger Sperry and associates at the California Institute of Technology launched a series of bold experiments. They explored a phenomenon observed since ancient times but that never had been rigorously investigated until Sperry's work.

Hippocrates, the Greek founder of medicine, had noted that soldiers struck on the left side of the head by a sword would suffer speech impairment, whereas those struck on the right side did not. From this he concluded that the two sides of the brain must function differently. Nineteenth-century doctors made similar observations, resulting in the identification of more specific functional areas, such as the two speech centers named after Paul Broca and Carl Wernicke, both found on the left side of the brain. But no one was able to explore this phenomenon experimentally until Sperry and his team conducted *split-brain* research on epileptics who had turned to a surgical solution for relief from their seizures. Sperry's team of surgeons had separated the two hemispheres of their brains.

Think back on our two-fisted brain model for a moment. Down the middle, where your fingernails touched, the brain

What's in the brain that ink may character?

WILLIAM SHAKESPEARE

In general, the left hemisphere is more important for language and certain motor skills. On the average, the right side of the brain does better with certain kinds of spatial functioning . . . that don't depend on verbal descriptions.

DR. RICHARD RESTAK

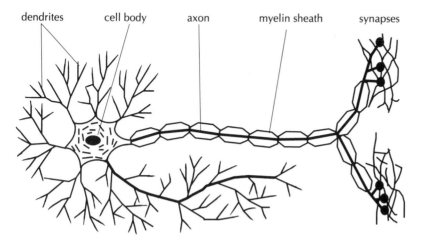

Simplified diagram of typical neuron. Electrical charges are received from other cells by the dendrites.

dendrites   cell body   axon   myelin sheath   synapses

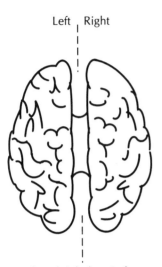

Left · Right

Left and right hemispheres of brain connected by the corpus collosum.

has a massive nerve fiber called the *corpus callosum* that connects the two halves. The two hemispheres communicate by sending signals through the corpus callosum. By disconnecting the corpus callosum in epileptic patients, Sperry was able to study the functions of the two brain hemispheres separately. Feeding information to just one side enabled him to observe what each half of the brain could and could not do.

In a typical experiment, a patient would put his right hand behind his back. He would then be handed a familiar object and asked to name it. Since the right side of the body is controlled by the left side of the brain, which is the naming, language-using side, it could interpret the experience verbally. The patient had no problem naming the object. However, when another, equally familiar object was placed in the patient's left hand, the *mute* right brain could not come up with a word for it. Since the hemispheres could not communicate via the corpus callosum, the right brain could not obtain help from the speech centers located in the left hemisphere. The right brain could often draw a picture of the object, or point to a similar object, but was essentially speechless.

Of course, Sperry's experiments included more complex procedures than this. But in sum, they provided a vivid new picture of our dual brains—a picture so significant that Sperry received a Nobel Prize for this work in 1981.

In the past decade, right–left brain experimentation and theory have made rapid progress. As one book on the subject, *Left Brain, Right Brain* by Sally Springer and Georg Deutsch, notes:

> Interest in this topic increased dramatically after the split-brain operations of the 1960s and led to an explosion of research seeking to characterize the differences and to explore their implications for human behavior. Considerable attention has also been directed to seeing whether these differences may be related to diverse phenomena such as learning disabilities, psychiatric illness, and variations in cognitive styles among cultures.

Since Sperry's time, we have begun to view each brain hemisphere as having distinctive areas of strength as follows.

Left	Right
analytic	holistic
verbal	pictorial
sequential	simultaneous
temporal	spatial

Sperry welcomed this broad and diverse follow-through on his findings. Summing up the significance of his discoveries, he wrote:

> The main theme to emerge . . . is that there appear to be two modes of thinking, verbal and nonverbal, represented rather separately in left and right hemispheres respectively, and that our educational system, as well as science in general, tends to neglect the non-verbal form of intellect. What it comes down to is that modern society discriminates against the right hemisphere.

I would go without shirt or shoe . . . sooner than lose for a minute the two separate sides of my head.

RUDYARD KIPLING

Think about Sperry's conclusions for a moment. We've known for thousands of years that most people favor one hand over the other for most tasks, although a minority are ambidextrous, meaning they can use either hand equally. This preference for one side or the other is called *dominance* by scientists.

Although there are many theories about why dominance evolved in our brains, the important point is this: there are actual, physical differences, sensory and motor-nerve connections, in the side of the brain that control the dominant hand. Such differences may be similar to what happens when we train certain muscles for sports. If we naturally use and train one side of the brain more than the other, the functions of that side might grow stronger. Hence, dominance may imply that we have preferred styles of *thinking* too, not just preferred hands for pitching a ball or writing. In the light of Sperry's results, that would mean some people might prefer—and be better at—one particular style of learning rather than another. As a relatively crude example, one person might wander through a museum simply staring at paintings without being concerned about artists' names or periods, while another might

21

It is this new development [of the neocortex] that makes possible the insight required to plan for the needs of others as well as the self, and to use our knowledge to alleviate suffering everywhere. In creating for the first time a creature with a concern for all living things, nature accomplished a one-hundred-eighty-degree turnabout from what had previously been a reptile-eat-reptile and dog-eat-dog world.

DR. PAUL MACLEAN

prefer to follow the catalog listing or view the paintings in order, from the earliest to the most recent. Neither approach is right or wrong; both can involve learning.

Here is our first major breakthrough based on brain research: learning is *not* a single process. People may be better learners when they use the kind of thinking controlled by their dominant brain hemisphere. I will return to this idea in the next chapter, which considers psychological blocks to learning.

THE TRIUNE BRAIN

Another, different functional division in brain areas, proposed by Dr. Paul MacLean, a senior research scientist at the National Institute for Mental Health's Laboratory for Brain Evolution and Behavior, also points to the complexity of our brains. Based on his studies of the evolutionary development of nervous systems in many species, including man, Dr. MacLean proposed a vertical, three-point distinction in brain areas.

The R-Complex. According to MacLean, as our human brains evolved they added new lobes and functions onto an original basic brain similar to one that developed in reptiles. This oldest area is still present in our heads. It includes a number of parts—the brain stem, basal ganglia, reticular activating system, and midbrain—in the lowest part of the brain, closest to the spinal cord. This root brain, which MacLean calls the R-complex, deals with instinctive behavior, including self-preservation, claiming territory and status, and fighting and mating.

The Limbic System. A newer, second section of the brain evolved after millions of years, as mammals developed from reptiles. This part of the brain, the limbic system, literally wraps around the reptilian brain area. Its functions, Dr. MacLean believes, are closely related to emotional behaviors, such as play and rearing young, to the sense of self, and to memory. It also controls the autonomic nervous system, which regulates many bodily functions—including sweating, blood flow, digestion, and dilation of the eye's pupils—that go on continually, without our conscious knowledge.

Dr. MacLean points out how great a role the limbic system plays in sense perception and memory, something that makes this area vitally important for learning. The limbic system monitors all our sensory input, converts it into appropriate modes for processing, and directs it to the appropriate memory-storage system. Neurochemicals in the limbic system also affect our ability to transfer memory from short-term to long-term storage. Unless this transfer takes place, we literally lose what we have learned within 30 seconds, which is the time it remains in short-term memory.

The second major breakthrough from the new brain research is the discovery that memory and emotion are related to structures and processes in our brains that are deeply interconnected and that this cannot help but have a significant effect on learning. While the interconnections are not yet fully understood, most learning experts agree that feelings play far stronger roles in our learning than the purely rational, logical processes we were confined to in school. Many of the methods you will learn in this book enlist emotions to help learning.

The Neocortex. The third part of the brain, according to MacLean, is the distinctively primate and human neocortex, the latest neurological roll of the evolutionary dice. It lies at the top of our brain, on both sides, surrounding the limbic system. Research has shown that this part of the brain is where most of our mental activity happens. Spatial and mathematical thinking, dreaming and remembering, and processing and decoding sensory information all function through this area.

The neocortex is where many sorts of specialized functions take place, such as understanding language and imagining a mental picture of things. These are obviously essential to learning, and so we'd expect any injury to have a serious effect. Yet almost miraculously, we often find that, with training, another area of the neocortex can substitute for a damaged area, taking over its functions.

The theory of the triune brain implies that emotion, memory, and the state of our bodies may be linked through the

THE TRIUNE BRAIN

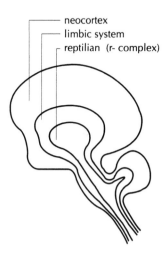

neocortex
limbic system
reptilian (r- complex)

middle section of our brains, the limbic system, in ways that crucially affect learning. Our ability to remember information for future use may depend more on our feelings at the time than we had realized. Also, rather than one smoothly functioning brain, we really have an often contentious committee, whose members are constantly striving for domination. Linkages between the newest part of our brain and its older relatives can play hopscotch with our learning. This might influence how easily we can keep cool under a threat, for example, or remain clear-thinking when faced with strong emotion.

The competition of organisms for survival in the external world mirrors a competition in the inner world among neurons to fashion the circuits that will be the most effective in the external world.

GORDON M. SHEPHARD,
*Professor of Neuroscience,
Yale University*

THE EVER-GROWING BRAIN

We used to believe that the brain developed to a certain age and then stopped and began to die. This made it easy to believe that learning was the province of the young and that, as we grew older, we began to lose our knowledge. Sperry and Mac-Lean showed that our brains were more complex than that. Our next bit of brain research explains why.

For much of human history we imagined that the brain was a passive receiver of sensations from the outside world, the

AREAS OF THE CORTEX

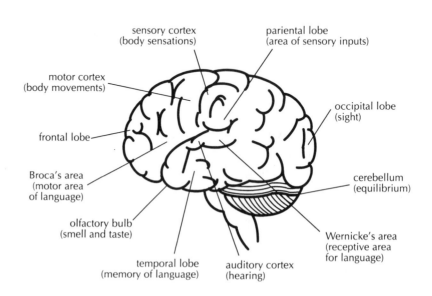

24

famed *tabula rasa,* or blank slate. But two trends of current research have erased that image and substituted a far more interesting one.

First, the brain is now pictured as constantly growing. "The structure and abilities of the cerebral cortex can be changed throughout life by enriching sensory environments," declares Professor Marion Diamond of the University of California at Berkeley. The implications of this newer, truer picture is that we actually can become smarter as we grow older, if we provide our brains with the right encouragement and environment in which to "do its thing."

Diamond has provided astounding evidence of the potential for brain growth in her laboratory at Berkeley, where she has continued a line of experimentation on rats that was started twenty years ago by Mark Rosenzweig. Her basic experiment was to place each of three comparable rats (often siblings) in one of three environments: standard, enriched, and impoverished. The standard cages contained the basic necessities of life: food, water, and adequate space. The enriched environments were larger cages with several rats, into which different toys, including objects to play with and treadmills, were introduced each day. In the impoverished situations there was little stimulation, and movement was restricted by a small cage size, resembling solitary confinement in a prison.

Diamond found that the enriched environment caused an actual increase in the weight of the rat's brain–about 10 percent—even in young adult rats whose growth *should* have stopped! Her findings astounded fellow biologists, especially hard-liners who had insisted, at first, that external conditions could not significantly influence the built-in development pattern of a rat's brain except in cases of major physical damage.

In recent years, Diamond and her associates have been so encouraged that they tried this experiment with rats equivalent in age to human beings in their sixties and seventies. Again, each of the old rats' brains grew by 10 percent when they lived with younger rats in an enriched environment.

As Robert Ornstein, a fellow brain scientist, has commented on Diamond's findings: "Specific changes in the brain

One of the profound miracles of the human brain . . . is our capacity for memory.

JEAN HOUSTON

25

Mental skills get rusty from disuse. Learning of any kind cleans off rust, and restores the gears to fuller functioning.

DENNIS THOMPSON

took place in the dendrites [the parts of neurons that connect at synapses] of each nerve cell, which thickened with stimulating experiences. It is as if the forest of nerve cells became literally enriched, and the density of the branches increased."

The crucial lesson here is that despite our traditional beliefs about old dogs learning new trick and our increasing apprehensions as we grow older about premature senility whenever something slips our minds, our brains can continue to grow throughout our lives. For that to happen, however, we need to create for ourselves the human equivalent of Diamond's enriched environment. For us, of course, that goes way beyond toys and treadmills; our enriched environment must include constant stimulation from new ideas and understanding, and from all the other challenges and opportunities offered by the best that humankind has thought, felt, and done.

A second new view of the ever-growing brain is that it is constantly active. In a complex, ongoing process, our brains organize sensory data into experience and experience into information. When we see something new, our brains take the effects of light on our eyes and construct the edges of the object. Discovering an author's views in a new book may lead us to reevaluate her earlier works. Thus, because our brains are constantly reorganizing our ideas and experiences, we are the source of our own learning.

The evidence for this comes from the world of artificial intelligence, commonly called AI. Neural networks are a recent field of AI research that uses computers to model how connections between brain cells operate. While it's not necessary to get into technical details, it is important to understand how this illuminates the way we learn.

A neural network is a computer simulation of a miniature brain, having anywhere from a dozen to a thousand or more artificial neurons. The computer is programmed so that each imitation neuron can, like the real ones in your brain, send signals to many of the others. Some fairly simple rules that mimic how real neurons alter their communication pathways on the basis of input are also programmed into the machine.

Once this mock brain is turned on, it's on its own. The experimenters feed it stimuli—words, pictures, even odors—and the mock neurons, following the simple rules of processing, begin reorganizing themselves on the basis of the input. For example, frequently used neuron connections will grow stronger, and new stimuli are more likely to be processed by the existing pathway. The artificial brain begins to build its own order.

NETTALK, invented by Professor Terrence Sejnowski of Johns Hopkins University, is a good example of a neural network. It can be trained to pronounce English words. At first, NETTALK operates almost randomly, much as a baby produces its first babble of sounds and talk. As it guesses at how to pronounce different words, rules ensure that a correct guess is reinforced, so that the associated connections between stimulated neurons become stronger with use.

After half a day of such training, NETTALK's pronunciation becomes clearer and clearer. Eventually it can recognize some one thousand words; after a week, twenty thousand! NETTALK isn't given any rules for pronunciation, just as a baby isn't taught such rules. It invents them afresh, based on its experience. Only after the fact can the researchers go in and find out how the system has organized itself.

"It turned out to be very sensible," Sejnowski told a reporter recently. "The vowels are represented differently from the consonants. Things that should be similar are clustered together."

Neural-network theory gives us a powerful new image of how the brain works when we are learning. The image is not that of the conventional classroom or student situation, in which tightly focused concentration *absorbs* a single piece of information. Rather, the image is that of combination New England town meeting or Turkish bazaar. Incoming information sparks literally thousands of neurons that shout, whisper, or mumble in ways in which lots of new data fit into patterns the brain has processed before.

This complex, ongoing, multineuron *conversation* has recently been described by M.I.T. Professor Marvin Minsky in his book *Society of Mind.* Reasoning backwards from computer programs to brains, he suggests that we are a more complicated committee than even that suggested by Sperry's two divisions or MacLean's three. There may be a myriad of small processes operating semi-autonomously at any moment, with our attention darting among them.

If the brain is a computer, then it is the only one that runs on glucose, generates ten watts of electricity, and is manufactured by unskilled labor.

DAVID LEWIS

27

THE BRAIN AND LEARNING

What do these findings add up to? The brain is much more than a passive lump sitting in our heads like a dumb switchboard system; it is as active an organ as our muscles. It processes the raw information sent by our senses and literally constructs the world we experience day by day.

What has been discussed so far about the brain suggests some important implications for how we go about learning. These were briefly summarized; now they can be described in more detail.

As the brain is part of the body, every brain shares its body's chemical and emotional environment, which influences learning. The physiological conditions of learning—such as light, temperature, bodily posture, state of wakefulness, and hunger—affect how well your brain works. Your brain even goes through time cycles of attentiveness and fatigue, some of which are unique to you.

The limbic system routinely checks out your physiological state whenever you call upon the brain to perform. You need to be in condition and warmed up for mental workouts just as much as for physical ones.

Brains can continue to grow throughout life. Your brain can continue to learn and grow for the rest of your life, barring trauma or grave illness. Aging per se does not undermine learning capacity; *attitudes* and *life-style* do that. "Use it or lose it" applies to your brain as much as to other parts of your body.

Brains are active, constructing organs. Your brain is constantly processing sensations and thoughts in myriad ways. "Normal brains are built to be challenged," says Dr. Jerre Levy of the University of Chicago. "They operate at optimal levels only when cognitive processing requirements are of sufficient complexity." To put it more bluntly, you can bore your brain to the point of sickness. Professor August de la Pena of the University of Texas has documented the deleterious effects of understimulation in his *Psychobiology of Cancer.* He found that information underload can trigger disease.

Your brain responds positively to being challenged by a rich environment and, as Dr. Diamond showed, can even continue to grow new cells and connections. It operates best when properly stimulated by interesting, complex materials, as long as it has methods for processing them effectively.

The brain has a large repertoire of functions and powers. In addition to being a magnificent biological computer, your brain is a source of rich and complex emotions, intuitions, creativity, and wisdom. It can operate in both an analytic/linear mode and a holistic/pattern-making mode. It can respond to information and situations with logic or feeling, rote instinct, blind emotion, or creative insight—or all of them at once.

But most of us become entrenched in only one or at most two kinds of thinking (rational versus emotional, for example). We grind away in our accustomed ways, with less and less return on the energy expended. If we merely changed to an alternative mode of thinking, we'd regain our energy and enthusiasm. Learning is most effective when we use the full range of our powers, not just the ones we use most.

Your brain is as individual as you are. Each brain is unique in physiological development, and it has distinctive preferences in how it functions. Some have to do with which side of our brain gets used most (dominance), or with the environmental conditions for learning; some with the way in which what we're learning is presented or organized; and others with the people factors in the situation. But most of us have never had the opportunity to arrange our learning to accommodate our personal preferences. When we are able to do that, learning takes on a completely different psychological flavor. Rather than being something imposed on the brain, against the grain as it were, learning occurs with ease and pleasure.

So much for the *hardware* side of learning, that is, how the brain works. What about the *software*, the process of learning itself? What is learning? To answer that question we must look beyond the physical nature of the brain, beyond even our as yet still limited understanding of its function. We must make a leap into the realm of the *mind*. This will take us to cognitive psychology and new theories of *how* we learn.

WHAT IS LEARNING?

For all our shiny new knowledge about the brain, the *mind* remains a mystery. How we, as humans, experience our world and change our actions as a result of that experience is far from understood. An excellent overview of the field of learning comes from Robert M. Smith's *Learning How to Learn: Applied Theory for Adults*.

The experimental subject, whether animal or man, becomes a better subject after repeated experiments. . . . He also, in some way, learns to learn. *He not only solves the problems set him by the experimenter; but more than this, he becomes more and more skilled in the solving of problems.*

GREGORY BATESON

> Learning has been variously described as a transformation that occurs in the brain; problem solving; an internal process that leads to behavioral change; the construction and exchange of personally relevant and viable meanings; a retained change in disposition or capability that is not simply ascribable to growth; and a process of changing insights, outlooks, expectations or thought patterns.

Noting that the above uses of the term *learning* can refer to a product, a process, or a function, Smith summarizes as follows.

> Learning, then, is an activity of one who learns. It may be intentional or random; it may involve acquiring new information or skills, new attitudes, understandings or values. It usually is accompanied by change in behavior and goes on throughout life. It is often thought of as both processes and outcomes. Education can be defined as "the organized, systematic effort to foster learning, to establish the conditions and to provide the activities through which learning can occur."

Now that we have a better definition of learning, we can ask how learning occurs. Malcolm Knowles, in his book *The Adult Learner, A Neglected Species,* lists more than fifty originators of learning theories from 1885 to 1980. Of these, I will focus on two different styles, or approaches to learning theory, a classification created in 1970 by two developmental psychologists, Reese and Overton. They grouped learning theories according to whether the theories assume a *mechanistic* model of the world or an *organic* one.

30

MECHANISTIC LEARNING THEORIES

A mechanistic worldview takes the machine as the basic metaphor for learning. From this perspective, complex events can ultimately be reduced to predictable and measurable interactions among the components, resembling the way the parts of your car engine work together to turn the wheels and get you where you need to be.

According to this approach, the model learner is reactive, passive, a blank slate responding to outside forces. Learning theories based on this model typically emphasize quantitatively measurable results, such as test scores. They try to explain complex learned behaviors by showing how they are built out of simple, more primitive ones.

These theories view learning as neurological *stimulus and response* and the process of *conditioning*. For example, when a doctor tests your nervous system by tapping your knee with his hammer, he's providing a stimulus; when your foot kicks up, it's in a reflex response. What is going on in this simple experience is that the hammer has stimulated a nerve that runs to the spinal column. Even without traveling up to the brain, the neurological circuit that is activated sends an automatic reflex reaction down through other nerves that makes the leg muscles kick out. The same sort of principle applies when you smell a delicious dinner cooking and start to salivate.

The Russian psychologist Ivan Pavlov discovered that if he regularly rang a bell whenever he fed a dog in his laboratory, eventually the dog would start to respond as if food were present whenever the bell rang. Pavlov called this process the creation of a *conditioned reflex*, a neurological response developed by associating a new stimulus, the bell, with a previous reflex, salivation in the presence of food.

The American psychologist B. F. Skinner, building on Pavlov's discovery, decided that behavior is completely determined by its consequences. He believed that rewarded behavior is more likely to be repeated and punished behavior is more likely to be stopped. Skinner suggests that if an environment can be completely controlled, any organism's behavior can be modified, or conditioned, by an appropriate pattern of

If men were the automatons that behaviorists claim they are, the behaviorist psychologists could not have invented the amazing nonsense called "behaviorist psychology." So they are wrong from scratch—as clever and as wrong as phlogiston chemists.

ROBERT A. HEINLEIN

rewards and punishments—and that this is essentially what learning is.

This process may seem quite similar to the standard types of schooling most of us were subjected to growing up. Correct answers on tests were rewarded; mistakes were punished with poor grades. Our development as learners was measured by how well we could produce the desired behaviors on command.

However, as we have seen, our brains are far more active and complicated than was previously supposed. The new brain-research results cast strong doubts on the blank-slate model. If the brain is actively constructing its own experience, learning is a more complex process than simply rewarding good behavior and punishing bad. Mechanistic learning theories do not seem to hold up against the recently discovered potential of our brains.

ORGANIC LEARNING THEORIES

The other side of the standard learning-classification system involves a different basic metaphor in which the world is seen as an interconnected, developing *organism*. From this perspective, the model learner is an active creator of new patterns and meanings. Theories of learning derived from this view focus on processes, organizing principles, and *qualitative* change. Complex learned behaviors may emerge unpredictably, like a flash of intuitive insight.

Organic theories of learning stress that it is more than simply associating a given stimulus with a desired response. Instead, the learner actively organizes experience according to both physiological processes (such as the way our brain organizes color, light, and shade into the objects we see) and psychological processes relating to motivation, needs, and personal meaning.

Humanistic psychologists such as Abraham Maslow and Carl Rogers developed theories about these inner, psychological needs that drive the learning process. For both of these men, the primary issue was not a passive reaction to outside events leading to modification of behavior, but rather a process of *self-actualization,* of self-initiated development of a person's skills and potentials to lead to a fulfilling life of challenge and growth.

Rogers formulated a set of hypotheses that defined a new kind of student-centered learning. These included emphasizing that one cannot be taught anything directly, and that teachers can only facilitate another person's learning; that significant learning happens only with those things perceived as maintaining or enhancing the structure of the self, (i.e., punishment does not lead to learning); that experience seen as inconsistent with the self can be learned only if a person feels sufficiently safe and unthreatened to relax its boundaries; and that the most effective learning experience is one in which a learner feels the least threat and is helped to make the greatest number of distinctions about the experience.

A more recent development in this type of learning theory is suggested by Bob Samples in his book *Openmind/Wholemind.* Drawing on the works of neurophysiologist Karl Pribram, physicist David Bohm, and chemist Ilya Prigogine, Samples has distilled a radically new model of the brain-mind as an open, holistic system interacting in a multitude of ways with the surrounding environment. I'd like to paraphrase some of his assumptions about how such a system could work, because these points are relevant to the understanding of lifelong learning.

If the brain-mind is an open system, then it is also intimate with what lies outside it.

BOB SAMPLES

- ♦ Each part of the brain-mind system experiences everything that other parts experience. The brain-mind system should be seen as a unified whole.
- ♦ Every part of the brain-mind system *knows* everything other parts *know.* We can find out what we know in many different ways.
- ♦ We can expand the range of what we pay attention to in our own brain-mind systems. We can choose to use more types of connections among our experiences.
- ♦ The more types of brain-mind connections we pay attention to, the more we expand our consciousness and increase the flexibility and fluency of our mental functioning.

33

Strange that I was not told that the brain can hold in a tiny ivory cell God's heaven and hell.

OSCAR WILDE

- The more ways of mental functioning we honor and ap-preciate, the more ways we have to express ourselves and, equally, the more ways to learn are available to us.
- We can't avoid using our whole brain-mind system. Our response to life both shapes and is shaped by all that we are and what we may become.

This has been a brief look at two different kinds of learning theory. The older, more traditional, mechanistic theories generally assume a passive learner and are close to what we may have experienced in our childhood schooling—learning governed by the reward-and-punishment system of grades and scores. The newer, organic learning theories, in agreement with recent brain research, assume an active, *empowered* learner participating fully in the creation of his or her own learning.

Now it's time to go back and connect these results with the earlier conclusions about the structure of the brain. Only then will it become clear how brain theory and learning theory will affect how we understand the process of lifelong learning.

LEARNING THEORY AND LIFELONG LEARNING

The best summary of the changes needed in theories of learning was developed at an unprecedented international conference, The Education Summit, held in Washington, D.C. in 1988, at which I delivered the keynote address. Researchers who produced the new findings listed above came together with innovative educators who have gone farthest in applying those findings in school and college classrooms. The conference was based on the principle that intelligence is not a static structure, but an open, dynamic system that can continue to develop throughout life, and that it therefore is possible for everyone at every age and ability to learn.

Here is the way in which these leading experts saw education needing to change to take full account of what we now know about the brain:

Traditional Learning Emphasizes	*Modern Learning Emphasizes*
Memorization and repetition	Excitement and love of learning
Linear and concrete intellectual development	Total human capacity in ethical, intellectual, and physical development
Conformity	Diversity and personal esteem
Individual/competitive efforts	Cooperative/collaborative efforts
Static and rigid processes	Thinking, creativity, and intuition
Content learning	Process learning of quality content
Teachers as information-providers	Teachers as learning facilitators
Departmentalized learning	Interdisciplinary learning
Cultural uniformity	Cultural differences and commonalities
Isolated teaching environments	Collaborative teaching environments
Technology as an isolated tool	Technology as an integral tool
Restricted use of facilities	Flexible use of facilities
Parental involvement	Extensive parental partnerships
Autonomy of the community	Community partnerships
The industrial age	An information/learning society

Nothing surpasses the complexity of the human mind.

FRANK HERBERT

The following chapters will demonstrate just how the shifts in emphasis of modern learning lead to a distinctive style and approach for adults wishing to reawaken a lost love of learning. You will come to understand why we must develop our personal learning programs around a flexible, exciting, holistic model of learning rather than using techniques developed for children and that may have helped us to lose our natural learning skills.

III

Entering the Flow State to Overcome Your Learning Fears

As was seen in the last chapter, recent brain research suggests that emotions and learning are strongly related. Feelings can determine how hard or easy it is to pay attention, or how well we can transfer information from short-term to long-term memory. Of course, we know this from personal experience: if we hated Latin, for example, studying for Miss Trout's test was sheer torture.

What we may not remember is that the opposite was also true: if we felt good about a subject, learning seemed almost effortless. We could become so absorbed that we never noticed time passing or the effort of studying. This and the following chapter will examine this relationship more closely. We want to understand how some kinds of feelings block the ability to enjoy learning or even to learn at all. More important, we want to understand the feelings that encourage learning and make it a joy and delight, because those are the feelings that can help make us peak learners.

The two key issues here are that your *feelings are important in learning* and that you *can* change your feelings. While the

There is a learner within you, able and confident, waiting to function freely, usefully, and joyfully.

MARILYN FERGUSON

first may seem obvious from our example above, what you may not realize is that feelings you developed during school, years ago, can block your learning today! That's why it's important to take some time to examine those early anxieties in order to understand what they mean, where they come from, and how to deal with them.

The second point, however, is the real kicker. If our feelings are locked in, beyond any hope of our changing them, then we're stuck and nothing can help. But that is simply not true. As we go through life, our feelings are continually evolving, based on our experience. We *know* that feelings can change, whether from discovering that we can develop a taste for something we once disliked or from realizing that someone we once thought was ideal has a few flaws.

Now, granted, choosing to change how we *feel* can be more difficult than changing our minds about other things. The reasons for this are complex. Simply put, feelings are *deeper* than thoughts, connected in complex ways to a wider range of experiences. We can think of emotions as extremely fast, subconscious evaluations of a situation. They happen so quickly we generally do not recognize where they come from. The result is that when we decide to change our feelings, we have to go through a process of retraining. We need to learn how to notice a feeling, name it, connect it to other experiences, recognize how our current situation differs from past ones, and decide to try a different and new approach, despite what the feeling tells us. If we can do this enough, we will discover that our feeling about the situation has changed.

You can begin that retraining process right now by examining the sources of negative feelings about learning and taking the first steps to dispel them. This chapter will explore why people have such fears, what they are, where they come from, and what to do about them.

CONQUERING THE
FEAR OF LEARNING

Chapter One discussed anxieties and negative myths about learning: the fear of not knowing *how* to learn and the feeling that learning is boring, difficult, passive, lonely, and unrelated to your real interests. Such fears and others like them are not new in human history.

The Greek philosopher Plato told a famous story comparing the human condition to life in a darkened cave, where people spend their time staring at flickering shadows on the wall caused by dim reflections of sunlight. (The image has an eerie similarity to the picture of today's couch-potato television addicts.) When a wise man suggests that people leave the cave and see the outside world in the full light of the sun, they refuse, afraid to leave the familiar shadows. They resist the opportunity to learn—to see and understand something new.

I believe a basic point this story makes is that many people are afraid, not just of the opportunity to learn, but of their own power to learn. They fear the responsibility such power entails, the need to face possible conflicts between one's own ideas and what others would prefer that one believe. After all, how many times have you seen a student get away with disagreeing with the teacher—especially if the student happened to be right? Most people would rather not rock the boat.

Another point here is the fear of change. As we grow up, we are taught by parents, peers, and teachers to believe in certain things. In many ways, these teachings define who we are, our relationship to the world around us, our community, our allies, and our enemies. Learning new ideas has the potential to change our comfortable picture of things, to force us to re-evaluate who and what we are. For many people, this is too disturbing to think about; so they stop learning.

Both these fears—of our own power to learn and of changing ourselves with new ideas—can lead to resistance to learning. Most of us can remember classmates in school who were always making trouble and being sent down to the principal's office—some were even pretty smart, when they wanted to be. But their unwillingness to play the game of passive students led them to break out and ignore any of the benefits of learning as well.

All of us have, to some degree, this blend of fear, discomfort, and resistance to learning. To become peak learners, however, we have to meet these fears, understand them, and work our way past them. Because you have taken the trouble to read

Let me assert my firm belief that the only thing we have to fear is fear itself.

FRANKLIN DELANO
ROOSEVELT

this far in the book, you are already well on the road to dealing with these basic fears of learning.

But these two areas are at the deepest level of our fears of learning. There are other negative feelings, closer to the surface, that grow out of those. Unfortunately, these more visible fears often arise directly from our experiences in school—the place where we're supposed to learn to love learning. Such negative feelings are produced because, in many cases, old theories of education were based on mistaken beliefs about how learning works. The result was to make learning more difficult—and much less pleasant—for most of us. When we experience problems with learning anything, when we feel blocked, bored, overwhelmed, or fearful, we are experiencing the effects of these past mistakes and our own reactions to them.

This is where you can start the process of retraining your negative feelings about learning into the joy and delight you can feel about Peak Learning. You will begin with an exercise, and then go on to consider some of the typical fears of learning produced by our school experience and the mistaken beliefs about how we learn that contributed to our fears. So brace yourselves: you're going to take a guided tour of the dark side of learning.

We are not troubled by things, but by the opinions which we have of things.

EPICTETUS

✦ ✦ ✦ ✦

Those Slow-Learning Blues

In the following exercise—the only negative one I will ask you to do—you will recapture the kind of experience that led to any present apprehensions you may have about learning. I simply want you to recall a typical day at school. When you recall such a day, it will evoke the feelings and sensations that you learned along with your subjects. These feelings shaped your current attitude toward learning—your self-confidence or lack thereof. Only by feeling once again what your attitudes were can you begin to transcend them.

Record your feelings and reactions in your learning log, in whatever form you like. You might jot down key words and feelings, draw a picture, or describe an incident you recall.

1. Sit in a chair, close your eyes, and relax. Picture yourself in a typical classroom from your school days or in a recent class

if you are currently in school. Feel yourself settling into the chair you remember from that class. Really try to feel your body in that chair. Picture the desk and the markings on it, too.

2. Now picture the teacher doing what you recall, probably talking to the class. Recall one specific moment that stands out in your memory. Does this teacher belittle you, another student, or the whole class for your ignorance or other supposed deficiencies? Recall what words are used.

3. Now consider these questions: How do you feel? Are you interested? Scared? Timid? Does the information you are being asked to learn relate to your life? Can you see how you'll use this information in the future? Do you feel smart? Energetic? Creative? Dead from the neck up? How about the passage of time? Does it seem to be going slowly or quickly?

How do you think the other students feel? Do you feel the support of the group, or do you feel alone despite the presence of the other students?

What would you rather be doing? How would you feel if you were doing that? Would you be learning anything if you were?

Do you feel that the experience you have recalled has been designed with your needs or feelings in mind? With the other students'? With anyone's?

How does this experience make you feel about learning itself?

♦   ♦   ♦   ♦

Groucho Marx recalled a conversation with his mother, when she learned he'd been cutting school: "Don't you want to get an education?" she asked. Groucho replied: "Not if I have to go to school to get it!"

WHAT DO PEOPLE FEAR ABOUT LEARNING?

When I present this exercise in my seminars, I ask people to discuss the things they felt. We do this so that everyone can understand exactly how the typical fears and anxieties produced by our schooling contribute to problems with learning. The effects of such feelings are dangerous in all stage of the learning process. When you *start* to learn anything new, they undermine your confidence in being able to understand and master the subject. *During* the learning process, they sap the energy you need, so that you bog down or lose momentum, becoming frustrated and despondent. And even *after* you have learned something, these feelings make it harder to remember or apply what you've learned, forcing you to start all over again—or give up.

Self-education is, I firmly believe, the only kind of education there is. The only function of a school is to make self-education easier; failing that, it does nothing.

ISAAC ASIMOV

Here are two typical examples my students produced of how their negative feelings blocked their ability to learn. Perhaps you will recognize some of your own anxieties from the exercise:

Dorothy K. had math anxiety. During the exercise, she recalled a feeling she often had during her school days: that she was unable to follow what was going on and feared she would never be able to catch up. The result was a vicious cycle. As each new math problem came up in class, she was still thinking about the last one and whether she had really *got* it. That was enough to distract her from the current problem. After the exercise, she realized that her attitude had become a self-fulfilling prophecy.

Arnold M. recalled an art class that had gone to a nearby park to do sketches of nature. All his life, he remembered, he had been told he had no talent in drawing. As a result, he felt uncomfortable with his new sketch pad and set of charcoals. This past conditioning was so strong that, even though he had tried to draw repeatedly in later life, he remained self-conscious about handling his artistic tools. He was unable to stop feeling that he would probably be unsatisfied with whatever he produced. He recalled how he was unable to draw anything the first three times he went out on his own.

From discussing hundreds of cases like these with my students, I've identified six major fears we commonly have about learning. Once you realize where they come from, these fears can lose much of their power over you, because merely describing feelings in words gives us a handle on them and reduces our anxiety. We'll cover each of the six and then go on to discuss the mistaken beliefs about how we learn that contribute to these fears.

Fear 1: I don't understand what I'm learning. We've all had that sinking sensation in the stomach upon realizing that we've lost our way in following a subject. Sometimes this feeling arises because a speaker or author uses words we don't understand. Other times, we understand all the words but can't seem to figure out what the *point* is supposed to be. At a lecture or in a seminar this can be even worse. People around us seem to be getting it. We can look and even sound like we are too, but deep down we know we're faking it. We feel lost, helpless, embarrassed, and unwilling to admit we don't know what's going on.

This universal experience often stems from the way we were taught in school. The pace and style of presenting information was determined by the teacher. If our own way of grasping things was different, little accommodation was made. Moreover, we were expected to master the same body of material as the other students in the class. It didn't matter what was really interesting to us, what parts we'd enjoy pursuing in depth, or what we didn't care much about. Finally, we seldom had the opportunity to process the material in our own ways, by applying it to our own interests or concerns or by making our own unique connections to other things we knew.

None of this needs to apply to the way we can learn now. As adults, we can and should be learning in our own ways, at our own pace, according to our own personal priorities. Only when we give ourselves permission to do that will the feeling of helplessness disappear—and, if they arise, we will have techniques to deal with them productively.

Fear 2: I'm not a person who can learn this subject. No matter how good a student you were in school, there is *something* you think you can't learn. For many people this is math; for others it may be foreign languages, the arts, athletics, salesmanship, or woodworking.

The reason we feel this way relates once more to the idea of our personal learning style. As has been seen, each of us has a unique brain. The combination of that brain and our experience of life produce certain talents, usually abilities we start to exercise at a young age. Those areas are where we each have our personal head start. In the same way, there may be things that are harder for us to learn because they did not come easily to us or we didn't start to practice them early in our lives.

Because our schooling tends to make only minimal concessions to different styles of learning or even differences in the subject matter, we often feel that learning in some areas is too difficult for us to ever accomplish. However, as peak learners we can call the shots. If one style of learning doesn't work for us

Some people never learn anything, for this reason, because they understand everything too soon.

ALEXANDER POPE

Learning is not a task or a problem—it is a way to be in the world. Man learns as he pursues goals and projects that have meaning for him.

SIDNEY JOURARD

in some subject, we can switch to other ways to pick up the information we need. If memorizing vocabulary lists and grammar bores us to tears, we can learn Japanese or Spanish by going to immersion classes where everyone uses the new language to socialize. If math textbooks make our eyes glaze, we can try an interactive computer program that will show us each step only when we're ready for it.

Fear 3: I don't know how to learn this effectively. As was mentioned in Chapter One, the typical pattern in school learning is the assignment to "go and learn this" with never a hint as to how you're supposed to go about it. There is little that can more effectively kill enjoyment than a challenge that comes with little direction, with no place to start.

It is as if you set out to meet some friends on a hike. They've told you where they'll be camping and where to park your car. You get out and look at the forest in dismay: Which trail should you take? What landmarks should you look for? But once you know how, it's easy and fun. You look for the white triangle painted on trees until you get to the stream, follow the current until you reach a tree with a yellow circle, and follow that marked trail to the campsite.

Peak Learning techniques will give you the *trail signs* you need to learn what you want to learn—and to have fun along the way. Once you have several options to try out in various learning situations, you need never feel lost with no place to start. And, as a peak learner, you will realize that anything one person learned can be learned by anyone else willing to put in the work.

Fear 4: I won't remember what I'm learning. Most of us can remember frantically cramming facts, dates, names, and so forth on the night before an exam. We got through the test and relaxed. The next day, however, we were lucky to remember half of what we tried so hard to learn.

Here again, school has given us a skewed picture of how learning should work. For school courses, we were tested periodically on how well we could regurgitate masses of information and we were graded on a curve that compared our retention to that of others. In that system, the fact that most students had forgotten as much as 90 percent of the information within a week of the test was irrelevant. What a waste of time and effort!

But in real life—which is what Peak Learning is about— you have the choice to retain as much or as little as you like, based on what *you* need, find relevant, or enjoy using. Once you have an overview of any subject, enough of a grasp of it to find your way around, it's far easier to go back and look up specific facts or brush up on whole areas if necessary later on. There's simply no *need* to retain everything in your head. No one is comparing how much you remember with what others remember. It is up to you to decide how much of what you're learning is merely nice to know *about* and which small parts are interesting, enjoyable, and useful enough to hold on to, think about, and build on.

Fear 5: I feel ashamed that I don't know something. Whenever we try to learn something, we have to start by *admitting we don't know it yet.* Often, that means we need some help to get started—even if it is only a book recommendation.

But ever since we first sat in a classroom and the teacher called on us for an answer we didn't know, we've been taught that admitting we don't know something is shameful. Most school situations assume that the teacher knows what is worth knowing and our job as students is to get it from him or her. If we didn't get what the teacher knew, we were punished for not knowing. Now, when we try to become *learners,* we revive all the resentment about being controlled, evaluated, and put on the spot as *students.*

But things are different for us now as adults. Unlike the constraints and obligations in other parts of our lives, as learners we have the perfect freedom to explore whatever we wish, when and how we want to. No one is going to ridicule us because we don't know something we're supposed to—the only evaluation that counts is our own.

To continue the hiking analogy I used earlier, as learners we can blaze our own trails, choose any path we wish, and camp wherever we like. As powerful and self-directed peak learners,

Learning is the very essence of humility, learning from everything and everybody. There is no hierarchy in learning. Authority denies learning and a follower will never learn.

J. KRISHNAMURTI

45

we can realize that anything we don't know is an exciting trail we've never been on. We can choose which trail to walk along and explore the new horizons we reach.

Fear 6: There's too much to learn. Here again, school experience gives us a mistaken assumption. In school, learning is organized around courses, a define body of knowledge. It is as if we had to eat an entire cow, even if we wanted only a quick hamburger. So we are left with the belief that to learn something means mastering every detail covered in the thick, heavy textbook. That image helps to kill any joy or interest we might find in the subject. We feel overwhelmed, tired before we begin, and decide to put things off until we are able to tackle them again.

But, again, the real world is totally different. There are no subjects, no courses, no fixed body of knowledge that is required. (When was the last time you saw a fence around a rock saying "Igneous Geology Required"?)

Instead, learning is an ongoing process in which you first identify the things that intrigue you, then find out about them to whatever degree you want. Next, you process that knowledge and build on it, fitting it in where it is useful for your purposes. You then make a decision about what's truly useful and worth keeping, while noting where you can find out the rest when and if you need it. Finally, you start the same cycle over again.

What matters is how much you've done and what you're doing with it, not someone else's idea of how much there is to learn about something. Day by day, month by month, your learning continues to grow in the directions *you* want, at whatever speed *you* set. At any moment, you are free to pass by something complex but irrelevant or to spend days on something simple but useful to you.

Remember that all of us have to contend with these fears when we decide to return to learning on our own terms. In order to change and grow and become able to use more of our potential, we have to let go of the parts of ourselves that get in our own way. The price we must pay for a happier, more fulfilling, and more rewarding life is stepping out of our caves and leaving behind the darkness and the pale, flickering shadows.

THE MYTHS OF LEARNING

For most of us, our years in school and college have also loaded us with beliefs about the process of learning that do not apply now that we are adults. During all those terms and semesters, you were absorbing a kind of mythology of learning. Whatever subject you thought you were studying, you were also being taught a subliminal curriculum that shaped your view of *how* you learn. For example, your learning was usually for someone else: for your parents, your teachers, or the school. *They* decided what was worth learning, how it could best be learned, and whether you'd learned enough of it.

There is no limit to the process of learning to learn. Indeed, once human beings have been bitten by the excitement of finding new ways to structure knowledge, they will never again fear being bored.

ROBERT THEOBALD

Here, again, as was the case with our fears about ourselves as learners, we can dispel much of the power of these myths simply by dragging them out of the dark corners of our mind and submitting them to the light of reason. The following section will run them down quickly by first stating each myth in its baldest form, then examining where it comes from, and finally formulating the truth of the matter.

Myth 1: Learning is a boring, unenjoyable activity. Being bored while learning stems from our being compelled to learn things we don't care about, in an uncongenial environment, without regard to our own needs and style.

Moreover, you were very likely too smart for the pace of learning that typically occurs in school and college, where classwork is often a lockstep dictated by the syllabus, the textbook, and the lowest-common-denominator pace of the group as a whole. "We descend to meet," wrote Emerson, meaning we slow down our natural rate of learning when we are in a group situation. Trying to slow down your brain makes learning tedious.

But learning is really one of the most natural and absorbing experiences you can engage in. Learning can move with

The best lesson anyone can learn from business school is an awareness of what it can't teach you—all the ins and outs of everyday business life. Those ins and outs are largely a self-learning process.

MARK MCCORMACK

the speed of thought, which outstrips any existing computer. Even when you are learning the rudiments of a subject by conventional studying (which can usually be avoided in favor of better strategies), your learning can be exhilarating once your are *doing* things with the information you acquire.

The Truth: Learning can be one of the most absorbing, compelling activities you can engage in—when it is the shortest path to what you want and need to know.

Myth 2: Learning deals only with the subjects and skills taught in school. The formal school curriculum is only a sliver of what's worth knowing. Properly designed, a personal education program gives you the tools with which to take your learning into your own hands. Once you have graduated or left school, your curriculum is entirely for you to determine.

The most successful people choose their own highly personal trajectory once they are on their own. Some throw themselves deeply into one field, skill, or area; others explore several realms. In many cases these subjects were not part of any school or college curriculum, and quite often they are literally created by the learners themselves as they move along.

The Truth: The best subjects and skills for you to learn depend entirely on what you want to make of yourself and your life. This is true because each of us has a unique range of interests.

Myth 3: We must be passive and receptive to "absorb" knowledge. This is an old-fashioned image of education best described as "pouring information into an empty vessel." It doesn't apply to adult learning. In the last chapter it was noted that the brain is an active, constructing organ. Learning by doing is a far more accurate picture than the one that views it to be passive and book-based. As an adult learner, you will increasingly discover the learning aspects of any actions you take.

A good way to understand this is to think of an inventor. He or she wants to build a gadget to do something and may try many different combinations of components to get the right result. With each trial, the person has to evaluate how close he or she has come. Each new trial *creates knowledge,* and it is knowledge that can't be passively absorbed from a textbook, because no one has built this gadget before. So each action of testing the gadget brings new knowledge, new learning. This is no less true if you're not an inventor.

The Truth: True learning is an active process of examining information, evaluating it for some purpose, and going on to the next action. You will get a direct feel for this with techniques described later in this book.

Myth 4: To learn, you must put yourself under the tutelage of a teacher. Education in most schools and colleges is based on the teacher as the driving, controlling force. The teacher decides the scope of the subject, the approach, the pace, the breakpoints, and the style. The teacher is the one who says whether or not you've learned satisfactorily and what to do about it if you haven't.

Of course, a good teacher can be a wonderful resource for your learning. But you will get the most value from teachers by using them at the right time and for the right purpose. For most of your learning, you will find other resources more convenient and effective: a tape cassette in your car during commuting time, a conference brimming with exciting experts in a new field, or a video or computer program that you can play as the mood strikes you—late at night, early in the morning, or on weekends. Generally, you will find that a live teacher is best used either as a last resort (when there's no other way to start a subject) or as a capstone (to provide a peak experience based on your other learning).

The Truth: As an adult, you are in charge of your learning. Teachers are one important resource for your use, but they should be on tap, not on top. It's *your* learning, not theirs.

Myth 5: Learning has to be systematic, logical, and planned. This myth derives from our having observed that our classes always had a curriculum or syllabus—a complete plan for learning a subject. This course of action was already preset when we entered the picture, and our job was to get through it. The syllabus dictated what needed to be covered, in what order, using what materials, and how we'd be tested. Since every course and, indeed, most lectures and laboratory sessions had their own

A [teacher] is like a fire. If you get too close, you get burned. If you stay too far away, you don't get enough heat. A sensible moderation is recommended.

FROM A TIBETAN PROVERB

plan, we naturally came to assume that whenever something was to be learned, the first thing to do was to plan out the learning in advance, in detail.

But research has now revealed that this is not the way learning takes place naturally—i.e., outside of a classroom. In the everyday world, and in the lives of the best learners, such as writers, artists, teachers, and higher-level business and professional people, learning progresses organically. When interviewed about their learning, people readily recall that much of it was spontaneous, even serendipitous.

In short, any subject has a myriad of entry points and a multitude of ways you can work your way through it. Each adult learner's path is a unique one, based on which directions and topics are most appealing and useful to the individual.

The Truth: Good learning balances reasonable planning with flexibility. Adult learning is sensitive to your changing interests and to the opportunities available.

Myth 6: Learning needs to be thorough, or it's not worth doing. In school, the criterion of success is to get a score of 100 or an A—meaning that you have learned virtually everything that the teacher presented in the course. But what if that's not your objective? Suppose that you found that just two topics in the entire course were of passionate interest to you and you spent most of your study time pursuing them, applying them, and building on them. You might actually have carried your study to the point where you had some original findings or thoughts of your own on those two topics. But, of course, you would fail the final.

The idea of *covering the subject* was invented by teachers and those who supervise teachers as a way of measuring whether or not they were doing a complete job. It rarely has relevance for the individual adult learner. Moreover, in many subjects and skills, you can learn 80 percent of what you want or need to know in the first twenty hours of study.

The Truth: One of your most useful decisions about any learning project is simply that of how much of the subject you want and need to learn—a decision that often is best made after you have started, not before.

FLOW LEARNING—THE MYTH-BUSTER

This section will explore the alternatives to the fears and myths of learning. It starts by examining a distinctive state of mind and feeling in which learning is effortless and delightful. This state has been studied intensively by psychologists for the past fifteen years. They have interviewed and tested students, blue-collar workers, professionals, and the elderly. The findings all agree: when our brains are working in this distinctive state of mind, we can overcome our fears about learning.

This state is called *flow,* and it is vital to our personal happiness. The term was coined by the pioneer researcher in the field, Mihaly Csikszentmihalyi (pronounced Chick-SENT-me-hi, though he prefers to be called Mike), head of the Department of Behavioral Sciences at the University of Chicago and author of *Flow: The Psychology of Optimal Experiences.*

"What do we mean by being happy?" Professor Csikszentmihalyi asks. "Is it just pleasure and the absence of pain? These are rewarding conditions, indispensable to maintain psychic processes on an even keel. But happiness also depends on something else: the feeling that one is growing, improving. That process is, by definition, a process of learning, broadly defined. One might conclude that learning is necessary for happiness, that learning *is* the pursuit of happiness."

Flow is the state in which learning and happiness are most completely merged. An article in the *New York Times Magazine* described it as "a state of concentration that amounts to absolute absorption in an activity. In this state, action flows effortlessly from thought and you feel strong, alert and unselfconscious. Flow is that marvelous feeling that you are in command of the present and performing at the peak of your ability. . . . research suggests that flow may be a common aspect of human experience."

Flow happens in every activity. In sports, it's that moment of reaching the *zone* where your ability and performance excel. In music, it takes place when you know your instrument and the piece so well that you just *do* it, as if you have *become* the instrument and the music. In dancing, painting, surgery, and even writing, there's a sense of control, a profound focus on

51

Humans can balance on strange surfaces. Even on unpredictable ones. It's called "getting in tune." Great musicians know it. Surfers . . . knew it. Some waves throw you, but you're prepared for that. You climb back up and go at it once more.

FRANK HERBERT

THE THREE LEARNING ZONES

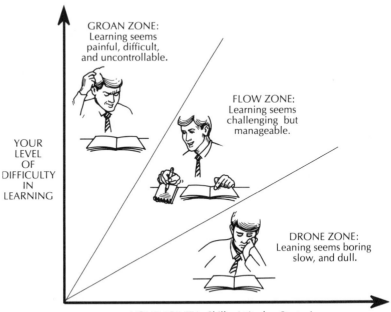

GROAN ZONE:
Learning seems painful, difficult, and uncontrollable.

FLOW ZONE:
Learning seems challenging but manageable.

YOUR LEVEL OF DIFFICULTY IN LEARNING

DRONE ZONE:
Leaning seems boring slow, and dull.

YOUR ABILITY - Skills, Attitudes, Strategies

what you're doing that leaves no room to worry about what anyone will think of your work. There are a number of features that characterize the flow state:

Flow can occur when perceived challenges match perceived skills. Perhaps the most crucial feature is the delicate balance between what you *perceive* to be the challenges in the situation you face and how you *perceive* your own abilities to meet those challenges. Perception is important here, because, as has been seen, the mind *actively constructs* the situations it faces. *Any* activity can be turned into a flow experience if viewed in the right way.

The first step in recognizing the conditions for flow is to *have something to do,* an opportunity for action, a challenge. The next step is to recognize that you have some skills you can use to decide what to do next. The balance between these two will start the ball rolling for flow.

Let's try to make this issue of balance clearer by comparing it to experiences in which there is an *imbalance* between challenge and skills. Imagine you had to take a beginners' course in what you currently do for a living. Your skills and experience are already far beyond what is being taught. Sitting through endless explanations of things you already know would be agonizing torture, immensely boring. That sort of experience takes place in the Drone Zone.

Alternatively, suppose you attended a graduate seminar in something you know nothing about—quantum physics, for example. The speaker goes on and on, but you sit there, comprehending about one word in a hundred, hopelessly over your head. You are now in the Groan Zone.

Flow happens in the region between Groan and Drone. It happens when you need to use all you can bring to the situation—and to stretch yourself just a little bit more. *For flow to occur, the balance between what the situation demands and your skills must result in an advance, an increase in what you can do.* This gives us our first crucial characteristic for flow learning.

Flow states involve a sense of control in the situation. With that perceived balance comes another characteristic of the flow experience: a sense of control. Imagine sitting down to play a game of chess for the first time. You have some idea of how the pieces are supposed to move, but as the game develops, it may be hard to figure out what you should do next. Yet as you play more, and learn more, you start to recognize certain kinds of situations that repeat. You don't fall for the same traps again. You have a better idea of what to do, and so you have an increased sense of control instead of feeling as if you're helplessly floundering.

Flow happens in situations in which one has clearly defined goals and feedback. Games provide a good model for describing other features of the flow experience. According to Csikszentmihalyi, it is important in learning to have a clear sense of the goals in a situation and clear feedback about the results of your actions. This knowledge of what you're aiming for and what difference your actions make encourages you to concentrate on what is relevant to the situation, to become immersed in it.

The ancient Greeks knew that learning comes from playing. Their concept for education (paideia) is almost identical to their concept for play (paidia).

ROGER VON OECH

Transformed perception could be called ordinary magic. . . . It is ordinary because it is hidden from us by nothing other than our reluctance to see it, by habitual beliefs. It is magic because such transformation of perception happens suddenly, without cause or condition, even though the training may be long, requiring great practice and energy.

JEREMY HAYWARD

In flow experiences, intense concentration on what is relevant develops the ability to merge unselfconscious action with awareness and to alter the experience of time. Think of kids who get involved in computer games, even the arcade shoot-'em-ups. What needs to be done to find the treasure or destroy the alien invaders is totally clear in each moment. And so it becomes easy to lose track of time, forget your hunger, and even ignore pain until you stop playing.

Thus in a clearly defined situation in which challenge is balanced by skill and there is a sense of control, it becomes possible to focus concentration intensely on the relevant cues, to merge action and awareness in a way that drops any self-consciousness and may even change how the passage of time is experienced. This feature is our next essential in the flow experience.

Flow experiences arise from intrinsic motivation, not from concern with external rewards or goals. Csikszentmihalyi has found that this feature is as important as the balance of skills and challenge. It is also the most important part of flow for us as peak learners.

As we saw before in discussing learning fears and learning myths, feeding back information for the sake of a good grade can rob learning of its joy and make it torture. Sure, you can be pleased by a good grade, but it is not likely to make the process of cramming for exams any more pleasant.

On the other hand, if you're jamming on a guitar with friends or perfecting your jump shot on a basketball court, what makes those things fun, according to Csikszentmihalyi, is that you're doing them for their own sake. You may wind up with a good riff for a song or the ability to sink a basket from mid-court, but while you're getting there you are just having fun. That is, the experience of learning is enjoyable in itself, not for what you will eventually get out of it.

Csikszentmihalyi believes that people who use flow actually use *less* mental energy than those who are struggling to concentrate because they're bored or anxious. He sees the flow experience as something that's a built-in part of being human, of having a mind that processes information. In his view, new challenges are enjoyable because they prepare human beings to be involved with their environment and to succeed. For Csikszentmihalyi, the joys of learning are as natural as the pleasures of sex, and both serve evolutionary goals for the human species.

LEARNING IN THE FLOW STATE

How does it feel to learn in a flow state? What would you experience if you could put yourself into this frame of mind whenever you chose? Here is how several clients and participants in my workshops have described it.

Helen, learning real-estate salesmanship

Flow learning was like scooping up sand at the seashore as a kid, and plopping it into place on a sand castle. Sure, there was an infinite amount to learn, an infinite amount of sand around. But I knew what I was after in those books, what I needed to build my castle, and just how to reach in for each handful and put it where I needed it.

Alice, learning pre-med organic chemistry

For me, the key was realizing that learning is a *feeling* thing as well as an intellectual process. Taking just ten minutes to enjoy and evoke my strong feelings about the subject, before each bout of studying, seemed to give me more energy and staying power. Also, keeping one favorite piece of music going whenever I turned to this subject helped evoke those feelings.

Jack, learning Spanish

After two previous unsuccessful attempts to learn Spanish in a classroom setting, I finally found a way that felt easy and safe to me: audio tapes that gave me confidence that I was making progress, and an immersion experience, where I simply talked Spanish at a party with other learners. The sense of being caught up in the social interactions, sometimes comically, as we all groped for words and grammar, left me too absorbed to worry about whether I was forgetting previous lessons while learning the next one.

Charles, learning astronomy

Nothing relaxes me more after a day's work in computer programming than to see things the average person will never see. It's a first-hand, direct experience of the universe. When the seeing is good, I find I often lose track of the hours I'm spending staring up at stars and planets. The experience becomes an end in itself.

Fred, learning to play a computer game

At first, there's some mild frustration in figuring out what you have to do to get the game to respond. But in a very short time I find I've mastered the basics, and then I get caught up in the game itself. I feel a tremendous urge to go further, surpass my past limits in the face of tougher challenges.

Susan, studying Chinese cooking

There is a sense of freedom and pleasure that I really enjoy about it. It almost feels as if I go into some kind of trance, deciding on ingredients and seasonings, mixing, stir-frying, or whatever. And then I can taste the results and decide what needs to be different next time.

GETTING TO FLOW: SOME FIRST STEPS

To approach the flow state, you can begin with two preliminary exercises: Relaxation and Activating Your Inner Learner. In the next chapter you'll discover several other Peak Learning techniques for getting more flow into your learning.

RELAXATION

Relaxation techniques have been around probably since the first cave dwellers got nervous about where they were going to find their next meal. A wave of attention on relaxation crested in the 1960s, when Transcendental Meditation got much media attention. Some people were put off by the religious

Damn braces. Bless relaxes.

WILLIAM BLAKE

trappings and Eastern flavor, but Harvard Medical School's Dr. Herbert Benson investigated TM scientifically and found that there really were measurable differences in improved performance as a result of using generic relaxation techniques. He wrote two books on the subject: *The Relaxation Response* and *Your Maximum Mind.* (Another good source is Lawrence LeShan's simple and straightforward *How to Meditate.*)

The benefits of relaxation involve the ability to get out of your own way. By regularly practicing relaxation exercises, such as the one below, you can cultivate the habit of letting go of daily stresses and strains and *reset* your mind for a new task.

Mike Csikszentmihalyi has noted the usefulness of ritual in preparation for a task, as a way to focus attention and help to create a situation in which the total immersion in flow can happen. But don't think you need to burn incense and chant spells in order to learn: *Ritual* here means only a set of steps you take for the purpose of clearing your mind in order to enhance your concentration. Surgeons, for example, may develop a particular way of washing their hands and putting on gowns that they repeat for every operation they perform. The consistency of the practice simply helps them to peel away mental distractions and prepare them to concentrate fully on their work.

A personal relaxation ritual can work the same way. Rather than sitting down to learn something and being distracted by whether you remembered to lock the car or by remembering something you left off your grocery list, spend a few minutes relaxing before starting your learning. The relaxation exercise lets you become calm, clears away mental clutter and static, and prepares you to devote full attention to making sense of what you have chosen to study.

There are many fine exercises for relaxation available today in books and on audiotapes. If you already have one that you like, continue using it. If this sort of exercise is new to you, take a short break right now and try this easy introductory exercise taken from Dr. Benson's research. When you're ready, you can go on to the technique of imagining you're *already* a better learner than you think.

◆ ◆ ◆ ◆

Learning Relaxation

> *The concept of contacting the inner guide . . . means going inward, quieting ourselves, opening to help, and asking for that help.*
>
> O. CARL SIMONTON

(repeat focus word on exhale)

1. Select a focus word or short phrase that's firmly rooted in your personal belief system. For example, a Christian person might choose the opening words of Psalm 23, "The Lord is my shepherd"; a Jewish person, *Shalom*; a nonreligious individual, a neutral word like *one* or *peace*.

2. Sit quietly in a comfortable position.

3. Close your eyes.

4. Relax your muscles; bend your head slightly.

5. Breathe slowly and naturally, and repeat your focus words or phrase as you exhale.

6. Assume a passive attitude. Don't worry about how well you're doing. When other thoughts come to mind, simply dismiss them and gently return to the repetition.

7. Continue for ten to twenty minutes.

8. Practice the technique once or twice daily.

◆ ◆ ◆ ◆

ACTIVATING YOUR INNER LEARNER

As peak learners, each of us has a hidden ace—an expert learner at our beck and call, whenever we need help. Where? In our minds' eyes. That's what activating your inner learner is about. It is the same kind of imaginative exercise that Olympic athletes use for training, a kind of mental rehearsal of peak performance called *visualization*.

This approach is being used more widely in sports and in many other fields as well. You no longer have to be training for the Olympics to get a videotape lesson on golf or tennis that tells you to picture yourself making the stroke.

The basis of visualization here goes back to the power of our minds and brains. Human beings have powerful imaginations. Why not use that power in positive, supportive ways rather than simply leaving your imagination focused on worrying about possible disasters?

Visualization works because when you take the time to picture yourself doing something well and bring to mind each detail of the process, you are strengthening the pattern of behavior in much the same way you do by actually practicing it. Visualizing is like knowing how to play a piece of music and being able to go through the motions of playing it in your head without even touching the instrument.

We can achieve our "personal best" much more often by vividly imagining what we feel like when we do it. We can also imagine what it might be like to be some master learner we revere. Excellence is contagious. The more time we spend in imagination, "playing" Socrates, Galileo, or Einstein as well as ourselves at our best, the more exciting our own real-life learning will become.

Don Lofland is a teacher of Power Learning. He advises his students to actually give their imagined ideal learner a name. Sometimes he has them actually wear name tags with the names of the master learners they would like to emulate and talk with each other as if they were those people.

Once, when I was using this technique in one of my own seminars, I went all the way and dressed up as Socrates, with a bed-sheet toga, leather sandals, and a soda can labeled "Diet Hemlock." I went around giving advice like "know thyself" and answering questions about "my" life and philosophy. It was great fun, but it also served a more serious purpose. What better way can there be to get people really thinking about the importance of an inquiring mind and challenging issues than to remind them of the great philosopher who insisted he was the most ignorant of men and merely sought to learn?

The following Activating Your Inner Learner exercise will provide a nicely balanced closing to the exercise that started this chapter, Those Slow-Learning Blues. Remember that that exercise also used the techniques of imaginative recall to bring back the worst of learning experiences. Now, we are about to look at the other side, the best of learning.

Life must be lived as play . . . then a man will be able to propitiate the gods.

PLATO

◆ ◆ ◆ ◆

Activating Your Inner Learner

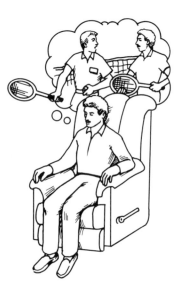

Take a moment to recall the state of mind you had during your best learning experience, a time when learning came easily, naturally, and most pleasurably. Don't think the experience has to be from school days. The state of mind is what is important, not the subject matter you learned. You can use anything, as long as you remember the learning experience as being fun. It might be cooking, learning a sport or hobby, or even exploring a new city.

It also might be one of the skills with which you earn your living. The activity can be relatively simple, such as learning to type or drive, or complex, such as learning the periodic table or financial equations.

1. Start by relaxing in a comfortable position in a favorite chair. Do some deep breathing, using a relaxation technique such as the one you learned in the previous exercise.

2. Now, recall the time when your learning went so well. Where are you? Can you bring back physical sensations, such as the light or the sounds or smells of the place? Who are you with? Picture the faces of people involved, and hear their voices. How do you feel?

    Does this moment stand out from the stream of your life? Do you feel a surge of satisfaction at "getting it"? Did mastering something new make you feel good about yourself? How do you think others felt—the other learners, if any, and the teacher, if there was one?

3. Dwell imaginatively on what you were seeing, hearing, and feeling during your experience. Enjoy this for as long as you like.

◆ ◆ ◆ ◆

That should start to give you a feel for what it means to be a peak learner and for the experience of flow learning. Remember that the key point here is *how it felt*. The more time you can spend feeling good about learning, imagining yourself enjoying learning, or imagining yourself as someone you respect who *did* enjoy learning, the easier it will be for you to enjoy your own learning—and, the bottom line, the easier it will be for you to learn anything!

At this point, you are nearly halfway through reading about those aspects of Peak Learning that deal with emotions. Consider what you have learned so far.

First, you have learned the why and how of the connection between feelings and learning: the many ways in which we can interfere with our enjoyment of learning by allowing out-of-date feelings to trip us up. Practicing the above visualization exercise offers a way to counter those past emotions. Use it whenever you experience any anxiety connected with learning.

You have seen some of the many deeply held fears that people have about learning and how they often arise because our past educational experience made a number of wrong assumptions about how people learn, assumptions that have been disproved by more recent research. You have also taken a tour through the unfortunate myths spread by the system of schooling we have experienced. Those beliefs were carefully distinguished from the type of learning we want to do as adults, as peak learners choosing to learn as much or as little of what we want in the way that suits us best.

You have taken your first steps toward encouraging yourself to be a better learner, toward retraining your feelings about learning by learning to relax and by activating your "inner learner." The next chapter will continue the retraining process by presenting two more powerful strategies for self-encouragement.

Everything begins . . . with belief. What we believe is the most powerful option of all.

NORMAN COUSINS

IV

Building Your Learning Confidence

This chapter continues the discussion of how to boost the power of the learning process. Once you recognize the negative, subconscious, and hidden beliefs that diminish your ability to learn, you need to take conscious steps to eliminate them.

The ability to learn was once natural for all of us. Watch a toddler poking around a new room, for example. She'll ask a hundred questions a day, want to experience everything, use all her senses, not care if she makes a fool of herself, and concoct her own zany ideas.

At that age, you learned more powerfully than at any period since. First, you had to make sense of that "booming, buzzing confusion," as the great psychologist William James called the world of the newborn. Later, you mastered your native language from scratch.

Two Peak Learning strategies, called affirmations and invocations, make it possible to bring back that power and delight. They cultivate a kind of positive, adventurous, energetic attitude that encourages intellectual abilities and senses. This

We are what we think. All that we are arises with our thoughts. With our thoughts we make the world.

BUDDHA

mental posture endows you with a state of mind that is open to learning and help you overcome learning fears.

AFFIRMING YOUR POWER TO LEARN

The first technique, affirmations, is based on the power of autosuggestion. This idea originated with a French doctor, Emile Coué, around the turn of the century. Coué was the person who invented the famous phase "Every day, in every way, I'm getting better and better." He believed that by repeating these words to oneself regularly, a person could cure all his or her ills. While his claims for the powers of autosuggestion to cure illness were probably exaggerated, more recent research on placebos and psychoneuroimmunology (PNI) suggest there is a basis in fact for improvements in mental attitude based on this technique, and that such improvements can also have benefits for physical health.

Autosuggestion allows you to internalize new attitudes about learning. It works because our subconscious mind is highly receptive to simple, positive statements that evoke our inner learner. When it hears that you are the kind of learner described below, it increasingly accepts that positive self-image, and that state of mind becomes more accessible to you. Think of autosuggestion as a kind of self-programming, a way to practice the habit of increased self-confidence about your learning abilities. You can also think of affirmations as a kind of ritual in the sense described by Mike Csikszentmihalyi in the last chapter—something you do regularly to encourage the focus and concentration of flow learning.

One of the leading teachers of the autosuggestion technique is Shakti Gawain, author of *Creative Visualization*. "The practice of doing affirmations allows us to begin replacing some of our stale, worn-out, or negative mental chatter with more positive ideas and concepts," she says. "It is a powerful technique, one which can, in a short time, completely transform our attitudes and expectations . . . and thereby totally change what we create for ourselves."

Nowhere is this truer than in the realm of learning, because we are dealing with the state of our own minds, not external conditions. I'm not sure about how effective affirmations may be in changing the external conditions of our lives—by bringing us riches or friends, for example—although a positive attitude in these areas can certainly be helpful. But I do know, both from my own practice and from the experience of my students, that affirmations can work wonderfully in opening the mind and making you feel more confident and positive about any learning experience.

The affirmations I'm going to suggest are simple and direct. In fact, they may seem simplistic at first. But be patient; they have to be elementary to have an impact on our subconscious minds. As you fill them with your own feelings, these affirmations will have surprising power.

Something we were withholding made us weak Until we found it was ourselves.

ROBERT FROST

♦ ♦ ♦ ♦

Peak Learning Affirmations

1. Choose a time when you will have complete privacy and no interruptions for at least half an hour.

2. Recall your best personal experience of Peak Learning, the one you used in the exericse on Activating Your Inner Learner in the last chapter. Let yourself reexperience the state of mind and its associated emotions deeply.

3. Now, read each of the following statements slowly to yourself, thinking about how each of them was a part of your recollected experience. After reflecting on each statement for as long as you like, speak it out loud in a gentle voice.

> My learning is exciting to me.
>
> The more I learn, the more exciting it gets.
>
> I find each step in my learning enjoyable.
>
> I understand easily and deeply.
>
> I enjoy adding to my knowledge and understanding.
>
> Learning is a pleasure.

Knowing and remembering are easy for me.

I love learning and knowledge more and more.

Learning keeps me mentally alert.

I am thrilled by the rich variety of my knowledge.

Every day presents me with opportunities for growth.

I am enthusiastic about learning.

Learning is a matter of attitude, not aptitude.

GEORGI LOZANOV

4. Now repeat the whole list aloud several times. You may want to make your own audio-cassette recording of the statements. Read them slowly, allowing ten to twenty seconds between them. Make any minor word changes you like, and skip any statements you don't care for or feel uneasy about. You can also add statements of your own, using the same simple, present-tense format.

5. When you've read the list through, put the recorder on pause, shuffle the affirmations, and read them again in a different order. This will help your mind to stay alert while listening.

6. Repeat until you have filled a thirty-minute tape this way.

Once you have created the tape, you can play it anywhere. You can use your driving time to encourage yourself to learn better all day, or you can play the tape softly, perhaps with a pillow speaker or headphones, just before you fall asleep. Set your own schedule. As with the relaxation exercise, however, it's best to use the tape on a regular basis until you notice enough improvement to feel it is no longer necessary.

♦ ♦ ♦ ♦

PEAK LEARNING INVOCATIONS

Invocations are calls for assistance. There is, in fact, a classical basis behind this collection of techiques, namely the myth of the Muses from Greek culture. This myth dramatized the fact that when you want your mind to work at its optimum, in any field from history to sports, you must deliberately put yourself in a receptive but energized state in which the *muse*—the spirit of excellence in that area—can add to your own efforts. The goddess summoned from outside, we now realize, was merely a symbol of a spirit that lies within each of us. But the *process* of summoning that spirit is essential. The following techniques are ways to do that.

These strategies prepare your mind for learning in many ways. You will find yourself relaxed, but braced for an invigorating mental workout. You'll feel your mental powers prepared for action. You will be keenly alert, but not tense. You will be confident of your capacity to rise to the occasion. Collectively, these techniques work to improve motivation, energy, concentration, understanding, retention, and even inspiration.

The invocations are:

Fall in love.
Stir your soul.
Use your experience.
Energize your brain.
Catch others' enthusiasm.

You may wish to experiment with each of these over the next few weeks. Then, whenever you need to evoke Peak Learning, you can use the one or two that fit your mood and the task at hand. Doing one or two of these warm-ups can take as little as two minutes. But, properly used, they will increase your productivity, efficiency, and performance.

Because each of us is unique as a learner, you will find some of these invocations more congenial than others. I have intentionally offered you *more* than you need, so that you can choose the ones you like. Each has its own purpose, as you will see. Some will be useful before, during, or after your learning sessions. For example, "Use your experience" will be useful in enlivening your learning or in thinking about it afterward. "Energize your brain" is helpful when you're actually sitting down to study or are about to start a class or workshop. "Stir your soul" can be done anytime, to regularly remind yourself of how powerful your mind is.

Invocation 1: Fall in love. The single most powerful thing you can do to foster learning is to fall in love with what you're learning.

The road to new interests is the natural route of fascination and delight.

HILTON GREGORY

Socrates insisted that learning begins with Eros—the same appreciation that draws us toward attractive people. In essence, the phrase *love of learning* is not merely a metaphor, nor does it mean simply a lust to understand. Rather, it is a truly profound emotion of respect, appreciation, or even adoration that is necessary to invigorate the process.

In our own times, the great philosopher Alfred North Whitehead described the first stage in any learning project as *romance*. The subject matter has the fresh impact of novelty, and the new learner catches tantalizing glimpses of something important gleaming through the mass of material. "In this stage, learning is not dominated by systematic procedures," Whitehead believed. Instead, you simply explore, randomly, whatever catches your eye, constantly delighted by unexpected treasures.

This feeling is familiar to most people. We often have such an experience when plunging into a new problem or challenge, discovering a new author or artist who illuminates our life, or visiting a foreign country. Perhaps this is the stage of learning that marks the beginning of flow, when we are captivated by something new.

It is worth noting that Whitehead's second stage, called *precision, does* involve a more systematic approach to organizing the new facts we are learning. But his final stage, *generalization,* requires "a return to romanticism with the added advantage of classified ideas and relevant technique." At that point, creative use of the learned material can happen—what we've called building on the relevant information in order to go further.

This invocation suggests the importance of becoming infatuated with our subject, something that traditional education seldom allows. When you tackle any new topic, think of the first, get-acquainted phase as one of discovery and delight. You need to explore those aspects of a topic that particularly appeal to you and use them as a springboard. Feel free to skip, scan, and read randomly. Cover only as much as you enjoy. Don't try to store or remember; just get a feel for the subject.

This phase may turn out to be more productive than you would expect. In fact, you may learn some of the most important points about your subject while roaming around it randomly. You often learn the most important points about any new subject at the start, before you know enough to develop pre-conceptions about it or fears about your ignorance. In many cases, your initial learning makes up more than 50 percent of what you want and need to know. And you learn these points much faster and more easily than the less important 50 per-cent that follows.

But your primary goal here is enjoyment. See how many and which angles you can find about your subject that delight, intrigue, amuse, and gratify you.

You may find it easier to fall in love with a person than with an abstract subject. So keep in mind that every subject, no mat-ter how cut-and-dried it may seem now, was once the passion-ate preoccupation of some fierce genius who created it out of his or her lifeblood. Discover one of those people, learn about his or her life, and you will find that your subject comes alive.

Tackle mathematics, for instance, by browsing in Eric Bell's *Men of Mathematics* to learn about one of the wonderful charac-ters who created the science of numbers. Or, if you're inter-ested in city planning, read a biography of Robert Moses or the creator of Central Park, Frederick Law Olmsted—men who championed the cause of livable cities against harrowing odds.

The overall aim and effect of this invocation is twofold: to create an attitude toward what you choose to learn that is eager, passionate, enthusiastic, and warmly appreciative; and, at the same time, to give yourself permission to *have fun* as you begin to strike up an acquaintance with your subject matter.

Invocation 2: Stir your soul. I assume that you already value and relish using your mind. But everyone can use a booster once in a while; we need to be reminded in a fresh, vivid way of what we already know. We also need to take time regularly to figure out how our learning can be fine-tuned to the changing cir-cumstances of our lives—to what has happened in the past week and to what we will confront next week.

So, whatever else you are learning, you should also be reg-ularly refreshing your awareness of the enormous potential of your mind. In doing so, you are opening a window through which the great thoughts of others can kindle a fire of inspi-ration.

For those who have ex-perienced it, the hour of the awakening of the passion for knowledge is the most memorable one of a lifetime.

COLIN WILSON

*That which is unique
and worthwhile in us
makes itself felt only in
flashes. If we do not know
how to catch and savor
these flashes, we are
without growth and
without exhilaration.*

ERIC HOFFER

The best way to do this is to dip daily into the classics. You will find that reading a page or two of them every morning or evening will give you an exhilarating sense of what humans can accomplish. It will also usually suggest some ways you can make your other current learning easier or more productive.

My basic list of such works includes the *Notebooks* of Leonardo da Vinci (perhaps the greatest learning log ever created!), Plato's *Dialogues,* and Aristotle's *Metaphysics.* Look them over the next time you're in the library, see which appeals to you most, and give it a try. You'll want to add the books that work to your permanent library. Other useful works might be found in the *Great Books* series created by Mortimer Adler, but don't feel you have to limit yourself to ancient classics. My own list also includes contemporary books about learning, creativity, and psychology. Even intelligent, well-written fiction can be mentally stimulating.

Another important way to stir your soul is to partake of the vast repertoire of magazines published today. Most of us are familiar with only a few national publications, but there are literally hundreds of provocative and thought-inspiring magazines that can introduce you to new ideas, social trends, and worldviews. Even when you disagree with the writers' opinions, they will challenge you to think and to develop a greater understanding of many issues than you may have had before.

To start with, I recommend that you read at least one periodical devoted to the subject of learning, growth, mental-stimulation techniques, or creativity. Here are some of the best. Sending them a self-addressed stamped envelope will bring you additional materials and possibly a sample issue, so that you can judge for yourself which ones suit your style.

Your Personal Best is a newsletter full of practical methods of enhancing your mental and physical well-being and performance. Rodale Press, 33 E. Minor Street, Emmaus, Pennsylvania 18098

On the Beam is the best newsletter on new teaching and learning techniques using the full range of senses, capacities, and potentialities. 4649 Sunnyside North, Seattle, Washington 98103

Adult and Continuing Education Today is a newsletter for professionals in the field, but useful to anyone involved in the lifelong learning movement as learner, teacher, or program developer. P. O. Box 1425, Manhattan, Kansas 66502

The Learning Bulletin is an excellent source on findings and practices in innovative learning. National Learning Laboratory, 8417 Bradley Boulevard, Bethesda, Maryland 20817

The Brain-Based Education Networker has superb coverage on ways to use your *whole brain* for learning. 449 Desnoyer, St. Paul, Minnesota 55104

Additionally, one of the most interesting and efficient magazines is the *Utne Reader*. This bimonthly magazine is a sort of *Reader's Digest* of the alternative press, in which each issue brings together articles and commentary on a major political or social issue of the times from a diverse group of nontraditional and smaller publications. Its publisher, Eric Utne, also recommends the following magazines and newspapers for those who wish to challenge themselves to alternative thinking:

East West	*New Options*
Extra!	*The Sun*
Granta	*Village Voice*
In These Times	*Whole Earth Review*
Multinational Monitor	*World Watch*
The Nation	*Zeta*

A good newsstand or your local library is bound to carry most of these, or you can write to the *Utne Reader* (1624 Harmon Place, Suite 330, Minneapolis, Minnesota 55403), who, for a small fee, will send you information on how to order the above publications.

Invocation 3: Use your experience. You already have an immense database for learning things to help you cope with your current problems. By reaching back for the most relevant prior experiences in your life, you can locate lessons learned then that apply in the present.

You do this already, of course. One of our most familiar experiences is to be reminded of something that happened in the past when we are going through something similar in the present.

Experience isn't what happens to you. It's what you make out of what happens to you.

ALDOUS HUXLEY

For example, suppose you're applying for a new job. You've made all the necessary preparations, got your resume together, and dressed appropriately, and now it's time for the interview. As it proceeds, you begin to feel a slight sense of uneasiness, not just the usual nervousness about whether your skills and experience will be acceptable to your potential employer. Your mind flashes to past interviews, to stories friends have told you about their own job interviews, or even to similar situations in TV shows or movies. You recall a friend who found herself handling executive-level responsibilities when she'd been hired as a secretary. Suddenly your hunch comes into focus: the way the interviewer is talking seems to suggest the position is a more demanding one than you had supposed, one for which you might have to travel or be available on weekends, if necessary. At the right moment, you can ask a question or two to confirm this, and adjust the salary you were going to ask for!

That swift, silent scan of previous experience has helped you to decide how to act in the present moment. You went from a vague hunch, to consulting your memories, to forming a theory based on past experience, to asking a question and changing your plans based on the answer. That's the same kind of learning process a scientist would use in the laboratory.

This process will be discussed in greater depth in Chapter Seven, when you will see how to make the most effective use of your recollections to enrich your present learning. For now, the key point is simply that you should allow those flashes from your past to be a part of your present learning. In fact, you should go looking for them.

One of the surest signs of active learning is the ability to take some new bit of information and *connect it* to the rest of your life experience. If you can see how the new data fits in *anywhere*, then you have anchored it in your mind's own cross-referencing system—which is more complicated than any library catalogue or computer—so it can be jogged back into awareness.

Invocation 4: Energize your brain. Whenever you're about to call upon your brain, it's worthwhile to check out the condition of

your body. The principle that learning depends on the state of
your body has been explored by several leaders in the field of
learning how to learn. Don Lofland, for example, insists in his
workshops on Power Learning that any study session or other
learning occasion "begins with your physiology." He urges his
students to do a quick check of their bodily state and make
whatever adjustments are necessary in terms of relaxation, the
temperature of the room, thirst, or hunger.

One practitioner who has probed this principle is
Washington-based Michael Gelb. He bases his High Performance Learning seminars on learning to juggle. "It's a way of
making participants aware of how they tense up their bodies
when confronted with the challenge of learning something
new," Gelb explains. "You wouldn't think people would be in-
timidated by something as unserious as juggling. I deal with
seasoned, thick-skinned executives. Yet you confront them
with this playful challenge, and you can see the change in their
bodies—and *they* can *feel* those changes! Juggling is just a metaphor, of course. But it gets right to the role of the body in
learning. The principle is that the bodily state of the learner is
the key to all learning. I want to free the body in order to free
the mind."

Gelb urges his seminar participants to notice when they
tense up their bodies in learning and to become aware of what
messages that sends to the brain. Basically, that message is usually "I can't do this. I'm afraid. I'll feel silly or stupid. But I probably *need* to feel this way in order to learn." When you get this
tense, your brain pretty well shuts down, and new learning is
even harder in that state.

As Gelb's work shows, this common, habitual body reaction
that interferes with learning can be caught, stopped, and
changed by consciously relaxing your body to a state more conducive to learning. The how-to details of such a procedure
should be learned in an experiential, hands-on workshop with
someone who can use nonverbal means of teaching (like juggling) and by watching your body for reactions you may not
even be aware of. But you can benefit even before taking such
training just by keeping your body in mind, as it were. The
basic principles are as follows.

Learning is movement from moment to moment.

J. KRISHNAMURTI

1. Be aware of your bodily state while learning. If you sense tensions, rigidities, or discomforts, take steps to alleviate them. You may need to go back and do the Relaxation Exercise described in Chapter 3. A change in temperature or ventilation, a brisk walk, a light snack, or a refreshing drink also can alter your state.

2. Use the active-learning techiques from chapters 6 and 7 to give your brain some enjoyable and varied tasks to perform on the material you're learning.

3. Be alert to signs of fatigue, tension, or irritation. Rather than suppressing them, attend to them, then throw yourself back into the learning process relaxed and refreshed.

The single most important part of your body for your learning is, of course, your brain, so taking care of it is paramount. The three essentials to this care are exercise, rest, and nutrition.

Exercise provides oxygen, which your brain needs and uses at a disproportionate rate given its size in comparison to other major organs. Weighing in at only 2 percent of your body's total, your brain consumes 25 percent of your intake of oxygen. When a person's oxygen supply is cut off, even if for only a few minutes, brain cells start to die. For these reasons, regular brisk exercise in the midst of your learning sessions (which include everything from reading to attending a workshop) is highly advisable. Regular exercise is also important in maintaining healthy circulation in the arteries leading to the brain, which deliver the needed oxygen.

Adequate rest is also important. Setting a consistent bedtime and wake-up time results in optimum functioning for most people. Disrupting your customary pattern is likely to result in reduced mental energy and acuity, as is experienced during jet lag.

It is now known that individuals differ in the *amount* of sleep they need to function at their best, and there's a good deal of evidence that most of us could reduce the amount we sleep by one or two hours a night with no negative effects. On the contrary, those who do so and make good use of the extra time in the morning or evening tend to feel better and have improved morale.

Finally, diet is important for the functioning of your brain. Just as the brain uses an amount of oxygen out of proportion to its size, so it is exceptionally sensitive to the effects of different nutritional strategies. It isn't too good an idea to try to learn something complicated after a big meal, for example; it is just too easy to nod off and nap. So much of the body's blood supply is involved in digestion that there's much less available to carry oxygen to the brain for alert learning.

The usual injunctions of nutritionists apply, of course, to learning situations as they do to a normal, healthy life-style: Eat a well-balanced diet of generally unprocessed foods, stress fresh fruits and vegetables, and avoid too many artificial ingredients along with sugar, starch, caffeine, alcohol, and unnecessary drugs.

If you want to explore more deeply how what you eat affects your brain, the best book I know is *Eat Right, Be Bright* by neurosurgeon Arthur Winter and science writer Ruth Winter. "A wise choice of food may actually improve your mental ability," the authors contend. While much of the book concerns matters not directly affecting your learning, the authors review all the available research on such matters as eating disorders, problems with dieting, the effects of food additives and of supplementary vitamins and minerals. They suggest, for example, that vitamin B-12, which can be obtained only from meat, dairy products, and eggs (foods that many cholesterol-conscious consumers tend to avoid) is vital to the growth and maintenance of a healthy brain and nervous system.

What kinds of foods can improve mental sharpness immediately? It's important to know this for selecting snacks and meals during periods of intense learning. Dr. Judith Wurtman of M.I.T., author of *Managing Your Mind and Mood Through Food*, asserts that "ups and downs, your mental energy or lack of it, are the result of changes in your brain chemistry." After seven years of research she has concluded that carbohydrates make you sleepy, protein increases your alertness, and fat dulls your ability to perform mentally. In her book she offers A, B, and C lists of foods—the A's being ideal for situations in which you want to sustain peak mental performance.

The general principles Wurtman promotes are to eat lightly—just enough to satisfy your hunger; avoid or minimize carbohydrates to avoid drowsiness; use coffee (in moderation) to keep you wakeful and positive-minded (two separate effects); and take a modest amount of protein to sustain alertness.

To keep the body in good health is a duty . . . otherwise we shall not be able to keep the mind strong and clear.

BUDDHA

◆ ◆ ◆ ◆

Exercising

The single best way to adjust your physiological state for learning is to do some brisk exercise. Therefore, follow this simple regimen when you want to get your system geared up for learning.

1. Take a vigorous walk for fifteen to twenty minutes.
2. While walking, focus your eyes regularly on the farthest horizon or on the tops of buildings or clouds in the skies.
3. Also look *around,* taking in as much of the terrain as possible, giving your neck a nice workout.
4. Swing your arms, and take big healthy strides.
5. Breathe deeply.

If it's not feasible for you to leave your desk or room, do some stretching.

1. Stretch your arms above your head, as far as you can reach.
2. Stretch to the sides, revolving your arms.
3. Bend over—*sandpaper* the floor.
4. Twist your arms to touch hard-to-reach parts of your body.
5. If you're with someone else, have that person give you a little massage of the shoulders and neck, and return the favor.
6. Rotate your head.
7. Walk or run in place.
8. Breathe deeply.

Finally, when you get back down to work, check your posture. When I say that Peak Learning is a type of posture toward life, I mean it literally as well as figuratively. Your physical posture reflects and influences how well you learn. Win Wenger, author of *Beyond O.K.,* dramatizes this with the following exercise.

◆ ◆ ◆ ◆

◆ ◆ ◆ ◆

The Learning Stance

1. Stand before a full-length mirror, with your legs comfortably spread and your hands hanging at your sides.
2. Turn you feet toes-in, facing each other.
3. Turn your hands with the palms facing front.
4. Open your mouth and let your tongue rest against the inside of your lower lip.
5. Furrow your brow the way you do when you hear something you can't quite understand.
6. Now, say in a firm, loud voice: "I am a sharp, swift, penetrating learner."

By contrast, adopt this posture.

1. Sit comfortably in a chair, with one leg extended out a little farther than the other.
2. Rest your right elbow on your right knee.
3. Rest your chin against your forefinger; hold it with your thumb.
4. Rest your left hand against your left thigh to balance yourself.
5. Look into the middle distance the way you would when absorbed with a problem and getting ideas on solving it.
6. Now, say to yourself: "I'm just not very clever at this sort of thing."

◆ ◆ ◆ ◆

It didn't come out quite right, did it? Your posture worked against it, because you were in the posture of Rodin's *Thinker*, the archetypal symbol of thoughtfulness. The impact of adopting this posture is described by Edward de Bono, a pioneer in teaching people how to think.

> I want you to imagine that . . . chin-on-hand pose which is supposed to come to any thinker who is being more than just frivolous. As a matter of fact, I believe that thinking should

be active and brisk rather than gloomy and solemn. But the traditional image is a useful one for the moment.

Throw yourself into that pose—physically, not mentally—and you will become a thinker. Why? Because if you play-act being a thinker, you will become one.

Adopt the pose of a thinker. Go through the motions. Have the intention and make it manifest to yourself and to those around. Quite soon your brain will follow the role you are playing.

As de Bono points out, posture is one of many subconscious cues our minds read when we decide to learn. And I hope you also caught the similarity to the exercise in Chapter 3 called Activating the Inner Learner. (That's another example of making use of the invocation *Use your experience*). When we assume a role, we don't have to be on stage or before a camera for the features of that role to appear within us. Even if we have only the foggiest idea of *deep thought*, we can develop the capacity by assuming the physical stance.

Invocation 5: Catch others' enthusiasm. Remember that the purpose of any invocation is to heighten your enthusiasm, your zest for learning. You want to rekindle the adventurous and energetic attitude you had as a child. One way to do that is to *catch* enthusiasm from other people who are already swept up in your subject. Many of us learn most easily and powerfully from other people. And enthusiasm, like excellence, is highly contagious!

Getting involved with someone who's pursuing the same subject makes for companionable learning. Seek agreeable co-learners when you attend a class. Check for people looking for books in the same section at the library you use, and look for other possible intellectual liaisons.

In every community in this country you can find people who are excited about their favorite subject. They often meet, whether the occasion is called a luncheon, reception, or lecture. Just recall the following familiar offerings that you've doubtless seen advertised in your own community. Each of these brings together, as a one-time special event or on a regular basis, people who are eager to share the excitement of their field or skill.

To change the modality we must change the metaphor.

JEAN HOUSTON

Business networking breakfasts

Foreign-language societies such as Goethe House,
    Alliance Française, and Asian Society

Astronomers' sky-viewing nights

Marketing luncheons

Museum and gallery openings

Computer users clubs

Archaeological society lectures

Civil war roundtables

Medievalists or science-fiction fans

There are two kinds of knowledge: knowing something, and knowing who knows it.

SAMUEL JOHNSON

You can also find enthusiasts eager to share their excitement at specialty stores in virtually every field, from photography, dance, the occult, and music to cooking, computers, nutrition, writing, and stage magic.

Just for practice, take two subjects in which you'd enjoy meeting some fellow students or expert practitioners, hearing some good shoptalk, and seeing what local events are upcoming; then look up the specialty stores in these two areas in the Yellow Pages.

A second way to tap the enthusiasm of a field is to read the liveliest newsletter in that field. (The specialty store you just looked up will probably have sample copies.) What you're after here is the in-group chatter, the sense of camaraderie in which you will soon be able to participate.

Once you've found your source of enthusiasts, you may want to strike up a friendship and spend more time with one. Such people are usually delighted by a newcomer with a genuine excitement about their field; it refreshes their own energy to tell a bright novice what they're letting themselves in for. So it's often possible to strike a mutually agreeable deal, in which you serve a mini-apprenticeship by just tagging along and helping with some chores in return for the delights of a guided tour and some first-class instruction along the way.

In this chapter you have seen examples of solid techniques to help you release the full power of Peak Learning in your own life. Because learning is so individual, I wouldn't expect anyone to find that *all* the suggested techniques work equally well. But, without a doubt, you will find that one or more of these *will* make a substantial difference in the ease and enjoyment with which you learn. Do not neglect these techniques.

- ♦ Use affirmations to encourage your subconscious mind to find learning exciting, easy, and fun.
- ♦ Fall in love with a field you want to learn by *playing* in it, unsystematically, in order to get a feel for the parts that will be most pleasurable to you.
- ♦ Regularly seek stimulation, support, and inspiration from great examples of learning in the past.
- ♦ Use all of your past experience when you need it to help you in a present learning situation.
- ♦ Recognize that if you want your brain to function at its best in learning, you have to take care of your body as well. The right combinations of food and exercise can help make you a better learner.
- ♦ Remember that opportunities exist everywhere to find others who share your interests and will be happy to help you increase your enthusiasm for learning.

All of these techniques will help you become a peak learner. In exactly the same way that the negative emotions about learning hindered your progress, the positive emotions you develop using these methods will continue to make your learning easier and more enjoyable.

V

Discovering Your Personal Learning Profile

Many people are surprised to hear that they have a distinctive, personal way of using their minds. There are two reasons for their surprise.

First, we've all been taught to think that our schooling shaped our minds into the one *right* way to learn and think. That's what all those lessons on logical thinking, study skills, and test-taking strategies were all about. The teachers were supposed to be training us to use our minds correctly, at least as far as traditional education goes. However, the way of learning and thinking that we were taught in school is only one way. And it is not the one that is most congenial for the majority of adults.

The second reason why some people are surprised to find that they think in a distinctive way is that other people's thought processes are not visible to us. The brain is the ultimate black box, which we can't open. So we are unaware of how differently each of us thinks and learns.

But four decades of psychological research lead us to conclude that each person has a distinct, individual way of dealing

Exploration of the full range of his own potentialities is not something that the self-renewing man leaves to the chances of life. It is something he pursues systematically, or at least avidly, to the end of his days. He looks forward to an endless and unpredictable dialogue between his potentialities and the claims of life—not only the claims he encounters but the claims he invents.

JOHN GARDNER

81

with information and concepts. In fact, if our faces differed as much as the way our minds work, some of us would have eyes like magnifying glasses, others would have noses like an elephant's trunk, and still others might have ears like radar dishes!

Professor Robert Smith of Northern Illinois University provides an excellent analysis of learning styles, based on his years of monitoring the literature in the field.

> People differ in how they go about certain activities associated with learning. They differ as to how they think. They differ as to how they approach problem solving. They differ as to how they go about "information processing," or putting information through their minds. Some people like to "get the big picture" of a subject first and then build toward a full understanding of that picture by details and examples. Other people like to begin with examples and details and work through to some kind of meaningful construct or way of looking at an area of knowledge out of these details. Some like theory before going into practice. Others don't.
>
> With regard to method, one might hear a person say, "I don't like discussion," or, "I went to a workshop and we did role playing—it made me uneasy." With field trips, we might hear, "I fall behind and can't hear what the guide is saying." People differ with regard to the amount of structure and autonomy that they want. Some seem to prefer being told what to do at every stage of learning, while some [only need] some structure and some freedom of choice. People differ, too, in their reactions to competition. When they find themselves in a seminar where the instructor sets them against each other, some experience great anxiety and even drop out, while others appear to thrive. Environmental considerations also come into play—for example, preferred locations and physical conditions for learning. Some like it hot, some like it cold. The amount of light, background noise, and mobility permitted while learning are relevant factors to consider.

Here are three typical examples of differing learning styles.

♦ Andrew Soltise, a new sales representative in pharmaceuticals headquartered in Minneapolis, found himself sinking fast in the plethora of technical information provided by his company, and had difficulty keeping up with data on competitors' products.

♦ Barbara Paar, an attorney in St. Louis, was struggling to master a new word-processing program using legal lingo. "I felt mired in details in the manual," she explained. "I couldn't really get hold of the big picture, so all those details kept slipping away."

♦ Nicholas Naritz, a New York editor for an apparel-industry trade magazine, wanted to bone up on everything French—language, popular culture, trends in business—for an upcoming trip to Europe. But he felt uneasy at the "scraps of knowledge" he was accumulating, as he put it, from an assortment of books he had bought.

Variety's the very spice of life,
That gives it all its flavor.

WILLIAM COWPER

Andrew's problem was caused by a different aspect of his learning style from Barbara's. He had fallen into the habit of doing his technical reading in the evening, after his day of calling on doctors and pharmacies. But Andrew quickly discovered from the first exercise you'll be doing that he is a *lark*, not an *owl*—he learns best first thing in the morning, not late at night. When he swiveled his schedule around to get up an hour earlier in the morning, do his reading before breakfast, and just relax in the evening, he had no trouble in keeping current.

Another simple exercise you will do below revealed that Barbara prefers to learn "from the top down" rather than "from the bottom up." Her problems were readily solved when she called the manufacturer's 800 number, explained the situation, and was referred to a commercially available *alternate* manual, which explained the whole system in the top-down way Barbara prefers.

Nicholas's problem, too, derived from his preferred way of learning. He discovered from the brain-dominance exercise you will do that the way he likes to learn is to absorb the spirit of a field by talking with people in it. That's how he'd become so knowledgeable about the apparel business, on which there was little to read and study. So he found a more satisfying way to learn all about France. He put away his books and magazines and started going to evening events at the Alliance Française.

"I picked up what I needed to know, just by osmosis," he reported.

What does this mean for your learning? It reflects the simple truth that you can make your learning more productive by capitalizing on your personal learning style. Like these three typical learners, you can make your learning easier and more fun by discovering *how* you like to learn—and then adjusting things so that you learn that way.

In this chapter, you'll explore four important aspects of your personal learning style. The purpose of the exercises is to become more aware of how you like to learn. (As you go along, you might find it useful to make notes on each exercise in your learning log for use later in the chapter, when you put them all together to discover your personal learning profile.) Then, at the end of this chapter, you'll see how you can readily arrange to learn in the style best suited for you.

We all have times when we think more effectively, and times when we should not be thinking at all.

DANIEL COHEN

TEST 1: YOUR PEAK AND VALLEY LEARNING TIMES

Everyone has a favorite time of day. For some of us it's the early evening, when we are unwinding from work and are eager for the night's activities; we feel more alive and capable, ready to dance until midnight. For others, it's that quiet period at dawn, when few people are up and the day seems fresh and new. A whole new field within psychology, *chronopsychology,* is devoted to researching the patterns of time and energy for each person.

It is now firmly established that each of us is mentally alert and motivated at certain times during the day. Larks seem to wake up singing, mentally speaking, while owls take hours to warm up and may not reach their peak until late afternoon or evening.

Remember that one of Andrew's problems, as we mentioned above, was that his peak learning time came during the early hours of the day, just when he hit the office. But although this was the best time for him to be using his brain, he was beset by distractions. By realizing what was happening and planning around it, he dramatically improved his efficiency.

You obtain three benefits to knowing your own peak and valley times for learning and adjusting your learning efforts accordingly.

1. You will enjoy your learning more when you feel in the mood for it.
2. You will learn faster and more naturally, because you will not be fighting resistance, fatigue, and discomfort.
3. You will make better use of your "low" times by doing things other than trying to learn.

This exercise will enable you to determine your time preference in learning.

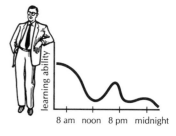

◆ ◆ ◆ ◆

Your Best and Worst of Times

The following questions will help you to sharpen your sense of what time of day you learn best. You may already be generally aware of your preferences, but these simple questions will help spur you on to act on them. The questions were developed by Professor Rita Dunn of St. John's University, Jamaica, New York. Answer *true* or *false* to each question.

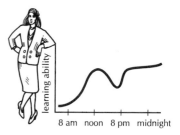

I dislike getting up in the morning. _____

I dislike going to sleep at night. _____

I wish I could sleep all morning. _____

I stay awake for a long time after I get into bed. _____

I feel wide awake only after 10:00 in the morning. _____

If I stay up late at night, I get too sleepy to remember anything. _____

I usually feel a *low* after lunch. _____

When I have a task requiring concentration, I like to get up early in the morning to do it. _____

I'd rather do those tasks requiring concentration in the afternoon. _____

I usually start the tasks that require the most concentration after dinner. _____

I could stay up all night. _____

I wish I didn't have to go to work before noon. _____

I wish I could stay home during the day and go to work at night. _____

I like going to work in the morning. _____

I can remember things best when I concentrate on them

    in the morning. _____

    at lunchtime. _____

    in the afternoon. _____

    before dinner. _____

    after dinner. _____

    late at night. _____

Carpe diem. (Seize the day.)

HORACE

◆ ◆ ◆ ◆

Your answers should provide a map of how you prefer to spend your mental energy over the course of the day. To interpret your answers, check whether you answered *true* or *false* for most of the questions that point to a single time of day: morning, noon, afternoon, evening, or night. That will be the period during which you feel that you either work your best or at your worst.

How can you use these results? There are two simple guidelines for Peak Learning that will give your mind an opportunity to work at its optimum.

First, seize your highs. Know when your mind is most likely to click into high gear, and prearrange your schedule whenever possible so that you are free to use it undisturbed during that period. Change appointments and hold phone calls to take advantage of the times when your brain does its best thinking.

Second, shut down before you run out of gas. Know when your mind is *least* likely to be ready for action, and plan ahead to do other useful or enjoyable activities at those times, such as socializing, routine work, or relaxing.

More specifically, if you have discovered that you are a morning person, you can enhance your learning by getting up an hour or so earlier than usual. Starting the day with some fast, pleasant learning will give you a good feeling of having met some of your own needs before you move into your daily work. It will also give you grist for thinking during *down times* about what you learned that morning.

On the other hand, if you found that you are an owl, you can make the most of the late hours each day. Think of your learning as the personal reward you've earned by putting in your daily round of work. Take a close look at your late afternoon and evening hours. How would you feel about targeting a specific piece of reading, thinking, problem solving, mental rehearsal, creating, or planning (all learning activities) for your commute home from work? If you know beforehand what you want to accomplish, you can have just what you need right at hand on the bus or train (or perhaps a cassette ready in the car). Instead of just nodding off or filling the time with the evening tabloid, you can get your second wind with something you really care about. And by the time you get home, some of the less rewarding TV viewing may not look as attractive as another half-hour or hour devoted to your favorite subject, whether it's reading further or making notes in your learning log. The result will be some fresh food for thought, to be integrated by your mind while you sleep. I guarantee you'll wake up in the morning with a feeling of accomplishment. Often, you're likely to wake up with some fresh ideas of your own about what you were learning.

TEST 2: DO YOU LEARN BOTTOM UP OR TOP DOWN?

Here's how Carolyn likes to learn something: Once she has determined what her final result should be—developing a personal accounting system, for example—she plans out what she needs to do to reach it. She lists the information she needs to keep track of and considers the ways she might sort receipts, create ledger books, or whatever. She might decide to investigate computer programs that will do the job for her, or she

The scientist atomizes, someone must synthesize; the scientist withdraws, someone must draw together. The scientist particularizes, someone must universalize.

JOHN FOWLES

might consider taking a basic accounting course from a local business college. But her first step is planning her campaign.

Joe learns differently. When he wants to master a new style of cooking, for example, he steers clear of courses and plans. Instead he goes to restaurants, talks to the waiters or cooks, and tastes a variety of dishes. Then he picks up a cookbook and, after a few experiments, gains a sense of what tastes together and how much preparation is needed. That's when he starts improvising his own recipes.

The following exercise, developed by David Lewis and James Greene of the Mind Potential Study Group in London, will reveal a basic aspect of your personal learning style. You will find out whether you prefer to tackle new topics from the bottom up, laying a solid foundation first, or from the top down, gaining an overall perspective before filling in the details. Then you will learn how to use this knowledge to design your approach to any learning task.

◆ ◆ ◆ ◆

Are You a Grouper or a Stringer?

Check the phrase in each pair that corresponds more closely to your preferred approach to learning. There are no right or wrongs ways to complete these statements; they're designed simply to distinguish your preferences.

When studying one unfamiliar subject, you
_____ (a) prefer to gather information from diverse topic areas.
_____ (b) prefer to focus on one topic.

You would rather
_____ (a) know a little about a great many subjects.
_____ (b) become an expert on just one subject.

When studying from a textbook, you
_____ (a) skip ahead and read chapters of special interest out of sequence.
_____ (b) work systematically from one chapter to the next, not moving on until you have understood earlier material.

When asking people for information about some subject of interest, you

____ (a) tend to ask broad questions that call for rather general answers.

____ (b) tend to ask narrow questions that demand specific answers.

When browsing in a library or bookstore, you

____ (a) roam around looking at books on many different subjects.

____ (b) stay more or less in one place, looking at books on just a couple of subjects.

You are best at remembering

____ (a) general principles.

____ (b) specific facts.

When performing some tasks, you

____ (a) like to have background information not strictly related to the work.

____ (b) prefer to concentrate only on strictly relevant information.

You think that educators should

____ (a) give students exposure to a wide range of subjects in college.

____ (b) ensure that students mainly acquire in-depth knowledge related to their specialties.

When on vacation, you would rather

____ (a) spend a short amount of time in several places.

____ (b) stay in one place the whole time and get to know it well.

When learning something, you would rather

____ (a) follow general guidelines.

____ (b) work with a detailed plan of action.

Do you agree that, in addition to specialized knowledge, a person should know some math, art, physics, literature, psychology, politics, languages, biology, history, and medicine? (If you think people should study four or more of these subjects, score an "a" on this question.)

Now total all the a and b answers.

If you scored six or more a's on the test, you are a *grouper;* if you scored six or more b's, you are a *stringer.* If your a's and b's were close to equal, you find both approaches congenial and can choose the one that better fits the subject at hand.

The higher your total of either a's or b's, the more specialized your learning style is. The descriptions below should illustrate your learning methods closely and clarify how you might follow a grouper or a stringer strategy.

◆　◆　◆　◆

GROUPER

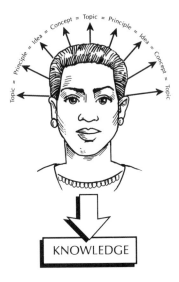

KNOWLEDGE

Groupers. You prefer to take a broad view of any subject under study. You like to search out general principles rather than meticulous details and to relate one topic to as many other areas of knowledge as possible. You are quick to find relationships and to draw parallels among different areas of study.

Because of this learning style, groupers learn most easily and effectively in unstructured situations and do less well if knowledge is presented according to some rigid plan. Because you are able to bring together a wide range of information, you are likely to prove more successful than stringers when an eclectic approach is used.

Very little current teaching is presented in this way. Lesson plans, textbooks, and training schemes, whether in the factory, university, or classroom, are usually designed in a systematic, step-by-step manner that favors stringers. This approach works to the disadvantage of groupers, who prefer to come to grips with overall principles before getting down to the finer details of a topic.

Jump right into the subject you want to study. Go to the library and skim through several books and magazines that look interesting. Feel free to explore several aspects or topics simultaneously. Don't worry about not being systematic, of not mastering the fundamentals first in order to have a solid foundation. You're not building a house; you're creating a rich configuration of facts and concepts that your mind will delight in connecting.

As a grouper, you should keep an eye open for *big ideas, basic concepts,* and *organizing principles.* But as you do this, keep a separate list of the detailed parts of the subject that you will want to master later. This is a necessary aspect of learning, although you can keep it on the back burner when you're starting out. As long as you have your list, you're not likely to get anxious about having too many principles but not enough practical techniques.

Stringers. A systematic, methodical approach best suits you, because you learn most successfully by mastering specific details before moving to more general concepts.

Your best approach is to establish a series of clearly defined goals that allow knowledge to be accumulated gradually. Only facts directly related to the topic under study should be considered, while less relevant information, no matter how interesting, can temporarily be ignored. Stringers tend to achieve good grades in college, because the highly structured nature of most academic work favors their particular style of learning.

Devote the initial portion of your time to developing a firmly structured plan with which you feel comfortable. Don't worry about taking all the time you need with this: you will more than make up for it once you get started, because you will have the confidence of a detailed road map for your study.

Consult the tables of contents of several good books in your field of study, so that you can define the scope and priorities in that field. Having acquired a rough map of the entire terrain, select those topics you want to master and arrange them in a sensible order.

As a stringer, you should learn about each subtopic fully before proceeding to the next. You will thrive on a feeling of mastery of each segment and on the cumulative sense of building solidly on the subject as a whole.

What should you do if a learning situation prevents you from using your preferred style? You may be a grouper who prefers to start with the big picture but are in a language course in which you're required to master vocabulary, word by word by word. Or suppose you're a stringer looking for a clear and methodical introduction to art, but your course takes lots of field trips to museums to view and discuss various paintings from many time periods. There are four things you can do.

First, check out whether an alternative arrangement can be made for learning what you want to learn. From our experience in school and college we are all conditioned to accept too readily that the class, course, or program we're in is not something we can control. But as an adult who's in the market for learning, you are much freer to pick and choose. Moreover,

STRINGER

KNOWLEDGE

there's almost always a range of providers—people and institutions eager to serve learners whose needs diverge from the conventional. If the result will be a more rewarding experience, it may well be worth a few hours devoted to a search for a more congenial learning situation.

If an alternative is simply not available, you can bring your preferred style into play by *wrapping* it around the less congenial tasks. In the case of art, you can indulge your strong need for a logical learning style by reading an entrancing book on the kind of artworks you are studying. Dealing with the same subject in an organized, verbal, and analytic way will enliven and inform your experience with the visual aspects. Or you can seek alternative ways to learn. In the case of foreign-language vocabulary, you can turn loose your skills at association and imagination to make up all sorts of connections between the words, such as sound associations (*frère* and *fair* or *there*). The holistic methods popularized in Sheila Ostrander and Lynn Schroeder's book *Superlearning* offer a way of mastering languages that is much more appealing to the grouper than word-by-word study.

Finally, if you find yourself dealing with learning tasks that call for a style with which you are not comfortable, recognize that fact and realize that you'll need to use some of the other Peak Learning techniques to overcome your resistance. Find additional ways to get excited about the subject, practice with friends, review what you want to derive from the learning situation, and so forth.

A Gestalt is a figure or pattern which can be distinguished against the background or field of perception. . . . But the term . . . carries stronger connotations of significance and meaning [and] applies whenever a significant pattern or construct (the "figure") emerges against the background scene or noise (the "ground").

OXFORD COMPANION
TO THE MIND

TEST 3: WHERE ARE YOU LOCATED IN THE FOUR LEARNING QUADRANTS?

Now that you've explored your preference for the basic grouper and stringer styles, you're ready to dig a little deeper. You also have preferences for dealing with facts or feelings, using logic or imagination, and thinking things through yourself or working with other people. This next exercise will make you more aware of these preferences.

The exercise is based on the pioneering work of Ned Herrmann, whose Herrmann Brain Dominance Instrument (HBDI) is one of the chief tools used by those interested in adapting learning to people's styles of thinking. Herrmann is a living example of the benefits of becoming aware of your brain's preferences and potential. At Cornell, he double-majored in physics and music. Later, while directing Management Education at General Electric, he became a successful sculptor and painter. Today Herrmann is chairman of the Whole Brain Corporation, which offers workshops on the brain and creativity to top corporations.

Herrmann has expressed his personal credo in a colorful book, *The Creative Brain,* in which he tells the story of how the idea of stylistic quadrants first came to him. It's a vivid example of how one's preferred ways of knowing can lead to fresh ideas. Herrmann had been intrigued by both Roger Sperry's work with two different brain-hemisphere styles and Paul MacLean's theory of the three-level brain, both of which were reviewed in Chapter Two.

Herrmann administered a homemade test to fellow workers to see whether he could correlate their preference in learning with the idea of brain-hemisphere dominance. The responses seemed to group themselves into four categories, not two as he'd anticipated. Then, while driving home from work one day, he combined his visual images of the two theories and had this experience.

> Eureka! There, suddenly, was the connecting link I had been searching for! . . . The limbic system was also divided into two separated halves, and also endowed with a cortex capable of thinking, and also connected by a commissure—just like the cerebral hemispheres. Instead of there being *two* parts of the specialized brain, there were *four*—the number of clusters the data had been showing! . . .
>
> So, what I had been calling left brain, would now become the *left cerebral hemisphere.* What was the right brain, now became the *right cerebral hemisphere.* What had been left center, would now be *left limbic,* and right center was now *right limbic.*
>
> The whole idea unfolded with such speed and intensity that it blotted out conscious awareness of everything else. I

Again and again, step by step, intuition opens the doors that lead to man's designing.

R. BUCKMINSTER FULLER

93

discovered after the image of this new model had taken form in my mind that my exit had gone by some time ago. The last ten miles had been a total blank!

Note how Herrmann's preference for visual ways of thinking led him to a spatial image, which sparked the new idea. Of course, he followed up on his insight by using his analytical and verbal skills to delineate how the quadrants might work. The moral, notes Herrmann, is that if we want to learn more creatively, "we need to learn to trust our non-verbal right brain, to follow our hunches, and to follow them up with careful, highly focused left-brain verification."

Before I explain the four learning styles Herrmann discovered, try the following exercise.

♦ ♦ ♦ ♦

Four Quadrants for Learning

Start by picking three learning areas. One might be your favorite school subject, the one you had the most fun with. Try to find another that was different—perhaps the subject you *hated* most. The third should be a subject you are currently starting to learn or one that you've had an intention to begin for some time.

Now, read the following descriptions of four learners' styles and decide *which one was (or would have been, for the subject you hated) closest to your most comfortable way of learning the subject*. Give that description the number 1. Give the one you like *least* a 3. Of the two styles remaining, decide which one might be slightly more enjoyable for you and number it 2. Do this for all three learning areas on your list.

Remember, there are no wrong answers here—all four styles are equally valid. Likewise, don't feel you have to be consistent; if one style seems better for one area but not as comfortable for another, do not give it the same number in both cases.

Learning Area

Style	1	2	3
A			
B			
C			
D			

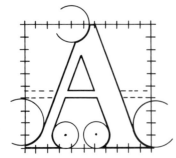

STYLE A: The essence of any subject is a hard core of solid data. Learning is built up logically on a foundation of specific knowledge. Whether you're learning history, architecture, or accounting, you need a logical, rational approach to get your facts straight. If you focus on verifiable facts on which everyone can agree, you can come up with more precise and efficient theories to clarify the situation.

STYLE B: I thrive on order. I feel most comfortable when someone who really *knows* has laid out what's to be learned, in sequence. Then I can tackle the details, knowing that I'm going to cover the whole subject in the right order. Why flop around reinventing the wheel, when an expert has been through it all before? Whether it's a textbook, a computer program, or a workshop—what I want is a well-planned, precise curriculum to work my way through.

STYLE C: What *is* learning, anyway, except *communication* among *people*?! Even reading a book alone is interesting primarily because you're in touch with another person, the author. My own ideal way to learn is simply to *talk* with others interested in the same subject, learning how they feel, and coming to understand better what the subject means to them. When I was in school my favorite kind of class was a free-wheeling discussion, or going out for coffee afterward to discuss the lesson.

STYLE D: The underlying spirit of any subject is what's important to me. Once you grasp that, and really feel it with your whole being, learning becomes meaningful. That's obvious for fields like philosophy and art. But even in a field like business management, isn't the important thing the vision in people's minds? Are they simply pursuing profit or do they see profits as a way to make a contribution to society? Maybe they have a totally unexpected motive for what they do. When I study something, I want to stay open to turning the information upside down and looking at it in a brand-new way, rather than being spoon-fed specific techniques.

◆ ◆ ◆ ◆

Even if you had trouble deciding between two or more styles, the tentative order you put down is important.

Herrmann associates Style A with a "master of logic and reason." The A style is devoted to getting the facts, figuring problems out logically, stating things clearly and precisely, reducing complex issues to simple decisions, and generating new ways of doing things more efficiently. Someone who is strong in this style to the exclusion of all others, Herrmann thinks, is likely to distrust ambiguity, intuition, and emotion.

Style B types are similar to A but place more reliance on what has already worked, on getting all the details right, and on procedure, order, and stability. They are more involved in answers and actions—doing things on time and on schedule—than on the questions and theories an A wants to analyze. Both are more verbal than emotional or intuitive.

Style C is primarily sensitive to moods, atmospheres, and attitudes. There is a greater awareness of things as a body process, rather than as visual or verbal information. There is a strong interest in people and communication; logic and theory take second place to feeling and experience.

Style D is where Herrmann finds the most emphasis on originality, ambiguity, and surprise, on the use of metaphor and the ability to picture things in preference to verbalizing them clearly. Style D types thrive on confusion and chaos, enjoying the challenge of many possibilities, and resist coming to final conclusions.

As Herrmann points out, these four styles are exaggerated. It is hard to find someone who uses only one of the four all the time. Even if all of your 1s, 2s, and 3s are on the same styles for all three subjects, your most favored learning style for all kinds of occasions is likely to be a blend of the styles you marked 1 and 2. On the other hand, if the numbers you assigned vary among different styles, you probably have a more flexible approach to learning. Most frequently we find ourselves strong in more than one of these styles and naturally pick the one that's appropriate to a given learning situation.

Your awareness of which of these styles feels most comfortable will enable you to adjust the conditions of your learning to make it more congenial. In much the same way as the grouper–stringer approaches, recognizing that you have a preferred approach allows you to seek learning situations in which that approach works best. Alternatively, you can choose a less comfortable style in order to stretch your learning muscles. And, when you can't find a useful match between what you want to learn and the style in which you'd be most comfortable learning it, you can use your preferred style at the same time. You might experiment with forming an intuitive picture of some subject while building and discarding several logical systems, or you might discuss the views of various authorities in conversation with other students.

Recall Nicholas Naritz, one of the learners mentioned near the start of this chapter. He was boning up on everything French but finding the experience frustrating, because he was trying to learn in Style A. Once he switched from trying to pick up facts from printed sources to plunging himself into a situation with other people (Style C), in which he could absorb the spirit of the subject (Style D), his learning was greatly enhanced.

TEST 4: WHAT ARE YOUR PERSONAL INTELLIGENCES?

YOUR SEVEN
INTELLIGENCES

Most people still believe that their capacity to learn is determined by intelligence. We all recall having our IQ taken at some point in our childhood, and most of us know the results. The IQ test was supposed to measure your capacity to learn and therefore to predict your success in school. However, contemporary psychologists have debunked this whole idea of a single capacity called intelligence. You have not one, but at least *seven* intelligences—and you can use most of them to enhance your learning.

Each intelligence in this sense is a particular kind of learning talent that seems to come easily. One person may excel at the eye–hand coordination of sports, playing a musical instrument, or solving math problems; another might find it easy to empathize with other's needs, build a birdhouse, or learn a language. The precise combination of skills can arise from a combination of talent and environmental factors.

The best guide to your multiple intelligences is *Frames of Mind* by Harvard psychologist Howard Gardner. Gardner's seven intelligences are:

1. Linguistic intelligence
2. Logical-mathematical intelligence
3. Spatial intelligence
4. Musical intelligence
5. Bodily-kinesthetic intelligence

6. Intrapersonal intelligence (knowing yourself)
7. Interpersonal intelligence (knowing other people)

Most of us have a pretty good idea of which of these intelligences we've cultivated the most and in which we feel strong. As a reminder, however, here's a simple exercise that will pinpoint some of your strengths.

♦ ♦ ♦ ♦

Which Are Your Strong Intelligences?

Circle the numbers of those descriptions that you feel apply to you.

1. You easily remember nice turns of phrase or memorable quotes and use them deftly in conversation.
2. You sense quickly when someone you are with is troubled about something.
3. You are fascinated by scientific and philosophical questions like "When did time begin?"
4. You can find your way around a new area or neighborhood very quickly.
5. You are regarded as quite graceful and rarely feel awkward in your movements.
6. You can sing on key.
7. You regularly read the science pages of your newspaper and look at magazines on science or technology.
8. You note other people's errors in using words or grammar, even if you don't correct them.
9. You often can figure out how something works or how to fix something that's broken, without asking for help.
10. You can readily imagine how other people play the roles they do in their work or families and imaginatively see yourself in their roles.
11. You can remember in detail the layout and landmarks of places you've visited on vacations.
12. You enjoy music and have favorite performers.
13. You like to draw.
14. You dance well.

15. You organize things in your kitchen, bathroom, and at your desk according to categories and in patterns.

16. You feel confident in interpreting what other people do in terms of what they are feeling.

17. You like to tell stories and are considered a good story-teller.

18. You sometimes enjoy different sounds in your environment.

19. When you meet new people, you often make connections between their characteristics and those of other acquaintances.

20. You feel you have a keen sense of what you can and can't do.

This above all: to thine own self be true.

WILLIAM SHAKESPEARE

If *all three* of any of the following trios applies to you, you probably are strong in that intelligence, even if you haven't cultivated it.

Questions 1, 8, and 17: linguistic intelligence

Questions 6, 12, and 18: musical intelligence

Questions 3, 7, and 15: logical-mathematical intelligence

Questions 4, 11, and 13: spatial intelligence

Questions 5, 9, and 14: bodily-kinesthetic intelligence

Questions 10, 16, and 20: intrapersonal intelligence (knowing yourself)

Questions 2, 10, and 19: intrapersonal intelligence (knowing others)

◆　◆　◆　◆

Whatever your strongest intelligences might be, by selecting among various methods you can assemble a repertoire of ways to learn that capitalize on them. By focusing your learning through your best areas you can make it easier, more rewarding, and more fun. You can build up skills without expecting too much from yourself by challenging yourself to learn something in an unfamiliar way; and by combining skills from as many intelligences as possible, you can learn in a way that is more complete and involving.

Whatever your thinking style, keep in mind that different does not mean defective. . . . Adapt tasks to your way of thinking and take on jobs that can best be addressed by your style.

ROBERT AND SUSAN
BRAMSON

Suppose you have a strong spatial intelligence and you're setting out on a study of philosophy. How might you link your learning with your predilection for visual forms, shapes, and patterns?

First, you might seek out the *facts* of the philosophers by obtaining photos of them and their habitats. Find films and videos such as Edward de Bono's series *Great Thinkers,* which feature mock interviews with historical philosophers, or contemporary videotapes of interviews with noted scholars.

You might also try to make diagrams about what you're learning, using varied colors for the aspects of each master's thoughts. The metaphor of vision as a symbol for insight and understanding will be of particular interest as you read, and you will come across some books that present philosophical ideas visually, such as *Maps of the Mind* by Charles Hampden-Turner. You will certainly want to create some fresh visual images of your own that portray the philosophers, problems, principles, or systems you are studying. A diagram comparing Plato to Aristotle, for instance, would be wonderfully illuminating.

DRAWING YOUR PROFILE

Now that we've explored several concepts of personal learning style, you are ready to bring your findings together in your first sketch of yourself as a learner. You will have fun filling out this personal learning-style profile based on the insights you have gained into the ways your mind works best.

Don't worry if your answers don't entirely satisfy you at this point; this exercise is an initial draft. You'll recall seeing in crime films how a police artist composes a portrait of a suspect from descriptions by victims. The first sketch is just a rough approximation, but only after seeing it can the victim say, "No, the nose is wrong. It was much shorter" and "You've got the eyes just right, but the eyebrows were bushier." That's the purpose of this first draft of your personal learning profile. Only by getting *something* down in words can you begin to say, "Yes, I do like to get the overall picture first. But I also like to know that there's a step-by-step way to go through the materials if I want to."

◆ ◆ ◆ ◆

Personal Learning-Style Profile

In your learning log, complete each of the sentences below, referring back to your findings from the previous exercises in this chapter. For example, your completed version of the second item might read: "I'm a stringer. I like to learn from the bottom up. I like to focus on solid facts about a new field or topic. When learning about managing for results last year, for example, I recall being bored by the theoretical articles and looking for case studies and concrete instances to begin with."

Continue in this way to complete each of the items. You should return to this profile periodically as you work your way through the book. You will continue to refine this first sketch, and as you do so it will become increasingly useful in planning your learning and diagnosing any problems you find.

1. *Drawing on your responses to the "Your Best and Worst of Times" exercise:*

   My best time for learning is _____, so I feel best when I can schedule my learning times _____.

2. *Drawing on your response to the "Bottom-up" or "Top-down" exercise:*

   I'm a (grouper/stringer/combination). I like to learn (bottom-up/top-down), so my preference is to approach a new subject _____.

3. *Drawing on your responses to the "Four Quadrants" exercise:*
   I like generally to learn through (facts/structure/people/feelings), so my preference is to approach a new subject

   _____.

4. *Drawing on your responses to the "Which Are Your Strong Intelligences" exercise:*

   My two strongest intelligences are _____, so I enjoy learning most when it involves _____.

◆ ◆ ◆ ◆

MATCHING YOUR STYLE AND
LEARNING RESOURCES

*The gifts of nature are
infinite in their variety, and
mind differs from mind
almost as much as body
from body.*

QUINTILIAN

Whatever you want to learn, you will be using certain resources. A resource in this sense is anything that feeds or provides the opportunity for your learning. The major resources from which we learn most things are:

- Printed matter, such as books, articles, and papers
- Experiences, particularly ones especially designed for learning, such as simulations, study or action groups, and conferences
- Media: TV, films, audio and videotapes, slides, and graphics
- Nature: Your own investigation of some aspect of your environment
- Other people, especially in situations designed to foster learning, such as lectures, classes, seminars, and workshops

Your preference among these, for any given kind of learning, is a crucial dimension of your learning style. If you can arrange for your learning to involve the resource—the mode or situation—that you prefer, you obviously will find the experience more pleasant and more productive.

Perhaps the most important dimension here is whether you prefer to learn on your own or with other people. Fortunately, it's also one of the easiest to ascertain, because you probably have a strong intuitive sense of your preference. Did you seek out others to study with in school? Do you like to go to classes in part because of other people there? Do you feel greatly deprived if you're reading a fascinating book and have no one to talk with about it? Obviously, if your answers were affirmative, you thrive on companionship in learning.

On the other hand, perhaps you relish exploring a new subject by yourself. Do you feel that the presence of other students in a class is likely to slow down your progress or distract from the things you'd like to learn most? Feelings like this suggest that, for you, learning can very satisfactorily be a solo flight with you at the controls.

There are ways to indulge your preference in either case. If companionship is what you want, there are ways to link up with other learners that are more flexible than having to sign up for a class. If you prefer to go it alone, there are new media and resources that can enrich your adventure in learning.

The following exercise has two purposes: first, to illustrate the broad range of resources you can apply to almost any learning goal; and second, to enhance your awareness of your own preferred learning resources.

◆ ◆ ◆ ◆

Matching Learning Resources and Personal Style

Suppose you want to learn more about endangered species. Below is a list of things you can do, each of them resulting in significant learning about this subject. Which *three* would you feel most comfortable with?

1. Reading a book or two on the subject
2. Participating in a simulation that models the administrative process of getting a species declared protected
3. Attending a series of lectures
4. Interviewing knowledgeable people in the field
5. Viewing videotapes or films
6. Visiting a game preserve, taking pictures, and acquiring relevant materials
7. Writing letters soliciting information and viewpoints on the subject from a range of interested people
8. Writing a paper, article, or speech on the subject, based on any one of the above experiences
9. Role-playing to dramatize the contrasting attitudes different people have about the problem
10. Joining a six-person task force to help plan a local campaign on behalf of an endangered creature
11. Working on your own to design a public information campaign that would spread the word about the general problem and solicit support for a nationally active organization in this field
12. Interning for a week with an zoologist at a nearby university

103

13. Determining what questions to ask on a survey of community attitudes toward the subject

♦ ♦ ♦ ♦

The person who seeks an education must involve himself in discovering the meaning of his own life and the relation between who he is and what he might become. Without that vision of a personal future and a hard look at the reality of one's own situation, the ultimate purpose of education itself— that is, to grow, to change, to liberate oneself—is almost impossible to achieve.

HAROLD TAYLOR

LEARNING MORE ABOUT YOUR LEARNING STYLE

If you would like to go even further in exploring your mind's way of working at its best, there are several approaches you can take.

The easiest and most useful is to make notes regularly on your learning style, along with your other ideas, in your learning log. You can distinguish these notes about your learning *process* by writing them in a distinctive color or enclosing them in a box or balloon. Once you get into this habit, you'll find that you quickly become quite sensitive to your distinctive kinds of learning behavior. Here are some typical notes my students put in their learning logs about their own learning processes.

The third hour after waking up in the morning is the best one for me. My two cups of coffee have taken effect, my head is cleared up and working in top form. But that's also the time I arrive at the office, and people start distracting me. Maybe for one or two days a week I could warn people away, tell them I have a deadline or something. I know I'd be able to review piles of materials then, much more efficiently than any other time.

Looking up into the sky is a great relaxer after I've been poring over a book. My eyes feel refreshed just from a couple of minutes of tracing clouds.

Discovered I'm the only one in our tennis class that's reading an instructional book outside of class. Guess I just like to get it put in words too.

The division I've moved into is a whole different ball game, and no one's taking the time to explain the rules. This reminds me of what happened when I first came to the company three years ago. But this time, I realize, I know what's wrong. At this point, I'm at a low point on the learning curve, so I've got to be wary while I wait for the upswing as people get accustomed to seeing me around and let their hair down. I'll catch on just by hanging around.

The second way you can learn more about your learning style is by taking workshops. These usually use one of the major learning-style tests in a group setting, with individual counseling about your own style. Among the learning experts who regularly offer such workshops in many cities around the country are Don Lofland, Rita and Kenneth Dunn, Bernice McCarthy, Elizabeth Ruedy, and proponents of such systems as the Myers-Briggs Type Indicator.

There is no book specifically on adults' learning styles. The best treatment of the subject you can read is *In Their Own Way*, by Thomas Armstrong, which focuses on discovering and encouraging children's personal learning styles but is well worth reading for its application to adults.

You now have a sense of how to capitalize on your preferred style to make your learning more enjoyable and efficient. You can organize materials and structure situations to fit your best way of learning; fine-tune your timing to capture your hours of maximum receptivity; and choose learning experiences that match your tastes.

Equally important, however, you can also flex your style by bringing into play those modes of learning that you now use least or find least congenial. If your primary intelligences are linguistic and spatial, you might adventurously tackle an appealing learning project that has a mathematical or musical flavor. If you're a grouper, you can experiment with a stringer approach to a project. If you're a morning person, you might stay late at the office one night and see whether there are tasks you can actually do more effectively during those hours. If you customarily take a class when you want to learn something, try organizing your own learning project instead.

But challenge yourself by occasionally trying something that doesn't come naturally. Everyone can stretch his mind, and it's worth a little effort to learn new thinking strategies.

ROBERT AND SUSAN BRAMSON

105

There are three advantages to experimenting with flexing your style. First, some subjects and situations strongly demand one or another style. When that happens, you are at a disadvantage if you can't switch into that mode and operate, if not at your maximum, at least effectively. One example is academic courses, which generally require you to take a stringer approach. Second, you may discover that an alternative approach actually works surprisingly well. Perhaps you have never really given it a try only because some early experiences convinced you that you weren't successful with that approach. All of us have neglected capacities of this kind. Finding yours can be a revelation and add a strong note to your intellectual repertoire. Thousands of people who "knew" they couldn't possibly draw or write—two powerful and gratifying ways of learning—have discovered that they can from two earlier books in this series, *Drawing on the Right Side of the Brain,* by Betty Edwards, and *Writing the Natural Way,* by Gabriele Rico. And third, practice with different learning styles will greatly improve your capacity to communicate with other people who operate in those styles.

Beyond applying it to your own learning needs, you may find your new awareness of learning styles especially useful with children, if you are a parent or a teacher, and in your career. In both of these areas, chronic problems can be solved through this approach.

In the world of work there is widening recognition of the need to capitalize on different learning styles within organizations. According to Dudley Lynch, in *Your High Performance Business Brain,* "we can use this powerful new way of understanding people to design better organizations, . . . do a more effective and productive job of hiring and placing people, and to frame our management messages so that they can penetrate the natural filters of the mind." That means you should be able to measure how well your learning style fits the tasks that compose your present job. You should also be able to recognize the styles of others, which will make for better communications.

In my workshop we illustrate this by forming a *hemispheric circle.* All the participants seat themselves in a semicircle so that each person's position reflects his or her degree of preference for either the stringer or the grouper style of learning. Those on the left side of the semicircle prefer to learn in a step-by-step, analytical, systematic way; those on the right prefer a holistic, top-down, big-picture approach. Then, we talk about how these two kinds of people can best explain things to each other or convey new information.

"Hold on, now," one of the left-side folks will say. "I'd really prefer it if you could start out by giving me some basic examples of what you're talking about. You seem to be all over the map instead of starting with first things first." But the next minute someone from the right side will complain, "Hey, I can't see the forest for all those trees you're throwing at me. Could we wrench ourselves up out of the details and get an overview of the subject? What's the point? Where are we headed?"

Often partnerships are profitably forged out of two individuals who complement each other's styles. In my workshops we often see two people who work closely together take seats on opposite ends of the hemispheric circle. In one recent case, a couple in the fashion business found themselves in those places; it turned out that one of them was the idea person and the other, the financial wizard. Together they made a dynamic duo indeed.

Creating teams to work together or to solve problems is an important area in which an awareness of styles can assure greater success. Some highly technical problems call for team members who all share the same way of processing information, seeking new facts, interpreting evidence, and coming to conclusions. A narrow fact-finding or problem-solving assignment, such as determining how to expedite the passage of orders through the billing department, might be such a situation. In other situations, however, your success may depend on having the right mix of styles. You may need one or two people who take the top-down, broad view together with others who like to work systematically and logically. Creating a plan for the next year's activities would be a task that could benefit from this mix of approaches.

Another area in which styles of learning and thinking can crucially affect the success of individuals or organizations is

Today's successful managers can't spend valuable time in unproductive seminars that are 60 percent old stuff or sit around waiting for someone to offer just the right course. Only those who can design their own learning can cope with constant change.

PAUL GUGLIEMINO

boss–employee relations. This typical situation occurs every day in business and industry: a supervisor will complain that a new worker can't seem to learn a routine task. When the suggestion is made that the newcomer might learn it if shown it move by move, the supervisor—clearly a grouper rather than a stringer—expresses dismay, exclaiming, "I *never* give instructions that way. It would be insulting and patronizing—*anyone* can pick it up if they really want to."

Such conflict based on differences in style can extend right up to the executive suite. In their book *Type Talk*, management consultants Otto Kroeger and Janet Thuesen tell how they helped straighten out troubled organizations by analyzing the disparities among the styles of the managers and executives involved. They even suggest developing a version of the organization chart in which each of the key individuals is identified not by his or her title, but by his or her learning style!

In this chapter you have learned how *you* like to learn. You've discovered how your brain prefers to process new material, which modes and media of instruction suit you best, which times are best for you, and how to flex your style. You have acquired an awareness of yourself as a learner, which is the first prerequisite of Peak Learning. Now you can make the best use of the powerful techniques and strategies that will make Peak Learning happen for you.

VI

Improving Your Learning, Reading, and Memory Skills

How can you enhance your learning as you are doing it, day-to-day, minute-by-minute? What can you do before, during, and after learning to increase your enjoyment of the learning process and assure the maximum benefits from the time you spend learning?

The techniques you will learn now are more specific than the general strategies you learned in the last chapter, such as adapting your learning tasks to your personal style and choosing resources. Those strategies set the broad course of your learning, determining where you want to wind up and your general approach to getting there. The new techniques, on the other hand, are your specific *tools*—the compass, sexton, and depth gauge—with which you pilot your learning, steering your path just as an expert navigator conns a ship.

You may have been stopped by that word *pilot* at the end of the previous paragraph. It's not the image we usually apply to the activity of learning; the words that more readily come to mind are *absorb* and *acquire*. Yet I chose the word *pilot* carefully.

What is a good learner? It seems useful to think of him as someone with a certain set of skills. He knows how to formulate problems. He can identify the relevant resources . . . that are available in his environment. He is able to choose or create procedures and to evaluate his results. Beyond this, there is a set of higher skills, which we may call "meta-skills." Stated very loosely, they include the ability to know what he wants (or needs) to learn; the ability to see clearly the process *of his learning; and the ability to interact with others to help learn these meta-skills. Out of all this, he is able to create useful knowledge.*

MICHAEL ROSSMAN

As you use these techniques, you will indeed be in charge of your learning, steering your course as you go.

There are three categories with two techniques each. After you've had a little practice with them, you may choose the technique in each category that most appeals to you. You may also adopt the one that might be most apt for the kind of learning you are doing.

LEARNING TECHNIQUES

I. Before Learning

Pro-Active Reading, a technique to get exactly what you want from books and articles.

The *Vee-Heuristic* technique, to preview in your mind the key questions you want to answer in any learning situation.

II. While Learning

Mind-mapping, a technique that encourages the use of your natural mental associations to organize incoming information.

Probes, the kinds of questions you can formulate to become actively involved with your information by creatively anticipating where it is leading.

III. After Learning

Memory Improvement, techniques to store factual data in your memory more easily.

Instant Replay, a technique for deep recall and review of any experience to increase what you learn from it.

BEFORE LEARNING

A principle stressed throughout this book is that the decisions you make *before* you start to learn are crucial for your success.

Your choice of what you want to learn, which resources you want to use, when and where you learn best are all decisive for your effectiveness and enjoyment.

There are also some *specific* techniques you can use when you are just about to start learning something. The two I have found to be most generally useful are pro-active Reading, when you are going to learn from a book, and the Vee-heuristic technique, when you want to enhance your learning from some other kinds of experience.

PRO-ACTIVE READING

From our experiences in school, most of us have retained a passive posture toward books. We feel faintly guilty if we don't start on page one and read through to the end. If we decide to quit before finishing, we feel we haven't really read the book. Most important of all, we let the author's priorities and choices of what to emphasize take command of our attention—we hand over control of the learning experience to the author.

The computer is teaching us a better way to read books, quite different from the way most of us were taught in school. That way is *active, self-directed,* and *creative.* When we sit down at a computer, *we* are in charge. We access the information and procedures we want, choosing from a variety of menus or commands to accomplish our task. We go directly to what we want. We can look over a whole program or database before getting involved, to get a feel for its contents and procedures. We skip around from one part to another. We call up various areas of interest to see what they're like.

When we adapt this style to using books, they take on a different character. Instead of being conduits of data going one way—from author to reader—they become interactive resources for self-directed learning.

Of course, I don't mean to apply this to *War and Peace.* Reading a novel for pleasure *is* an entertaining experience presented by the author for our enjoyment—even if we often learn quite a bit from it anyway! But for the majority of books most of us use to gain information and understanding, this method of proactive reading is more appropriate than reading straight through from page one to the end. Instead of tamely following the author's interests in presenting his or her information, we can browse for the exact tidbits of information *we* need to learn for *our* goals.

The following exercise, developed by Professor Robert Smith of Northern Illinois University for his pioneering course in learning how to learn, will teach you to do this.

♦ ♦ ♦ ♦

Pro-Active Reading

You will need writing material and a nonfiction book that you are not familiar with. The book should have a dust jacket, a table of contents, some front matter (foreword, preface, introduction), and an index.

1. Turn to the inside front of the dust jacket and read what the publisher has to say about the book.
2. Turn to the back of the dust jacket and read what the publisher has to say about the author and his or her qualifications to write such a book.
3. Turn to the front matter (foreword, preface, introduction) and read the author's or editor's orientation to the book.
4. Turn to the table of contents and see how the author has organized the information into parts, chapters, or other subsections.
5. Leaf through the book, rapidly scanning or reading the occasional paragraph or heading that interests you. Try to get the feel of the book.
6. Put the book down and write three questions concerning matters you have become curious about as a result of this preliminary examination.
7. Next, review your first question and find in it a key word or phrase that you think might be in the index. Go to the index and look for the key word; if you draw a blank, try to come up with a synonym. If the synonym isn't there, see if the table of contents leads you to where the question can be answered.
8. Now turn to that part of the book that deals with your question and look for the answer. If the author refers to material

in other parts of the book, follow the leads until you have enough information relevant to your question.

9. Use the same procedure with your second and third questions.

Questions

1. How differently did you feel about using a book as a resource for learning from the way you usually feel about a book?

2. Is there any difference in the quality of the information you have gained?

◆ ◆ ◆ ◆

The key point of this exercise is discovering when you formulated your three questions. It wasn't after you had read the entire book, cover to cover. Instead, you did a preliminary *scan* of the contents. At that point, you could readily decide whether or not this particular book was going to be useful to you—that is, whether the author had something to say that was important for what *you* wanted to learn. If not, there was no need to go further with that book.

Amazingly enough, however, if you have even a general idea of what you want to learn, such a brief scan can stimulate more specific questions that the book should answer. Of course, there may well be more information in the book than those answers, but *you* decide how much more of what the author wants to present is relevant to your needs. Perhaps digging out the answers to those three questions leads to your decision to read the entire book. On the other hand, those three answers may be all you need from that book and you can go on to your next learning resource.

How you choose to use the book is up to you. As you've seen, the key difference between a Peak Learning life-style and your previous, school-based learning is that, in Peak Learning, *you choose whatever you want to do.*

Now that you've gotten the feel of using a book as your personal learning resource, there are some more advanced things you may want to try. For example, you can check the contents of a book in much the same way someone might search through a computer's database information using key words. An easy analogy would be searching for the name of a client to find out when he or she was last billed. The name is the key word under which the transactions are filed. Many on-line information systems allow one to locate all articles that contain a particular key word.

In a book, of course, these key words are listed in the index. Here's an excerpt from a typical book index. Read it as a *graph:* the length of the listing for each item—i.e., the number of pages on which that term is mentioned—indicates how much attention is paid to that subject in the book.

> Educational need, concept of, 111
> Effort: as motivation indicator, 5, 279–280;
>   and self-concept, 97
> Einstein, A., 20–21
> Ellis, A., 68, 73, 87, 296
> Elstein, A. S., 236, 296
> Emotions. *See* Affect
> Empathy: and affect, 186; and attitude, 76;
>   defined, 24; by instructors, 22–28; and
>   learners' level, 26–27; and learners' per-
>   spective, 27–28; and understanding of
>   needs and expectations, 24–26
> Enjoyment, and motivation, 8, 279
> Enthusiasm: caring and valuing in, 32–33;
>   defined, 29; emotion, animation, and en-
>   ergy in, 33–38; indicators of, 34, 36–37; by
>   instructors, 28–38; loss of, 35, 38; research
>   findings on, 30

Of the items on this list, only *two* are covered in a major way: *empathy* and *enthusiasm.* If you took five minutes to scan the whole index this way, you'd end up with the twenty-five key words for this book. Usually these key words will constitute about 15 percent of the entries; the other 85 percent will have only one, two, or three pages following them. By reading a book's index this way, you can get an immediate answer to the following crucial questions:

1. What are the dozen most important ideas covered in this book?

2. Which of these important ideas might provide good starting points for me to get into the book because of my familiarity with them?

3. What ideas are covered that are entirely new to me, and do they sound intriguing and useful?

4. Given the above, and my learning goals, do I have enough reason to continue with this book or should I seek information elsewhere?

To summarize the value of the Pro-Active reading technique just described:

- A quick scan of the book's description, introduction, table of contents, and index can give you an immediate sense of whether the book will be useful in meeting the learning goals you have set. If the book is not going to help you reach those goals, you can safely discard it.

- If you quick scan suggests questions you'd like the answers to, you can read only those parts of the book that provide those answers (and any cross-reference necessary to understand them) and go on to the next learning resource. There's no need to feel any guilt because you haven't read the entire book—no one is testing you on it!

- Analyzing the index of a book can help you decide whether to spend any further time on it and where the best place for *you* to start might be. There is no danger that the "book police" will catch you because you didn't start on page one!

> *The mere formulation of a problem is often far more essential than its solution, which may be a matter of mathematical or experimental skill. To raise new questions, new possibilities, to regard old problems from a new angle requires creative imagination and marks real advance in science.*
>
> ALBERT EINSTEIN

TURNING ANY EXPERIENCE INTO A LEARNING OPPORTUNITY

It is sometimes said that the experiences we go through in life make us what we are. That's not entirely correct, however—it's what we manage to *learn* from those experiences. Few people have developed a method for learning from their experiences in a systematic way. The best we do, most of the time, is try to be alert to what's going on during the experience, then think about it later—if we ever find the time to do so. The result is that we fail to gain the full learning value from many of our most significant experiences. There's a simple technique by which we can do better. The "Vee-heuristic" technique enables you to:

1. Identify upcoming experiences from which you want to learn.
2. Marshal your existing knowledge and understanding, so that you can draw on it during the experience.
3. Formulate interesting, useful, powerful questions you want to answer by learning from the experience.
4. Plan your own behavior so that the experience yields the answers you are looking for.

The original Vee-heuristic technique was developed for students in school by Joseph Novak and Bob Gorwin, two Cornell University professors who explain it in their book *Learning How to Learn.* (The term *heuristic* refers to techniques that help

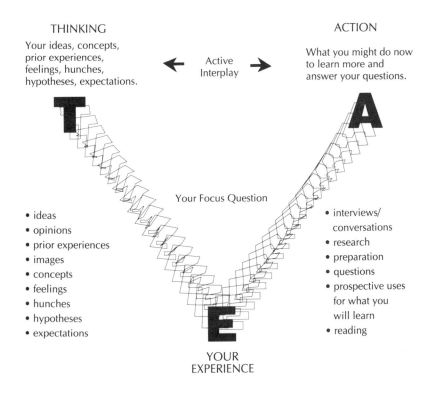

THINKING

Your ideas, concepts, prior experiences, feelings, hunches, hypotheses, expectations.

← Active Interplay →

ACTION

What you might do now to learn more and answer your questions.

Your Focus Question

- ideas
- opinions
- prior experiences
- images
- concepts
- feelings
- hunches
- hypotheses
- expectations

- interviews/ conversations
- research
- preparation
- questions
- prospective uses for what you will learn
- reading

YOUR
EXPERIENCE

us find or discover something.) The diagram that follows is my simplification and modification of theirs, based on the needs of adult learners.

The *Vee* provides a framework that enables you to think creatively about what you might learn from an upcoming experience. You can explore how to pose questions or to behave in ways that will yield the knowledge or understanding you want from the experience. You can use the technique to learn from a meeting you will be attending in two hours or from a stint of jury duty that starts in three weeks.

Use the example of jury duty to see how we might enjoy it more and learn more from it by using the Vee. Start by drawing a sample of the Vee diagram in your learning log. On the left side, write down what you already know or feel about jury duty—facts, impressions, opinions, and questions.

One of my workshop students' entries for this exercise included remembering the classic film *Twelve Angry Men*, a textbook she had used in college on the American legal system, a magazine article on the jury's role in a recent newsworthy trial, some rules of thumb she had learned about how leadership emerges in small groups, and her feelings about this intrusion on her family and professional life. Each of these pieces of past knowledge or feeling could be the basis for deeper learning from this actual experience of jury service. For example, you might note the differences and similarities between the actual experience and the dramatized portrayal of a jury in *Twelve Angry Men*. Or you might formulate three or four theories about how a leader emerges in a small group like a jury and see which ones are borne out. It might be interesting to discuss, during break times, the jurors' different attitudes about taking time away from their families and jobs.

That's where the focus question comes in. Once you've identified what you already know and feel (left side of the Vee) and decided what you'd like to learn from the experience, you can formulate the question you'd like to explore.

The following questions are but a few that have been formulated by my workshop participants. An anthropology major who is now in market research asked, "How does a jury trial serve the same function as rituals in primitive societies?" A question posed by a secondary-school teacher considering a

While information may be infinite, the ways of structuring it are not. . . . Your choice will be determined by the story you want to tell.

RICHARD SAUL WURMAN

Clustering taps the childlike, wondering, innocent, curious, playful, open-ended, flexible, pattern-seeking design mind, allowing us to play with language, ideas, rhythms, images, sounds, and patterns creatively before committing ourselves to a fixed course. In short, we avail ourselves of choices.

GABRIELE LUSSER RICO

career shift into industrial training was, "How does a 'natural' leader emerge in a small group, and how does he or she relate to the officially designated leader?" An actor-director in a regional theater asked, "How does a theatrical portrayal of a courtroom differ from the mundane reality?" And this question was posed by a manufacturer with an accounting background: "Are there ways the trial process could be expedited without a loss of integrity, in order to increase its efficiency and speed trials?"

Having identified your own question, go to the right side of the Vee and list some actions you can take to gain the information you seek. For example, you might do some preparatory reading or even see the movie *Twelve Angry Men* again. Or you might decide you want to watch the behavior of your fellow jury members to see whether you can predict which one will most affect how the others decide. Or perhaps you will want to talk with other people in advance about their own jury-duty experiences.

Sometimes the preparation you do will cause you to rethink your focus question. Often you may recall some bit of relevant experience you forgot to list initially, or you may come up with some new sources of information to pursue during or after the experience. The key feature of this technique is that *any experience to which you apply the Vee-heuristic method is one in which you are actively involved in the process of learning as much as you can.*

Most people spend most of their lives simply going from experience to experience. However, as active lifelong learners—as peak learners—we can use *any* experience we have in the cause of furthering our learning and enhancing our enjoyment of life. With just a little advance planning, your life can become a rich storehouse of potential learning experiences.

DURING LEARNING

While you are engaged in learning—whether you are reading, listening, or discussing—your mind should *not* be passively trying to absorb information. Rather, it should be *active*. You should be posing questions to yourself, organizing the incoming information to fit your own interests, learning goals, and needs.

Two of the best techniques I know for activating your mind while learning are mind-mapping and probes.

MIND-MAPPING

Mind-mapping will appeal most strongly to those with high visual intelligence, who may feel stifled by the need to outline subjects in a linear order, one topic after another. They, like groupers, will prefer to see a more complex overview, with branches in many directions. However, mind-mapping is a simple enough process to be easily used by the rest of us as well, and therefore it's a good way to flex your own learning style in the visual, top-down direction. Even if your preferred style is highly linguistic or mathematical, you will find mind-mapping an intriguing alternative way to look at information and ideas.

Mind-mapping was first popularized by Tony Buzan, a leading British learning coach, in *Use Both Sides of Your Brain.* Gabriele Rico, in her book *Writing the Natural Way*, pioneered using the technique to make writing easier and more enjoyable; she calls it *clustering.* The idea has been applied to problem-solving and idea generation in business and industry by Charles Hess and Carol Colman, Anne Robinson, and Dudley Lynch, who call mind maps *brain webs.* In modified form, it has also been recommended by many educators for teaching youngsters in school.

Mind-mapping is also suitable for advanced learning: one of the most dazzling mind maps in my personal collection organizes connections among the main thinkers behind contemporary culture. Created by Maurice Stein and Larry Miller at the University of California at Santa Cruz, this giant map links such figures as Sigmund Freud, Karl Marx, and Charles Darwin with more recent figures such as Herbert Marcuse and Marshall McLuhan. Following is an example from Tony Buzan of a British student's mind map of concepts in economics.

If the brain works primarily with key concepts in an interlinked and integrated manner, our notes and our word relations would in many instances be structured in this [mind mapping] way rather than in traditional "lines." Rather than starting from the top and working down in sentences or lists, one should start from the center or main idea and branch out as dictated by the individual ideas and general form of the central theme.

TONY BUZAN

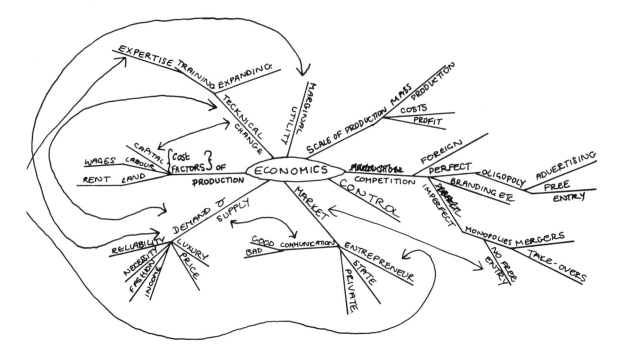

At first glance it may look confusing, a hodgepodge of branches and arrows and labels. But as you study the map, it starts to make more sense. The place to start is in the center, where you will start shortly when you make your own mind map. The central circle, labeled *economics,* is where this map begins.

As we move away from that center we see a series of labeled branches for concepts, in no particular order. These are the first few terms that occurred to the student in connection with the idea of economics. There is no rule that requires this list to be complete or academically accurate; after all, it's the student's *own* map! Some of these secondary ideas spun further branches, others didn't—again, the amount and distribution of information is up to the person making the map. One can always return and add new branches anywhere. Finally, the arrows around the outside show links between various branches that this student wanted to stress.

You may wish to go back to page vi, preceding the table of contents, and review the mind map of this book.

Sometimes people ask why mind-mapping is superior to

the standard outlining technique we all were taught in school. There are several reasons why it is more effective and enjoyable for most people.

1. It's *visually* pattern-oriented, and therefore it activates an additional area of our brain in the service of our learning.

2. It's open to creative additions at any point, thus encouraging us to think about a topic in more directions than simply *before* and *after.*

3. It invites use of color and design in ways that make it easier to remember later.

4. It allows us to see connections among widely disparate elements of the subject (since they're all right there on the same page). Interconnecting arrows can suggest complex relationships among parts of some idea or field we might otherwise have missed.

The following exercise will be your guide to creating a mind map.

◆ ◆ ◆ ◆

Mind-Mapping Something That Matters to You

Develop a mind map for an idea, issue, problem, or situation of current concern to you. Your area of focus might be a business problem or a subject you are studying in school or on your own.

To start your mind map, put the key word you want to work with in an oval in the center of a sheet of paper that is 8 by 11 inches or larger (the larger the better). In Peak Learning workshops, participants work on flip-chart-size sheets of paper (27 by 34). At first they are daunted by the size, but once they get rolling they find they have so many ideas that they can hardly fit them all on the page. Work in pencil so you can easily erase and change items as you find more precise words for your thoughts.

Now, begin to create branches to other ovals that are your main sub-ideas. (Initially, it is easier to read the labels for sub-ideas if each one has its own oval rather than simply assigning the label to the branch itself, as our earlier example did.) It generally helps to arrange the sub-ideas you think are most closely related to your central concept as direct branches from it; less significant ideas can then branch from those sub-ideas. However, don't worry about you're sure an idea is important enough or not—you can always erase it, move it to the periphery, and insert a new, more important idea in that oval. And leave room for new ovals that will occur to you later.

Each time you create an oval that interests you, add spokes to it to capture related ideas. These may be specific examples, references, or thoughts implied by the sub-idea. Note that in some cases these spokes will themselves develop spokes, as in the lower right-hand corner of our example, where *competition* led to *imperfect* and on to *monopolies,* which subdivided into *mergers* and *take-overs.*

As you can see, the rules of mind-mapping are made to be broken; the whole point is to create and capture your own thoughts in your own way, reflecting your personal image of the idea you are mapping. Use any resources and techniques that appeal to you.

I like to use three to five colored pencils (or felt-tipped pens) when doing a group mind map or when I want to further distinguish the kinds of branches into types. For example, I might use one color for all the people who have written about my subject, another for sub-ideas that come from my own experience, and a third for connections I need to research.

Feel free to use visual symbols as a conceptual shorthand. You might use a little cartoon image of a brain to refer to all the ways in which brain functions relate to your idea, or a drawing of a book next to a name might suggest a text for reference. You may want to create special symbols for how you feel about various ideas sparked by your key term. Benefits and promising applications, for example, could be flagged with a smiling face, a rising sun, a light bulb, or a dollar sign. Danger points or reservations could be designated by a question mark, a downward-pointing arrow, or a skull and crossbones.

♦ ♦ ♦ ♦

Don't be surprised if one mind map leads to another. The way this usually happens is that one of your ovals begins to emerge as very important to you. It has a lot of spokes, many of them are important ideas that generate their own spokes, and the whole thing looks like it's going to get out of hand! That's the time to start another map, with the sub-idea from your original map in the center.

Naturally, you'll have to do a few mind maps just to get the feel of the process before it comes naturally. You have an interesting experience to look forward to. The creative climax of mind-mapping at its most successful can actually give you more information than you started with! You may find, while connections are spilling onto the page and radiating from the center, that something suddenly strikes you that you hadn't seen earlier. As Gabriele Rico describes it in *Writing the Natural Way:*

> You are clustering, seemingly randomly, when suddenly you experience a sense of direction. The moment between randomness and sense of direction is the moment of shift. . . .
>
> You suddenly perceive a direction to follow. Something stands out as significant for you here and now. . . . it is like looking through the eye of a camera at a total blur only to discover, as you turn the focusing mechanism, a sudden broad vista . . . or a grouping of clearly defined figures. Not only is the image focused, but it is *framed* to give you a sense that the objects you are focusing on somehow belong together.

That is the point at which Rico advises her students to start writing a brief summary paragraph describing what insight has just occurred.

Notice what is going on here. We started with a subject—whatever it is we have decided to learn about. We gained some information about it, one way or another. By mind-mapping or clustering we created our own personal pattern, an image of a network showing how our various bits of knowledge might relate to one another. Then, when the moment felt right, we returned to our usual style of verbal thinking and wrote a summary paragraph that captured the new insight.

We have actively used more of our brain's capacities to make connections that help us learn. How?

We can now approach our newly learned information from several directions. We can use the image of the map, and any secondary maps we create, as a literal map that reminds us of

Were all maps in this world destroyed and vanished under the direction of some malevolent hand, each man would be blind again, each landmark become a meaningless signpost to nothing.

BERYL MARKHAM

. . . shall I teach you what knowledge is? When you know a thing, to recognize that you know it, and when you do not know a thing, to recognize that you do not know it. That is knowledge.

CONFUCIUS

the overall territory we've traveled. A list of the concepts used in the map can supply key words to guide our search for further resources (which can be used, for example, to check the index of a book). Even the pattern of connections shown by the map—the branches and arrows—can tell us what we need to check further or assist us in reformulating a focus question to gain new information.

The pattern can also help us to organize data in a way more suitable to a standard outline or report, where our summary paragraph can find a proper home. If you wish to write up what you've learned in an essay or article, the summary paragraph will probably (but not always) be easier for others to grasp than your personal map would be.

You will find mind-mapping useful when you are:

- planning a speech or an article, as an alternative to standard outlines;
- taking notes from reading, lectures, workshops, seminars, TV documentaries, or meetings;
- bringing your prior knowledge, ideas, and feelings about a new subject to the surface;
- summing up or recalling what you've learned about a subject so far;
- generating new ideas about a problem, situation, or issue that concerns you; and
- brainstorming applications of new concepts you have learned.

PROBES

Probes are ideas and questions you develop while you are learning but *before* you have learned much about any new field. The idea of probes affronts most people, because we all learned in school that you needed to learn what had already been established in any field before you could even think about contributing an idea of your own. On the contrary, you can and should come up with ideas of your own right from the start for two reasons. First, they will help you learn the subject by keeping your mind actively involved with what you're studying.

That would be a good enough reason in itself, but there's a second, even more intriguing justification: occasionally, one of these early probes in a new field will contain an insight you would have missed if you had waited until you knew more.

This is called the *novice effect,* which Michael Hutchinson identifies in his book, *Megabrain.* One's first exposure to a new field, Hutchinson points out, causes changes in the brain's chemistry. He cites the frequency of "late bloomers" who made original contributions to a field, even in the sciences, where the usual pattern is that the best discoveries are made early in one's career.

Leo Szilard, for example, was a leading physicist who became a biologist as he approached fifty. Szilard suggested that scientists could actually harness this novice effect by changing their fields every five or ten years, plunging into something about which they know nothing. A similar pattern is found in the career of Gregory Bateson, who combined the fields of biology, anthropology, systems theory, and psychology (among others) to produce intriguing new insights in each field.

"Subjected to a novel barrage of experiences and stimulations," Hutchinson writes, "the brain is forced to grow, to make neural connections, to forge new chemical pathways, to retain its youthful plasticity, to see the world with fresh eyes." In that youthful freshness lie the seeds of insights that are not likely to come to those who have been mired in the same field for twenty years.

A more mundane use of your own probes is to learn more effectively by actively engaging your mind with the material. Your mind works faster than you can read—and much faster than any lecturer can talk. It likes to keep busy, so after it takes in what's being conveyed, it looks around for something else to do. The result is that you experience distractions. Eventually, you could get so irritated by the difference between your own speed of comprehension and the rate that information is being presented that you lose track of what you're reading or hearing.

A powerful remedy is to put your mind to work in a productive way. Give it something to chew on to keep you focused, to spark your own creative responses, to leap *ahead.* I call such leaps *probes.* You can think of the word as standing for *propositions before*—that is, before the text or speaker gets to the point, before the facts and arguments are presented, and before you get distracted.

Consider probing whenever you begin to sense that the argument is moving along a little too slowly for you. Start to go beyond simply *taking* notes on what's being said or read; instead, start to *make* notes about what's coming next. Just *guess* what the speaker or writer is leading up to. I call these *prenotes*—notes made *before* you're exposed to the material.

Then, as you proceed through the text, watch for how you need to modify your proposition in light of what you're reading. You will, in effect, become a co-creator with the author, absorbing what he or she has to say as well as exploring your own ideas and expectations. The result is an active dialogue, a conversation, which tends to be far more absorbing, stimulating, and pleasurable than passively absorbing information as it is handed out.

Probes are such a powerful learning tool that they are often used by authors as they write. An author will formulate an initial proposition, present it as a hypothesis, and then examine the evidence to see how well it stands up.

For example, Professor David Perkins of Harvard uses this as the organizing principle of *The Mind's Best Work: A New Psychology of Creative Thinking.* Here's how he explains its usefulness:

> I have found it helpful to organize most chapter sections around "propositions" and "revised propositions." A proposition, which usually occurs near the beginning of a section, is a concise statement of a familiar or plausible view about creating. The revised proposition, arriving near the end of a section, is another statement on the same issue, sometimes a direct contradiction of the original proposition and sometimes a qualification of it. The text of the sections is mostly a journey by way of evidence and argument from the original to the revised proposition. This device has helped me to keep the issues explicit and focal.

Thus, Perkins opens one chapter with this simple proposition: "There must be something special about the mental processes that lead to discovery." He explains why this is a proposition worth investigating: "Extraordinary outcomes like moments of discovery ought to involve extra-ordinary means."

Later in the chapter, Perkins shows how creative discoveries can often be adequately explained by quite ordinary mental processes such as remembering and noticing. By the end of the chapter he is revising his initial proposition. If there *is* something special about the mental processes that lead to discovery, he realizes, it's *not* what we usually think: some unusual, hidden work of the unconscious or some special mode of mental functioning. He then gives his revised proposition:

> Revised Proposition: Discovery depends not on special processes but on special purposes. Creating occurs when ordinary mental processes in an able person are marshaled by creative or appropriately "unreasonable" intentions.

Which happens to be a good description of what happens when you put Peak Learning principles to work.

As you can see, using probes is a superb way of making sure that you have a clear idea in mind of what is being discussed. It's no accident that this is essentially the basic method of scientific experimentation: formulate a hypothesis and test it.

Probes can also be developed from your prior knowledge and awareness of the subject you are studying. When you bring such prior knowledge to the surface by using mind maps and/or the Vee-heuristic technique, you may then find a variety of ways to formulate and reformulate focus questions that you can use as probes to be tested as you continue to learn. The following exercise will help you in developing your own probes.

Asking a question is the simplest way of focusing thinking . . . asking the right question may be the most important part of thinking. . . . A fishing question [is] exploratory (like putting bait on a hook but not knowing quite what might turn up). . . . A shooting question [is] used to check out a point and [has] a direct yes or no answer (like aiming at a bird and hitting or missing).

EDWARD DE BONO

♦   ♦   ♦   ♦

Developing Probes

This exercise has two parts. In the first, you'll go over a sample text and explain the steps you might use to formulate probes about where the author is headed. In the second, you'll cover some guidelines you can use on a text you choose for yourself.

PART 1

This sample text is a selection from a chapter called "Role Playing" in Edward De Bono's book *Six Thinking Hats,* which will be returned to in the next chapter. Read the following two paragraphs.

People do not mind "playing the fool" so long as it is quite clear that they are just playing a role. They even take pride in putting on a good performance and playing an extremely foolish fool. That now becomes a measure of achievement and excellence. The role has taken over and the ego is now the stage director.

One of the problems with Zen Buddhism is that the harder the ego tries "not-to-be-there," the more present it becomes in its "trying." One style of actor loses his or her ego identity and takes on the ego of the role (method acting). Another style of actor directs his or her own performance. Both are good actors. Both are having an ego holiday. One is having a holiday abroad and the other is having a holiday at home.

Now turn to a fresh page in your learning log and formulate a probe. Your first one might be "What is this author talking about?" Is it about being a fool? About problems with Zen Buddhism? About acting styles? The role of ego?

When you have an answer that feels right, make a guess about where this might be leading. How is it going to relate to styles of thinking, which would seem to be the topic of the book? Here are some possibilities, but take a few minutes to think up your own.

- He's going to argue that ego gets in the way of thinking.
- He wants to show that there are different styles of ego-development in playing a role.
- He is trying to convince us that playing a role is a process in which we rate our performance in a different way than we would if we felt our *self* was being judged.

Now close this book and think of your own probe and answer. When you are ready, return to the selection and read the next two paragraphs.

To play at being someone else allows the ego to go beyond its normal restrictive self-image. Actors are often quite shy in ordinary life. But a role gives freedom. We might have difficulty in seeing ourselves being foolish, wrong, or outsmarted. Given a well-defined role we can act out such parts with pleasure in our acting skill rather than damage to our egos. There is prestige in being considered a good actor.

Without the protection of a formal role, the ego is at risk. That is why habitually negative people claim the role of devil's advocate when they want to be negative. This means to imply that they are not normally negative, but that it is useful to have someone play this role and that they intend to play it well. . . .

How well did your probes match up with the next selection? Clearly, De Bono is saying more than "ego intereferes with thinking." These paragraphs provide a further explanation of why playing a role is a way to allow the ego to feel safe. Instead of feeling guilty for continually pointing out why something won't work, a nay-sayer can feel pride for scrupulously playing devil's advocate, because *someone* has to tie down excessive optimism and enthusiasm in order to prevent thoughtless mistakes.

Now revise your probes. You are still trying to understand how this issue of role-playing might be relevant to how we think. Write any guesses in your log. Here are a few possibilities.

Questions are the creative acts of intelligence.

FRANK KINGDON

- ♦ Maybe he wants us to believe that actors make the best thinkers.
- ♦ Perhaps he is going to tell us that looking on the dark side of any idea is a bad thing, because the people who habitually do it pretend they're being "devil's advocates" as an excuse.
- ♦ Perhaps this is a similar kind of role-playing to that in the exercise in Chapter Three about "Activating Your Inner Learner." (Using a Vee-heuristic technique might help to recall this and other past experiences that could be relevant here.)

Now that you've revised your probes and leaped ahead, read some final paragraphs from De Bono.

To role-play being a thinker in the general sense of that word is a valuable step towards becoming a thinker." *[Aha!]* "But we can go further by breaking down that large role into more specific parts. These become character parts like the character parts in a good pantomime, a good TV soap opera, or a traditional Western movie. . . .

The broad-thinking hat role is broken down into six different *character roles,* represented by six differently colored thinking hats.

You choose which of the hats to put on at any one moment. You put on that hat and then play the role defined by that hat. You watch yourself playing that role. You play the role as well as you can. Your ego is protected by the role. Your ego is involved in playing the role well. . . .

129

Thinking now begins to flow from the *acted parts* and not from your *ego*. . . .

How did you do? This is not a question of whether your guesses about where the author was going were correct—such a question would turn this into a *test*. My question is about whether you gained more from the material by actively anticipating what would be presented and noting not just what you read but what these passages *suggested to you as new thoughts to follow up*. My bet is that using the probes enriched your reading immensely.

The true art of memory is the art of attention.

SAMUEL JOHNSON

PART 2

For the second part of this exercise, pick a new text on your own—perhaps an editorial from today's newspaper or a nonfiction book you're about to start reading. Do all the pre-noting and Vee-heuristic work you'd like to before reading a short opening section of the piece. Now stop, turn to your learning log, and begin to create the same sort of probes just used.

- ◆ What is the point of this first section? What is the author trying to say?
- ◆ What past knowledge of or experience with this subject do you have that leads you to suspect where the author is going?
- ◆ Is the author taking a stand on some issue? If so, what kind of supporting evidence or argument do you think will be presented to justify that stand? If no definite position has been presented so far, do you think the author is leading up to some position? How?
- ◆ What kinds of information do you expect the author to present next as relevant to the topic discussed? (Who, what, where, or when something happened? How or why some situation came to be?) What kind of result can be expected with this issue?

As you can see, each of these general patterns for probes can spawn many more, all specific to whatever you're reading or hearing. Even considering a small fraction of the possible probes you can raise will keep your mind happily occupied while waiting for the next bits of information to arrive.

◆ ◆ ◆ ◆

This section has covered two important Peak Learning tools for becoming actively involved with what you're learning while you're learning it. Mind maps let you build personal pictures of the relationships you can see in the material, while probes allow you to anticipate where your learning is going and correct your understanding "on the fly." Now it's time to turn to the tools you can use to *retain* what you learn.

AFTER LEARNING

No matter how clear we are about our learning goals, no matter how well we've matched a learning plan to our personal style, and no matter how carefully we take notes and keep them organized, sooner or later we all have to remember something of what we've learned so that we can put it to effective use. What can you do to strengthen your retention of what you're learning or have just learned?

For factual material, there are numerous techniques to assist memory retention. These mnemonic devices are an intriguing and enjoyable way to improve your memory. When you've had a rich experience from which you feel there's more to be learned, the instant-replay technique will enable you to distill further learning from your recollections.

MEMORY IMPROVEMENT

We all tend to be uncomfortable about remembering. From our school days, most of us recall having to memorize material that seemed boring, irrelevant, and uncongenial—whether vocabulary lists or mathematical equations. Naturally, we had trouble doing so. From that experience we overgeneralized the difficulties and unpleasantness of the process.

However, it's entirely different when you are working with information that you know you want and ideas that excite you. When you use the Peak Learning approach and techniques in your self-directed learning process, remembering becomes astonishingly easy. Learning in these active, multisensory, personally congenial ways, your mind absorbs information without strain. The following strategies and techniques can help to make your learning more memorable.

Choose your own goals. This assures that you know *why* you're learning and have immediate uses to which you can put your knowledge. What you're learning isn't an alien mountain of material you are trying to cram into your head. Your keen interest, by itself, will facilitate recall. Understanding your subject in some depth will further strengthen retention, and your immediate use of your new knowledge will make it stick. "Understanding the subject, and relating what you learn to something you already know, makes for powerful memory and storage," declares Toronto psychologist Endel Tulving.

Employ techniques that activate your mind. This enlivens what you are learning and makes it more personal and memorable for you. You are asking questions, responding creatively, and processing new information in other ways. In doing this you are automatically storing the information in a richer, more elaborate form, connecting it with other data. "The more you organize information, the greater the likelihood that you will be able to retrieve or remember it," says Dr. James Staszewski, research psychologist at Carnegie Mellon University.

Three other Peak Learning approaches and techniques previously discussed also further reinforce your retention.

Get into the "flow" of learning. As you saw in Chapter Three, flow learning sidesteps any resistances or anxieties, thereby opening your mind to input and understanding, which promotes maximum retention.

Invoke your enthusiasm and commitment. Invocations stir your feelings and emotions in support of your learning, thereby giving the material a more powerful impact.

Use your strongest style. This permits you to approach learning in the way that's personally most comfortable and efficient, thereby facilitating study.

The result of all these factors is less struggle and easier learning. "My favorite word about learning is *ease*," declares Elisabeth Ruedy, who conducts "Learning How to Learn" workshops in New York City. "The right attitude and the right skills result in ease in learning. Easier learning is largely a matter of changing self-limiting attitudes and acquiring more effective skills."

Of course, there are special occasions when you need to rely on your memory *per se.* You might want to remember the names of a number of people you are introduced to at a party or meeting or need to memorize a list of items being rattled off in a situation in which you can't take notes. Or perhaps you want to memorize your long-distance telephone credit-card number and others you use often. These aren't parts of learning projects, and you can't use most of the strategies and techniques that have been discussed. For such situations, there are two powerful techniques you should add to your repertoire. These techniques will also be useful when you *are* involved in a learning project.

Association. The first is association in its many various forms. By association, you aim to associate meaningless names or numbers with something significant that will help to recall them to mind.

Tony Buzan, who was introduced earlier in connection with the technique of mind-mapping, lists several key principles for making memory associations easier. They include:

- Involving as many senses as possible. Create colorful, moving, three-dimensional mental images, complete with sound, rhythm, touch, and even scent to associate with the thing you want to remember. Writing, speaking, drawing, touching, listening—the more you can use all of these in the process of memorizing something, the better your recall will be.
- Creating an organized sequence of associated images for a list of things to be remembered. You can simply number the items or use the ancient method of imagining each item in a particular place. This allows you to create a state-specific kind of recall—if you lose your place, you can go back to the start of the sequence and work forward again.
- Using exaggeration, absurdity, or even sexuality to give your associated image an impact you won't forget soon.
- Keeping it simple. Too witty or convoluted a link between your image and what you want to remember is confusing; make the link direct.

What memory has in common with art is the knack for selection, the taste for detail. Memory contains precise details, not the whole picture; highlights, if you will, not the entire show.

JOSEPH BRODSKY

133

Here are a few examples of these principles for the association method of memorization.

To remember the name of a new person you meet, say it a couple of times during your conversation (which adds the physical act of speaking to the sense of hearing), learn something distinctive about the person, and associate the name or face with something visually fanciful. Harriet Goddard will be much more memorable when you have worked her name into the conversation once or twice, learned that she studies comparative religions as a hobby, and pictured her parachuting out of a plane as a kind of "goddess with long hair" ("Hair" and "God-ard").

To remember a set of unrelated items, such as groceries on a shopping list, try associating each of the items with a part of your house or room. Picture a bunch of carrots sitting on the table in the foyer, a can of coffee right next to the phone, bananas hanging from the standing lamp, and so forth. If you have trouble recalling an item, you can start at a familiar spot and mentally walk through your house until you find it.

To recall an important formula or list, devise a sentence with words based on its first letters; for example, you might remember the planets via "My very excellent mother just sells nuts until Passover" (Mercury, Venus, Earth, Mars, Jupiter, Saturn, Neptune, Uranus, and Pluto) or the familiar "Roy G. Biv" for the colors of the spectrum (red, orange, yellow, green, blue, indigo, violet). This is called the *acronyms* technique.

To remember important numbers, link them to patterns that are meaningful to you. An avid cross-country runner might turn the formula for her bike lock, 3-4-3-9, into 3:46.39, close to the world record for the mile.

Sophisticated test-takers use state-dependent learning by studying in the room in which they will take the test or by calling up the visual look of the book and the page on which they read the material. The brain apparently encodes much of the context together with what you are learning, and any one of the contextual pieces can serve as a key for unlocking the rest of the information.

If you wish to develop a more systematic approach to this kind of memorization, there are a number of fine books available, such as Tony Buzan's *Use Your Perfect Memory.* However, I urge you to examine such books before you get lured into their intriguing systems. Pay particular attention to the examples offered, and decide whether you really want to be able to do these stunts. Whole chapters in Buzan's book, for instance, deal with memorizing an entire pack of playing cards, lists of telephone numbers, historical dates (three chapters), birthdays, and anniversaries. Will doing this be useful or enjoyable to you?

Mental review. The second approach to better memory, mental review, also enables you to retain more complex data with remarkable reliability. In fact, you can actually reverse the *curve of forgetting* and increase your recall over time. The usual curve is shown top right.

It sweeps distressingly downward: after only five minutes, a significant amount of new learning is lost; an hour later, about two-thirds; and a day later, you have lost 90 percent.

The good news is that this curve can be turned around. You can train yourself to recall *more* with the passage of time. Much of what's forgotten in five minutes can actually be recalled in an hour, and the loss on Day One can be rectified on Day Two. The resulting curve is shown below right.

Your remembering can peak after a couple of days, and you can end up retaining, instead of forgetting, 90 percent of what you want to memorize.

The discoverer of this phenomenon, and of the technique that follows, is Professor Matthew Erdelyi of the City University of New York. Memory review is most effective for "nailing down" well-organized expository presentations, such as speeches, workshop presentations, or classroom lectures. Following is an exercise to help you learn how to use this memory technique.

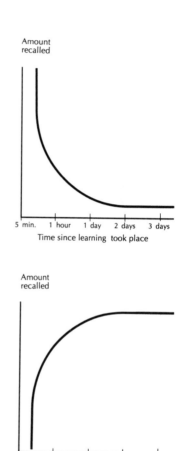

Amount recalled

5 min. 1 hour 1 day 2 days 3 days
Time since learning took place

Amount recalled

5 min. 1 hour 1 day 2 days 3 days
Time since learning took place

♦ ♦ ♦ ♦

Mental Review

1. Select a task. As you read, listen, or participate in a meeting or conversation, make a mental note (or written note) of the

key points. (Because this technique does not require taking written notes, it is a favorite of many top executives, who often need to keep track of important information in conversations over lunch or at other social occasions where taking written notes would be awkward.) Keep a running total of how many points you want to remember.

2. Five minutes later take two or three minutes by yourself, undisturbed, and go through those main points. Say each one to yourself, but just once. Relax and enjoy this session. Don't worry about or strain to recall anything you've forgotten, but "guesstimate" what the missing points might have been.

3. About an hour afterward hold a second session, doing exactly what you did before. Again, relax and simply say each item once to yourself. Note that these sessions are only a couple of minutes long and can be done anywhere, including in the car going home after a lecture or during a commercial while watching a documentary on TV.

4. About three hours later, hold a third session.

5. About six hours later, hold a fourth.

6. Hold a final session right before going to sleep.

7. Repeat this procedure three times on the second and third days, spaced evenly throughout the day.

8. From then on, you can keep the material fresh in your mind by having a recall session every three or four days.

Needless to say, the above procedure can be enhanced with any of the mnemonic tricks covered earlier. You can associate your items with visual images, particularly unusual and vivid ones.

◆ ◆ ◆ ◆

It was a mental state of happiness about as complete as I have ever known in life. Ideas came in an uninterrupted stream and the only difficulty I had was to hold them fast. The pieces of apparatus I conceived were to me absolutely real and tangible in every detail, even to the minutest marks and signs of wear. . . . When natural inclination develops into a passionate desire, one advances towards his goal in seven-league boots.

NIKOLA TESLA

INSTANT REPLAY

After going through some new experience, you may feel that you missed some of the significance of what happened. You realize that there were facts, insights, or new ideas that you were aware of but didn't quite pull into focus. Perhaps events were moving too fast or you were understandably preoccupied with the task at hand. It's not review that you need—you're concerned with catching important things you simply didn't learn the first time around.

Fortunately, there's a straightforward, enjoyable way to extract such learning from any experience, after the fact. You can replay your experiences, recapturing what you might have missed the first time around. In fact, you can often perceive and understand *more* than you possibly could while they were occurring. While similar to the visualization technique we used in Chapter Three to activate your inner learner, this approach works by recalling subconscious images in all their detail. Because you recall *pictures,* this exercise may seem a little difficult at first. Most of us tend to remember *words.* But with a little practice, you will find that the technique becomes easier and is well worth it.

INSTANT REPLAY

The benefits of instant replay are similar to those of instant replays of ball games on TV. You can see the experience from angles that were not observable at the time it occurred. You also can analyze it to understand the structure and process, as the TV commentators do by highlighting the nuances that you couldn't follow while watching the action. The key is summoning up as clear a picture of the experience as possible.

"Instant replay isn't merely recall," notes Win Wenger of Project Renaissance. "You will actually *increase* your perceptions and insights from the experience by three to five times."

The following exercise will guide you in learning the instant-replay technique.

♦ ♦ ♦ ♦

Instant Replay

Select a recent experience, preferably from the past 48 hours, which you feel has additional significance to be plumbed. It might be an encounter with a person, a movie, or a television show or simply a moment of observing a scene or an image.

Close your eyes and describe this experience aloud to someone else or to a tape recorder, following these guidelines.

1. Begin with sensory details and your feelings—what you saw, heard, felt, touched, or otherwise perceived. Stay in the present tense throughout this exercise. ("I am having lunch in the company cafeteria with the marketing team.")

137

2. Describe the items in such detail that the person listening will almost see, hear, and feel what you did. ("Bill is wearing a plaid shirt and has loosened his tie. Janet's blouse is yellow. Frank is fiddling with a pen. I see strong sunlight reflecting off the next table.") Make a real effort to plumb the reality of the experience. Devote three to five minutes to this.

3. Having done your best to evoke the scene and the situation, try to move in closer. Ask yourself questions about half-glimpsed details. ("In the corner of my eye, I see Frank's fingers suddenly clench around the pen. Was there something wrong?") Try to connect these new details with your other recollections in several ways. Often some new insight about the significance of the experience will present itself. ("Bill laughed at Janet's choice of colors for the new packaging. Maybe Frank agreed with Janet, or maybe he was irritated by Bill.")

4. Continue for at least ten minutes, or as long as half an hour, if you like.

5. Review the tape or jot down any notes you have about your new perceptions and insights.

♦　♦　♦　♦

At such points where deep human emotion, identification with other beings, and perception of reality meet lies the crux of creativity—and also the crux of the most mundane thoughts. Spinning out variations is what comes naturally to the human mind, and is it ever fertile!

DOUGLAS R. HOFSTADTER

Once you have mastered instant replay, you can add another angle to it. It's called the SubjuncTV and is the imaginary invention of Douglas Hofstadter. The SubjuncTV is an imaginary TV set on which you can dial alternative *possibilities*—what might have happened. Here's how you might use this technique.

1. Select a recent experience you'd like to have had happen differently. Follow the same pattern as with instant replay: close your eyes, start with sensory details, stay in the present tense, make the situation vivid and real for the listener. "I approached that interesting person at the party, noticing particularly his tweedy professorial jacket and smelling the pipe tobacco."

2. Now, imagine reaching out and switching the channel to an alternative version of the same incident. "Instead

of pausing awkwardly, reconsidering whether to say something or walk past him to refill by plate, I caught his eye and went directly up to him, and said . . . .")

3. Now, be just as concrete about what happened, as you were with the version that actually occurred.

4. Finally, enjoy the feeling of how the incident went this time.

This chapter discussed several key Peak Learning tools you can use to make your self-directed learning more powerful and effective. It covered techniques you can use before you start in on a learning project, such as pro-active reading and the Vee-heuristic technique, to ensure that you get the most out of the time you spend. It also covered things you can do while you are in the midst of learning, such as mind-mapping and probes, which keep you actively involved in your learning process and help to make the process itself a creative and enjoyable activity. Finally, I've mentioned several techniques you can use after having learned something to retain the information you want to keep. With these tools at your command, you're well on the way to your Peak Learning pilot's license!

VII

Developing Your Critical and Creative Thinking

Most of us unconsciously *narrow* the range of mental powers we use when we learn. One reason for this is that we were taught in school to concentrate on what we had to learn, and that process often stifles the broader range of mental powers we have available: imagination, intuition, making associations and connections to relevant (and irrelevant!) experiences, questioning, and synthesizing new insights. Ignoring all these natural responses tends to drain our energy and undermine our learning.

In this chapter, you'll learn how to bring the full spectrum of your mental skills to bear on what you choose to learn. Tapping these additional learning tools is as easy as knowing the *right* way to use such thoughts as:

"I have a gut feeling about this topic . . ."
"I could imagine it working this way if . . ."
"This reminds me of the time I . . ."
"I still have this nagging question about . . ."
"When I put it all together, I think the bottom line here is . . ."

Intellectual independence at the earliest possible age should be the object of education. . . . The initiative should be transferred to the student himself at the earliest practicable stage. . . . The educational ladder should hoist the climber up from the child's passive role to the adult's active one.

ARNOLD TOYNBEE

The following techniques will show you how to do that. You are going to explore ways to think about your learning experiences that will let you focus the power of your whole mind to make your learning even more your own. Using these strategies, you will be able to:

- *do more with what you learn,* by evaluating your learning in terms of outcome.
- *generate penetrating and insightful questions* derived from all of your past experience.
- *spark your creative flow of ideas* through conceptual strategies such as morphological forced connections.
- *orchestrate your mind's full range of powers,* including your imagination, intuition, and feelings, in a coordinated way.

CLIMBING THE LADDER OF LEARNING OUTCOMES

As was seen earlier, *learning* means different things to different people—even among teachers and experts in education. These differences provoke heated debates about what schools and colleges should be doing. Some people feel the focus should be on basic facts; others want the emphasis to be on general training and life skills; still others stress understanding or analytical abilities. The debates rage from local schoolboard meetings to national presidential campaigns.

Fortunately, when it comes to our personal learning as adults, we don't have to choose. And we shouldn't! *All* kinds of learning are vitally important to us, at different times and in different situations. Moreover, becoming aware of the different ways to think will enable you to expand your abilities in any learning situation.

There are six major outcomes of learning, according to Professor Benjamin Bloom of the University of Chicago and his associates. Their taxonomy is widely accepted as the most useful way to think about the results of learning.

1. *Recall.* Remembering bits of information, terminology, techniques, usage, etc.

2. *Comprehension.* Understanding what you read or hear, so that you can summarize or explain it.

3. *Application.* Using what you've learned in concrete situations.

4. *Analysis.* Breaking a subject down into its component parts, so that you can see how they fit together and spot any logical gaps where you might need more information to understand the subject better.

5. *Synthesis.* Putting all the pieces back together in a new, personal way that combines information from many different sources and creates new insights and ideas about the subject.

6. *Evaluation.* Judging the value of material for a given purpose.

Happenings become experiences when they are digested, when they are reflected on, related to general patterns, and synthesized.

SAUL ALINSKY

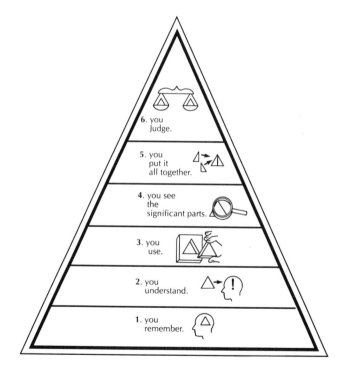

*One learns from books . . .
only that certain things
can be done. Actual
learning requires that
you do those things.*

FRANK HERBERT

I prefer to turn this list upside down and see it as a ladder of increasingly complex outcomes of your learning.

These steps are listed in rough order of complexity, of course. You have to absorb some facts before you can begin to understand a subject, and understanding usually precedes application. However, this hierarchy is remarkably comprehensive; almost any cognitive outcome of your learning can be fitted under one of the six categories. It is therefore useful in thinking about what you really want to get out of any learning situation.

For example, we're all familiar with the kind of person who "learns more and more about less and less" but never gets to the point where the learning becomes *useful* in his or her life. Such people are stuck at the lowest level of this hierarchy of learning outcomes: simply remembering facts.

Recognizing the need to move up the list to more complex learning outcomes gives rise to some of the most accepted truths about learning. Everyone agrees, for instance, that at a certain point in one's study of anything, the best learning experience is to *teach* what you've learned to someone else. This principle applies to every kind of learning, from learning to be a gourmet cook to mastering differential calculus. In shifting from learning to teaching, you also have to climb the ladder. You are moving from remembering and understanding to *using*. Moreover, to teach you have to go even higher: you must *analyze*, or break the subject down into its parts, and *synthesize*, or put it together again. Finally, if you're doing a conscientious job of teaching, you will need to *evaluate*—to judge not only which parts of the material will be most useful to the person you are teaching but also how well you are conveying information.

Consider the application of this hierarchy to your reading. Suppose you've read a popular treatment of some scientific subject and a friend asks you about it. What would you say?

You might start with stating whether or not you liked the book and why—in other words, giving your *evaluation* of the book, focusing on how useful it was in explaining the subject. You then might offer a short summary of the author's message—that is, provide your own *synthesis* of the book. (This is probably the best test of whether you really understood the book.)

Responding with several significant parts of the author's argument would let you explain how the conclusions you or the author reached depended on certain facts or assumptions. This would be your *analysis* of the book. If the book is, for example, the instruction manual for building a ham radio, showing that you understand it would involve actually building it, or *using* the information.

Finally, you may *remember* only bits and pieces, specific facts or interesting points raised. Depending on your goals, that may be all you need to absorb from the book.

Other ways to practice and use these learning processes will occur to you once you start looking for them. You will benefit from knowing how to *adjust* the kind of learning you are doing, so that you can advance from merely learning more and more facts to beginning to cultivate insights, applications, and new ideas from what you are learning.

PLAYING WITH CATEGORIES

At the upper end of the learning ladder, when you turn to analysis, synthesis, and evaluation, there is an important skill you can master that will help you to think more clearly about your subject: categorization. It seems to be a natural human function, and one which has paid off in a big way for civilization! We all make categories about simple things in our lives, such as what foods to buy or what clothes to wear, but when it comes to learning we may take that skill for granted. Whether we are explicitly learning or simply experiencing events, becoming aware of the categories we use—and revising them whenever we choose—is the key to being able to analyze a subject, synthesize new insights about it, and evaluate how suitable something is for our purpose.

We must remember that our categories are not rigid pigeonholes, but useful tools. They provide a way to make a tentative organization of a mass of data, much like the mind maps discussed in Chapter Six. It is usually a mistake to apply an old category to a new experience without considering what

Most [scientists] have never considered how it is that human perception and categorization underlie all that we take for granted in terms of common sense, and in more primordial ways that are so deeply embedded that we even find them hard to talk about. Such things as: how we break the world into parts, how we form mental categories, how we refine them certain times while blurring them other times, how experiences and categories are clustered associatively, how analogies guide our intuitions, how imagery works, . . . and so on.

DOUGLAS R. HOFSTADTER

is different about the new situation. Likewise, we must be careful not to assume that our tentative categories cover all aspects of a subject and never have to be revised.

Here are two examples of ways my wife and I taught our children to use categorization.

One fall when they were about seven or eight, we wanted Peter and Elizabeth to notice the wonderful differences among leaves—shape, color, and so forth. But instead of trying to *teach* them that, or even urge them to look closer, we went on a leaf hunt, looking for as many different kinds of leaves as possible. You scored points by finding a leaf that was different from any that others had already found.

Then, instead of just urging them to look carefully at the leaves to detect differences, we set them to devising a *classification* system for them. It could have any criteria they wanted, as long as they could both agree on where each leaf belonged and provided that every leaf fitted under some category. The categories had to do with such factors as size, color, shape, and number of points.

Suddenly, by operating on the *analytic* level of breaking the leaves down into categories, the children were keenly observing and comparing. This was, of course, an introduction to the basic scientific process of *taxonomy,* which resulted in organizing the elements into the periodic table and classifying animals and plants into different species.

Later on, when we wanted the children to learn about the propaganda techniques they were seeing in TV ads, we turned again to this climbing-the-ladder approach. Instead of trying to teach them the techniques abstractly, we just asked them to identify any one technique used in each ad as it came on, giving it whatever name they liked. When they had generated ten or so categories, we scrawled them on a piece of cardboard and taped it to the side of the TV set. Some of the categories they came up with were "Famous Person," "Fear of Smelling Bad," "Having a Better Car Than Your Friends," and "Everybody's Doing It."

Then the game changed. When each ad came on, the challenge was to figure out what category it went under or to devise a new one. Within a week, the kids themselves—using the learning skills of analysis, synthesis, and evaluation—had refined their own set of propaganda categories. You can imagine how much more interested they were, then, to see what the books said on the subject. They were intrigued to find out where the experts' categories duplicated theirs and where they had come up with different ones, or just different names. Needless to say, they hadn't come up with textbook terms like *argumentum ad vercundiam* (meaning "an appeal to an authority"—their "famous person"), *argumentum ad populum* ("everybody's doing it"), or *argumentum ad misericordiam* (an argument from fear or weakness). But you can imagine how delighted they were to discover that these were the Latin tags for the same categories they had created.

This game of categories can be played in all kinds of situations, from the frivolous to the serious. The important feature is *not* whether your categories are "right," nor is it whether the experts agree. Categorization is *your* analytic tool to serve *your* learning purposes. Actively categorizing your experience is a way to pay attention to what's happening so that you can learn from it.

Educators and employers tend to ignore the immense amount of learning that almost everyone does outside of school and college. This is often a personal tragedy, and it prevents our society from benefitting from the "hidden credentials" which Americans could be contributing to business and social life. We are blighting lives and hobbling our progress by failing to find ways to discern, harness, and reward these "hidden credentials."

PETER SMITH

LEARNING FROM YOUR EXPERIENCES

You have an immense database from which you can learn things to help you cope with current problems. By reaching back for the most relevant prior experiences in your life, you can locate lessons learned then that apply in the present.

You do this already, of course. One of our most familiar experiences is to be reminded of something that happened in the past when we are experiencing something similar in the present. Many of us inevitably remember a particularly unpleasant elementary-school teacher every time we happen to see the wicked witch in the classic movie *The Wizard of Oz*. We can also be reminded of a friend's experience with a certain store when we are about to decide whether or not to make a purchase there.

This process of being reminded of a relevant past experience was identified as basic to all learning by the great psychologist William James. A contemporary psychologist, Professor Roger Schank of Yale University, was as intrigued as James with this simple "reminded-of" phenomenon. He collected examples from coworkers, asking them for recent instances in which they had found themselves using past experiences to learn lessons that applied in the present.

One of Schank's coworkers reported seeing a TV commercial for a new video game in which an announcer offered the viewers a free game for buying two games at the normal price. The first thing it reminded him of is that the flip side of a hit record is often an awful song that nobody wants to hear. Then he thought of the free tickets offered to subscribers to our regional theater, which are usually to a play they can't sell out. He also remembered how the excerpts from new movies used in TV ads are sometimes the only part worth seeing. Putting all those together, he remembered an aunt of his who used to take him shopping and warn, "The strawberries on the top of the basket are the best ones you're going to get in that basket."

Schank points out that this person has created a whole category of events he can mentally access. This category might have a label like "getting stung when promised something for free," "examples of the principle that you get what you pay for," or "sellers who mislead you by featuring the only good part of their product." Having created such a file in his mind, and fitting experiences into it, the viewer made his past experience as a consumer useful in the present.

While such "reminded-of" experiences occur constantly to all of us, we usually do not consciously learn from the information. We are reminded of past situations on a random basis, and often the accessing mechanism is subconscious. Sometimes the past experience is clearly relevant, as in the case just cited; but more often, the past experience that comes to mind appears irrelevant: observing the color scheme of a room, smelling a man's cologne or a woman's perfume, hearing a tone of voice or noting a quick turn in the weather, for example.

What we really need, Schank explains, are techniques to *control* which past experiences are called up. By making our recollections more conscious we can benefit far more from the lessons learned. He continues:

If we can find ways to be reminded *when we want to,* we can have a very powerful set of data available to us at any time we wish, not just at the whim of our unconscious. Our own experience, when called upon at the right time, can allow us to learn a great deal. . . . We can come across events in our past that allow us to compare current events to ones in our past. What we want is to be able to take full advantage of history, both personal history and cultural history. [my italics]

The following exercise is based on several ways in which Schank suggests you can access your own past experiences more powerfully and consciously, using the analysis of a past event to help you understand more deeply a current event or solve a problem.

Time present and time past
Are both perhaps present in
time future,
And time future contained in
time past.

T. S. ELIOT

♦ ♦ ♦ ♦

Using Your Past Experiences for Present Learning

Identify a current situation, opportunity, or problem in your life that you feel might be understood better on the basis of your past experiences. It might be dealing with a troublesome person, deciding on a change in your work life, or understanding why you feel so positive or negative in a certain kind of situation.

Write or speak into a tape recorder in free-association style for two to five minutes about the situation you have identified. Your purpose is to bring it vividly to mind in all its aspects, bringing thoughts, feelings, assumptions, and projections to the surface. You might start by completing one of the following sentences or an appropriate version of your own:

What makes this problem hard to solve is . . .
What bothers me about this situation is . . .
It would help if I could think of ways to . . .
I'm wondering why I'm reacting by . . .
What's going on here might be explained by . . .

Now choose one or two of the following kinds of reminding that are most appropriate to your situation, and use the questions below to stir up recollections of comparable experiences you have lived through. Write a sentence or paragraph on each of them.

Era-Based Reminding
Focus on a past era in your life. Recall past experiences that are relevant

149

from when you were in college or high school; in your first job; in one of your early relationships; a young child; in one of the places you've lived for an extended period of time; on a vacation or trip; beginning child-raising; living through a historical period that meant much to you; or listening to certain popular songs or performers of a past era.

Question authority.

TIMOTHY LEARY

Live the questions now.

RAINER MARIA RILKE

Feature-Based Reminding

Focus on what features are important about the present situation. Recall past experiences that involve the same kinds of people or problems, and ask yourself the relevant questions:

- ♦ When did you deal with a person or people who share this dominant characteristic?
- ♦ When were you involved in the kind of organization that had the features of this one?
- ♦ When do you remember feeling the same kinds of emotions as you feel now?
- ♦ When did you face the same kind of pressure as you see in this situation?
- ♦ When did you hear the same words or terms that you are hearing in this situation?
- ♦ When did you feel in the same position vis-à-vis the problem as you do now?

Goal-Based Reminding

Ask yourself if the goal you are after now has been pursued by yourself in other situations or by others you know of.

- ♦ When and how have I pursued this goal before?
- ♦ Who else do I know who has pursued a similar goal?
- ♦ Whom have I read about or seen portrayed in plays, on TV, or in literature or the press who shared this kind of goal?
- ♦ How would people I admire for their skills and abilities go about reaching this goal?

Explanation-Based Reminding

Ask yourself what similar situations you have experienced in which you sought to explain things in a similar way. How might your strategy in those situations be helpful here?

- ♦ How have I explained this situation before?
- ♦ What explanations of this kind of situation have I read or heard about?

- What explanations of related situations might be applicable here?
- How could this situation be explained using various theoretical perspectives, such as psychological or philosophical systems, political beliefs, or business principles?

Once you have exhausted all the questions you can come up with that remind you of related past experiences, apply them to the present situation. Which reminders have the strongest similarities to your current subject? Can they help to resolve the problem? Can you find parallels between how you behaved in a previous situation and what you might do now? How would you have to change your past approach to meet the differences in the present problem?

For example, if you are uncertain about whether to suggest some idea to your boss, you may be reminded of her reaction to a previous suggestion made by a colleague. You might remember how that suggestion seemed tentative or half-hearted and how it opposed a policy your boss had endorsed strongly. Thus you might decide to approach her firmly, but only after first finding out whether she is open to the kind of modification you want to suggest.

♦ ♦ ♦ ♦

You will derive benefits from using this technique that go beyond insights into your current problems. Getting into the habit of accessing past experiences will affect the way you store your current experiences. You will actually begin to classify experiences and situations more and store them in more detail—thus developing your skills of contrast and comparison.

ASK PENETRATING QUESTIONS

A questioning attitude is the prime factor in the incredible learning we do in our early years, notes Professor James Adams of Stanford University in his classic *Conceptual Blockbusting.*

> Everyone has a questioning attitude as a small child because of the need to assimilate an incredible amount of information in a few years. The knowledge that you acquire between birth and the age of six, for instance, enormously exceeds

what has been consciously taught. A great amount of knowledge is gained through observation and questioning. Unfortunately, as we grow older, many of us lose our questioning attitude.

But that attitude is basic to Peak Learning. If I had to define the primary characteristic of a peak learner, it might well be the capacity to ask lots of questions, good questions, and know how to get answers. The model for this is, of course, Socrates, who launched our Western intellectual tradition not by propounding a new set of answers, but by insisting on asking penetrating questions.

Can we regain that questioning attitude and thereby turn our learning curve back, toward the way we learned as a child? Adams is convinced that we can:

> You merely need to start questioning. An emotional block is often involved here, since you are apparently laying your ignorance out in the open. However, it is a block that will rapidly disappear once you discover the low degree of omniscience present in the human race. No one has all the answers and the questioner, instead of appearing stupid, will often show his insight.

One of the best guides to developing this questioning attitude is Roger Schank, who was introduced in the reminding section. His book *The Creative Attitude: Learning to Ask and Answer the Right Questions* is full of useful advice and explanations.

One of Schank's most interesting points involves the degree to which creative thinking is based on failure. He suggests that the *cycle of understanding* begins when an expectation we have fails—something doesn't occur the way we thought it would. As a result, we ask why. Then we create an explanation, which often reminds us of another event. These lead to another question: How are these two events similar? This in turn suggests a new, more general explanation for *both* events. Since that generalization leads to a new expectation, we've gone back to the beginning of the cycle.

In summary, *failed expectation* leads to *question* ("Why?"), which leads to *explanation* ("Because . . ."), which leads to *reminding* ("Seems like when . . ."), which leads to *new question*

*'Tis a lesson you should heed
Try, Try again.
If at first you don't succeed,
Try, try again.*

("How are these the same?"), which leads to *generalization*—and that sets a new expectation.

This might seem like an exercise in futility. Why come up with explanations if our expectations fail? But that isn't how it works in practice. Some expectations *don't* fail—and then we can add the explanation for their success to our personal knowledge. The key issue is this: by actively creating many explanations throughout the learning process, you have a better chance of finding one that works. Every failed explanation rules out some possibility, and every successful one is worth trying again in similar circumstances.

As Schank suggests, your ongoing Peak Learning process involves actively explaining things to yourself, applying those explanations that work in one situation to new experiences, and evolving still more accurate explanations that can, in turn, be tried out again in the future.

This idea will be applied in the next exercise, "Questioning an Expert." It's an opportunity to sharpen the Peak Learning skill of creating and discarding explanations to enhance your learning.

In "Twin Peaks," *David Lynch and Mark Frost have understood that America, as we live it every day, is . . . an environment of anomaly.*

MICHAEL VENTURA

◆   ◆   ◆   ◆

Questioning an Expert

Through this exercise, created by Adams, you will experience the power of working with a *questioning attitude* instead of merely listening to an expert tell you about his or her field. Questioning is especially important in problem-finding and problem definition.

To do the exercise you need a cooperative person who is in a profession with which you are not very familiar. This exercise may take a certain amount of time, but if the person is a friend of yours or is interested in activities such as this, he or she probably will not object.

Begin by asking questions until you have isolated and defined a specific problem in the person's profession. Don't be satisfied with a vague, overly general, big-picture problem (for example, "medical care for the aged" would be too broad). Try for a specific problem statement that is obviously solvable with a small amount of effort, such as "Why does the sight of a hypodermic needle scare people?").

As you ask your questions, be aware of where your difficulties lie. Are certain types of questions more difficult to ask than others? What is your subject's response to different types of questions? Were you able to go from a very general problem statement to a specific one? Did you work with several problem statements on the way to your final one?

◆ ◆ ◆ ◆

Now, having had this practice in using the questioning attitude, you may want to learn more about how to formulate, hone, and answer questions. Schank points out that understanding can arise only from *not* understanding. For him, the key to creative thinking is something we don't understand, an *anomaly*. (As I wrote this, I found the word *anomaly* itself anomalous, so I looked it up in a dictionary. The word derives from Latin and Greek roots meaning "irregular, uneven, or incongruous.")

We've all seen those children's puzzles that ask for the number of things that are wrong with a picture. With great glee, a child will start counting upside-down cows, fish flying through the clouds, and so forth. That's a fairly simple example of training someone to spot anomalies. A somewhat more sophisticated example of the same principle is found in various psychological tests that ask you to decide which object is out of place in a group. Schank emphasizes anomalies because:

> To be creative in an area, you must learn to find anomalies in that area and make explanations of those anomalies. New ideas will start flowing. What does it mean to try to find anomalies? It means taking the experiences of a normal day and turning them around, treating them as if they were new. It means discovering why the normal day wasn't normal at all. . . .
>
> We can *decide* to see nearly anything as anomalous. When we do this, we effectively take *active* control of the understanding cycle, employing it in situations where previously it operated only unconsciously and passively.

Schank has a good point, one that is basic to the questioning attitude that peak learners develop. If you are able to find anomalies in everything instead of seeing daily events as just the same old stuff—the status quo—your experience of life is immensely richer and you develop a broader attitude toward learning. I also hope you noticed a recurring theme in both the Adams exercise and Schank's explanation of the importance of anomalies: *active control.* The more we are able to consciously direct our questioning and reminding skills, the easier it is to refine both our questions and our explanations. It is also quite a bit more *fun* to be learning in this way than to be a passive sponge only soaking up whatever an expert thinks we ought to know!

The following exercise will offer some ways to help develop your skills at picking up on subtle anomalies.

Thinking, willing, and judging are the three basic fundamental activities. They cannot be derived from each other and although they have certain common characteristics, they cannot be reduced to a common denominator.

HANNAH ARENDT

◆ ◆ ◆ ◆

Hunting for Anomalies

Schank presents four tools to assist in spotting anomalies. Select any three things that happened to you over the course of your day. They can be perfectly normal and ordinary things, events you might never think to question. Using the tools below, describe each of these events as if they were anomalies.

1. Assume everything is anomalous until proven otherwise. Ask questions such as:

    "What makes spicy Mexican food different from spicy Thai food?"

    "Why would someone open a new restaurant on that corner?"

    "How is that TV commercial trying to get me to buy their product?"

2. Propose alternatives to everything:

    "What if I used Oriental hot peppers in a Mexican salsa?"

    "Where would *I* open a new restaurant in this area?"

    "What information in a TV commercial *would* get me to buy their product?"

3. Reject standard explanations. Remember that the goal here is not simply to criticize everything, but rather to come up with new alternatives. Something "everybody knows" is a great target for your own original thinking.

4. Pretend you're a foreigner or a person from another planet. This is one of my favorites. How would you explain to ET, for example, such common earthly events as traffic jams or soap operas? What would you have to make clear?

◆ ◆ ◆ ◆

Most people think about things in only one way. Yet there are different types of thinking for different situations. Learning to distinguish and choose the right style of thinking is an art that can enhance your success, help you achieve your goals, influence others, and avoid making errors.

ALLEN HARRISON AND
ROBERT M. BRAMSON

SCHANK'S MAXIMS

This section closes with a final list from Professor Schank, one that sums up the best strategies for creative question-asking, as well as for Peak Learning as a whole. Some of them may appear obvious, something you already do from time to time. But that's the point here: while none of the following points is very hard to follow intellectually, Schank believes that *social* pressures keep us from being as creative as we can be. Either we're afraid of showing ignorance and looking dumb or we feel under pressure to accept what we were told without questioning—the don't-make-waves feeling that often seems so pervasive. As Schank puts it, "The difficult part is changing one's attitude toward one's own ability to think."

If you like, you can invent your own exercise to go along with Schank's Maxims, following the same pattern we used in the last exercise. In the following list, any comments I've added are in square brackets.

SCHANK'S MAXIMS

1. *Look for anomalies.* Anomalies are where the action is, creatively speaking.

2. *Listen.* You can't find anomalies if you weren't paying attention to what was going on in the first place.

3. *Find data.* Before you make a theory [or an explanation], look to the world around you, ask yourself what is happening. [Starting with a theory can prevent us from seeing important data.] The more you know, the more you can create.

4. *Classify, and invent new classifications.* Their real value is the generalizations they capture. [We can know why a category makes sense if we created the explanation behind it.]

5. *Make rash generalizations.* The idea behind making a rash generalization is not to be right, but to be thinking.

6. *Explain.* When we learn something, it's because we have invented an explanation for it. We have explained it to ourselves.

7. *Refuse to learn the rules.* You must pick your spots for rebellion, be sure that you have reason on your side, and be prepared to take the consequences. [Being creative depends on discovering things for yourself.]

8. *Reject old explanations. Ask why.* [Authorities tell us to believe simple answers to complex issues.] . . . it is important to learn to distrust these explanations, not because someone is trying to fool you, but because the standard wisdom might be wrong.

9. *Let your mind wander.* . . . the process of letting your mind go where it wants can be useful if where it wants turns out to be an interesting place to go. . . . If you don't give your mind a little freedom every now and then, it may stop wandering.

10. *Fail early and often.* Failure is a good thing. We learn from failure. Take a chance. Have an idea and allow the possibility that it might be a bad idea. [Wisely, Schank also adds the following to his list:] The Eleventh Maxim: *Reject all the above maxims.* Who says I know what I'm talking about? Can we really enhance our creativity? That's a good question.

Nothing is so useless as a general maxim.

LORD MACAULAY

ORCHESTRATE YOUR MIND'S FULL RANGE OF POWERS

To understand is to invent.

JEAN PIAGET

Most of the techniques that have been covered in this chapter and the last are *cognitive;* that is, they refer to ways of improving the knowledge we get from our thinking process. What about the other ways your mind functions? Some of them were explored earlier in this book, but here you will learn how to *coordinate* them—to orchestrate them to get the best from each.

Take, for example, your emotions—how do you *feel* about what you're learning? What's your "gut reaction" to new knowledge, new ideas? You always have *some* strong feelings about whatever information you are dealing with. Becoming aware of these feelings—and using them as cues to your instinctive reactions—can often be crucial for good learning.

Similarly, what about your imagination? Your mind is never constrained by the facts at hand. It's human nature to make multiple connections to other things. How can you enlist fantasy, metaphor, humor, and other uses of the imagination to enrich your learning?

Then there is *intuition,* which is derived from a Latin word that means "to see within, to consider or contemplate." Intuition generally refers to a process of knowing that seems more like a feeling than an intellectual response—it is immediate, it "feels right," and we don't know (consciously) how we arrived at our knowledge.

The next few sections will explore several techniques to weave emotion, imagination, and intuition in with our more rational, cognitive learning tools.

SPARKING IDEAS WITH IMAGINATION

Creativity might be defined as getting lots of *different* ideas about something. Yes, I know we are all taught to believe that one *good* idea is worth a thousand bad ones, but how can you tell which is the good one if you don't have a considerable number to choose from? In short, real creativity means allowing your mind to generate as many ideas as possible, without prejudging their worth.

Another aspect of creativity is the ability to generate as many ideas as possible across a *broad* spectrum, not just one or two narrowly relevant lines of thinking. In an exercise in which you are asked to think of as many uses as possible for a brick, you could, for instance, generate *lots* of ideas by listing such activities as "build a home," "build a shopping center," and "build a garage" and continuing along this line, but you'd be lacking in diversity. You'd be outscored by someone who came up with "make an artwork," "break a window," or "reach higher."

How can you get ideas about what you're learning that are numerous and different—and also relevant and perhaps important?

One of the best methods is Morphological Forced Connections, a forbidding name for a delightful procedure. Here are the rules and an example of the procedure, as laid down by the inventors, Koberg and Bagnall, in their offbeat, life-planning manual *The Universal Traveler.*

1. State the problem.
2. List the attributes of the situation.
3. Below each attribute, place as many alternates as you can think of.
4. When your list is completed, make many random runs through the alternates, picking up a different one from each column and assembling the combinations into entirely new forms of your original subject. (After all, most inventions are merely new ways of combining old bits and pieces.)

EXAMPLE:
Subject: Improve a ball-point pen.

ATTRIBUTES:

| Cylindrical | Plastic | Separate Cap | Steel Cartridge, etc. |

ALTERNATES:

Faceted	Metal	Attached Cap	No Cartridge
Square	Glass	No Cap	Permanent
Beaded	Wood	Retracts	Paper Cartridge
Sculptured	Paper	Cleaning Cap	Cartridge Made of Ink

INVENTION: A Cube Pen; one corner writes, leaving six faces for ads, calendars, photos, etc.

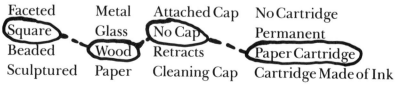

When I am, as it were, completely myself, entirely alone, and of good cheer, . . . it is on such occasions that ideas flow best and most abundantly. Whence *and* how *they come, I know not; nor can I force them.*

WOLFGANG AMADEUS MOZART

Another useful starting point to stimulate new ideas about your subject is a book called the *Strategy Notebook,* published by Interaction Associates in San Francisco. They present sixty-odd thinking strategies that can apply to any project you have, helping you to generate ideas. Any time you find yourself at a dead end, at a loss for where to go next, you can pick one of these notions at random and see what your imagination does with it. Here's their list and a sample of how you would use one of the strategies to generate ideas in a common business situation.

Build up	Display	Simulate
Eliminate	Organize	Test
Work forward	List	Play
Work backward	Check	Manipulate
Associate	Diagram	Copy
Classify	Chart	Interpret
Generalize	Verbalize	Transform
Exemplify	Visualize	Translate
Compare	Memorize	Expand
Relate	Recall	Reduce
Commit	Record	Exaggerate
Defer	Retrieve	Understate
Leap in	Search	Adapt
Hold back	Select	Substitute
Focus	Plan	Combine
Release	Predict	Separate
Force	Assume	Change
Relax	Question	Vary
Dream	Hypothesize	Cycle
Imagine	Guess	Repeat
Purge	Define	Systemize
Incubate	Symbolize	Randomize

Strategy for *Eliminate*

ADVANTAGES: The advantage of the technique of elimination lies in the possibility that you may be more sure of what you don't want than of what you do want. This strategy requires beginning with more than you need or want in the solution and eliminating elements according to some determined criteria. There is an element of safety in this strategy, because you have not overly extended yourself by deciding what you don't want in the solution.

LIMITATIONS: This strategy assumes that within the realm of possibilities you are considering, there is a good solution. However, after you've finished eliminating, it's possible to end up with nothing. Another difficulty is that it is easy to infer that you want the opposite of what you have eliminated (i.e., you don't want rain, therefore you must want sunshine, leaving out the possibilities of snow, fog, hail, etc.). Thus elimination must be tempered by caution and good judgment.

The following exercise presents a structure for the stimulation of new ideas.

The readiness is all.

WILLIAM SHAKESPEARE

◆ ◆ ◆ ◆

Who Needs Our Product?

Have each member of your group make a list of all the possible customers for the product you want to make. Don't leave out any ideas or associations anyone suggests, no matter how remote or incongruous. Write down all the ideas.

When everyone agrees that they cannot think of any more possibilities, each member of the group should go through the total list of ideas you've recorded. They should eliminate any potential customers they don't consider reasonable and write down their own personal lists of whoever is left. When all members have completed their own elimination lists, pin up all the personal lists on a display board so that everyone can share one another's ideas. This exercise has the advantage of allowing participants to get personally involved in the subject by using the strategy of elimination, and it can be modified to encompass a variety of subjects.

◆ ◆ ◆ ◆

By now you should be aware that generating a great many ideas about some subject is a good deal more like a game than like following some rigid formula or set of rules. Imagination involves *play*, letting the mind wander and seeing what it comes up with on its own. Since imagination is crucial to creativity, it should come as no surprise that creativity is just as playful.

Both of our previous examples referred to *conscious* processes—things you do with your mind. We now turn to what may be the greatest storehouse of creativity we all possess: the mysterious unconscious processes of intuition.

USING INTUITION

Precisely because our intuition operates outside our conscious awareness, it remains difficult to say much about it that can be scientifically verified. Intuition also lies on the border between the *emotive* learning techniques discussed in Chapter Three and the more cognitive skills covered above.

For the purposes of this book, however, I want to emphasize only that using your intuition can make a significant difference to your learning. It allows you to leap over detailed reasoning steps to reach a conclusion, emphasizing what your whole brain tells you is right without slowing down your thinking by forcing you to check each minute detail for flaws. Intuition can give you that sudden flash of insight that is the key to solving the whole problem. In many cases, this may be all you need for some learning project. As self-directed peak learners, the in-between steps just may not do much for you, but if and when necessary you can always go back and fine-tune the details later.

The keystone to intuition in Peak Learning is the recognition that learning is not just something you do, it is also something you *allow to happen.* Chance and luck can help your learning, if you let them. So you shouldn't be afraid to follow your hunches, even if you can't completely explain how they will work out in advance. How can you encourage this attitude?

First, welcome serendipity. We've all had experiences where we learn something new, such as an unfamiliar word, and suddenly find several opportunities to use it in the following few weeks. If you remain open to the opportunities fate sends your way, chances are at least some of them will be helpful. This is why peak learners make a habit of trying new things, reading books on subjects they never thought to study, talking with chance-met acquaintances like fellow passengers on a plane trip, and generally keeping an eye out for interesting anomalies. All these things help keep us open to serendipity and luck. When we take the time to think over such experiences, to consider what they might mean to us, we can find amazing treasures we would never have thought to look for.

Second, use your learning log to record any faint stirrings of thought that you might ordinarily dismiss as irrelevant, odd, or unproven. Remember, we've all been conditioned to believe that we have no right to our own judgment in some subject until we've mastered what the so-called experts already know. As you've seen in Chapter Six and in Schank's Maxims, the "Novice Effect" can actually deliver new insights *because* we are looking at some subject with fresh eyes.

Writing down such traces of creative thought may lead to useful new insights, because your intuition can function as an early warning system. You will have plenty of chances to test out the ideas as you learn more, and you may learn more from a wrong idea than from one that proves to be correct.

Third, consult your intuition. Explore how you *feel* about a learning project, the goals you set, the resources you consider, and the actions you are preparing to take. If you find yourself uneasy about any of them, look more closely and see if you can figure out why.

For example, you may be trying to solve some business problem and get a sudden flash about how to do it while taking a shower one morning. Your intuition may be telling you to try that solution first, rather than investing several hours in preliminary research. Why not give your sudden flash a try? Or you may be browsing in a bookstore when a particular cover suddenly strikes your eye. It may not be a book you would normally choose, but your intuition may be suggesting this book is worth looking at. In short, your intuition is a direct channel to the combined skills of your entire mind, a subtle whisper telling you something that you didn't realize you knew.

Initially, this may take some effort on your part. All through our school years, we were told to disregard feelings of discomfort; after all, learning was supposed to be hard work, not feel good. We were supposed to adjust our preferences to the teacher's plans. Happily, that is no longer true for us as adults.

The main difficulty of thinking is confusion. We try to do too much at once. Emotions, information, logic, hope, and creativity all crowd in on us. It is like juggling with too many balls. What I am putting forward . . . is a very simple concept which allows a thinker to do one thing at a time.

EDWARD DE BONO

Our feelings can serve as informative meters, providing feedback based on clues that escape our conscious gaze. Learning to make the most of this information—by letting it come to the surface of our minds without prejudging what it "should" be—is a valuable habit. The more we can do this in our learning, the more we encourage ourselves to exercise our intuitive skills on our own behalf.

SIX THINKING HATS

I'll close this chapter with one of the best ways I know to orchestrate feelings, imagination, intuition, and rational thinking in learning, a process developed by Edward de Bono called Six Thinking Hats. De Bono is generally regarded as a world pioneer in directly teaching thinking as a skill. He is best known for his term *lateral thinking,* which refers to the process of coming at problems *sideways* instead of following a strict, step-by-step approach in order to stimulate creative solutions.

De Bono has a unique capacity for devising simple, *usable* methods for better thinking. Of the Six Hats system, he says: "I could have chosen clever Greek names to indicate the type of thinking required by each hat. That would have been impressive." (De Bono was a Rhodes Scholar at Oxford and holds a Ph.D. from Cambridge, so he wouldn't have too much trouble doing it.) "But it would have been of little practical value, since the names would be difficult to remember. I want thinkers to *visualize* and to imagine the hats as actual hats."

De Bono asks you to imagine (or actually obtain) six colored hats, each representing one of the major roles your mind plays in its learning process. Each of these hats encourages you to see your subject in a unique way. Used together, they enable you to choose the best ways to think about your subject, to switch from one way to another, and to know that you've covered all the major ways by the time you've finished.

Hats are a familiar metaphor in our learning history. From our school days, most of us can still remember allusions to the dunce cap that early American schoolteachers made slow pupils wear, or to the injunction to "putting on your thinking caps." In this case, we're using the hats to stand for roles. (You may wish to go back to Chapter 6, pages 128–130, to review De Bono's explanation of mental role-playing as part of the exercise on probes.)

Now, start by forming a mental picture of the six hats, each one representing an essential way of thinking about any problem or issue:

- *White hat*—used to think about facts, figures, and other objective information. (You may wish to associate the color with a scientist's white lab smock.)
- *Red hat*—used to elicit the feelings, emotions, and other nonrational but potentially valuable senses, such as hunches and intuition. (Think of a red heart.)
- *Black hat*—used to discover why some idea will *not* work; this hat inspires logical, negative arguments. (Think of a devil's advocate or judge robed in black.)
- *Yellow hat*—used to obtain the positive outlook; sees opportunities, possibilities, and benefits. (Think of the warming sun.)
- *Green hat*—used to find creative new ideas. (Think of new shoots sprouting from seeds.)
- *Blue hat*—used as a master hat to control the thinking process. (Think of the overarching sky, or a "cool" character who's in control.)

The hats are particularly useful when you're attempting to solve a problem or make a decision, such as whether to take a certain job, rent an apartment, vote for a candidate, enter a relationship, or select a vacation spot. In situations like these, keep the hats in mind as you gather information for your decision and again at the point when you actually make it.

The following exercise provides a taste of the benefits you can gain with de Bono's playful *hat trick*.

♦ ♦ ♦ ♦

Using the Six Hats

1. Select a problem or issue on which you need to make a decision based on the facts, your feelings, what might happen in

Things learned on earth we shall practice in heaven.

ROBERT BROWNING

the future, and risks—in other words, virtually any significant decision from making an investment to entering a new relationship.

2. Express in one sentence what you'd like to accomplish in this little thinking exercise. Use your learning log or a pad, but be sure you have at least six separate sheets—one for each hat.

3. Decide which of the hats would be good to start with for this problem. Do you need to bring your real feelings to the surface? Figure out what you need to learn next about the situation? Project the future consequences of a decision? Clarify the risks that are bothering you? (These first three steps are, of course, made using the blue hat—you are deciding what to think about and how to approach your problem.)

4. Using one page for your notes on thoughts prompted by each hat, go through all six hats. Take as much time as you like, but put down at least three items under each. Your thoughts should address the following questions.

WHITE: What facts would help me further in making a decision? How can I get them? (From whom? Where)

RED: How do I really feel? What *gut* feelings do I have about this situation?

BLACK: What are the possible downside risks and problems? What is the worst-case scenario?

YELLOW: What are *all* the possible advantages? What would be the best outcome?

GREEN: What completely new, fresh, innovative approaches can I generate? What creative ideas can I dream up to help me see the problem in a new way?

BLUE: Finally, review your thoughts. Sum up what you've learned from this comprehensive display of your thinking about your chosen subject, and decide what your next steps need to be.

When you finish, collect all six sheets and look them over. You will probably discover that "putting on the hat" led you to generate more ideas in each area and to do so with greater freedom.

♦ ♦ ♦ ♦

These last two chapters have presented the meat and po-
tatoes of the Peak Learning system—proven exercises for significantly increasing your ability to learn and to actively manage your learning. From pro-active reading and probes to
anomalies, categories, questions, and hats, it has been a whirl-
wind tour. If you've been reading straight through for an overview, I hope you'll take the time to go back and try at least those
exercises that intrigue you.

With this chapter, we have covered two of three areas of
Peak Learning we set out to explore: the affective, or emotional, aspects of learning (chapters Two, Three, and Four),
and the cognitive, or thinking, aspects of learning (chapters
Five, Six, and Seven). What's left?

In the next two chapters, we'll deal with *environmental* aspects of learning in two ways: First, we'll see how you can design your best learning space, and second, we'll explore how
some new technology can assist your learning.

Finally, in chapters Ten and Eleven, we'll go back and put
all the pieces together by explaining how to develop your own
Learning Project plans, and how you can find learning resources.

VIII

Designing Your Optimal Learning Environment

There probably has been a time when you've gone into some-one's study or workroom and thought, "This place *works*! No wonder she's so productive. *Anyone* would be up for learning and creativity in this environment." The right learning place can do the same thing for you. It can be anything from an elaborate office in your house to a room in your apartment or a corner of your bedroom. However modest at the start, a comfortable learning place is an important step in taking command of your own growth. When asked, "What does a woman need in order to be able to write?" Virginia Woolf responded with a phrase that became the title of one of her books: "A room of one's own."

Perhaps that's why the word *study* means both the *process* of learning and the *place* where it occurs. Many of history's greatest learners created for themselves an ideal place to learn. Even today's most effective executives are known for the care—and the flair—with which they have designed their offices to facilitate learning, thinking, and decision-making. When you're serious about something that requires study, you want to be

I spent a lot of time creating the environment where I work. I believe people should design a world where they will be as happy as possible.

B. F. SKINNER

The best office space will be a space where you want to work. We all have our idiosyncrasies and preferences, and the right place for one person can be a disaster for another.

PAUL AND SARAH
EDWARDS

in a place where you can be at your best, where you can retire to your own thoughts and ideas.

The dual meaning of the word *study* expresses an important truth: when you go to your study, you go not only to a specific place but also to a mood and attitude that is productive of a state of mind—Peak Learning. The way you design and arrange the space can help greatly to evoke both the feelings and state of mind conducive to high performance, making learning easier and more enjoyable. Environmental psychologist Franklin Becker puts the principle well in his lively book *The Successful Office.*

> Plumbers have wrenches; surgeons, scalpels; carpenters, hammers and chisels: the tools of their trades. Good tools make for good work. For knowledge workers—lawyers, writers, executives, accountants, professors, managers, therapists, stockbrokers, journalists, people who work with ideas and information rather than with wood, pipe, concrete, or steel— the tools of the trade are the office and all its equipment and furnishings. In fact, your office can be as important to your job as a scalpel is to a surgeon. When you realize this fact, you will take your office more seriously. You will become aware of the whole psychology of workspaces and workstyles that extend far beyond the conventions of decoration or design.

Whether you are designing an executive corner office or one corner of the dining-room table after the dishes are cleared, the act of dedicating a certain space to learning and arranging it to your specifications is crucial. It can mean better concentration and discipline, more ease of learning and enjoyment, and less interruption from others.

Over the years, I've had the privilege of visiting with some of the most notable learners of our times, among them futurist Alvin Toffler and philosopher Sidney Hook. What always strikes me is the way their learning/working environment expresses so much about their style.

Toffler's study is an immaculate high-tech room with state-of-the-art word-processing and computer equipment from which he can monitor and tap into information sources throughout the world. On the other hand, philosopher Sidney

Hook's study is an old-fashioned, cluttered professor's hide-away, with books, magazines, and manuscripts strewn about in a system known only to the proprietor. Both of these environments work for their creators. Both are ideal learning places. Both say: "This place works."

Learning in the right environment has made a major difference for participants in my Peak Learning workshops. In one participant's words: "I never realized how much support a learning environment would give to my reading and thinking. Now that it's set up, I feel it calling to me first thing in the morning for some brain aerobics, then again in the evening to do some journal writing. And on the weekends for some of my larger projects."

Another participant noted, "Before I created my learning environment, everyone seemed to feel they could interrupt me for any reason if I was *only* reading or writing or listening to tapes. Now, I get much more respect for the fact that I'm engaged and shouldn't be interrupted."

And a third participant had the following comment: "I simply get twice as much work done in the same amount of time from having everything I need—including the proper attitude—right at hand."

Designating a place as your study and making it your own is a way of taking yourself seriously. In effect you're saying to yourself and others, "The growth of my mind is as important a part of my life as eating, sleeping, socializing, and working— and I need a special place to do it." It strengthens your sense of yourself as a self-directed learner and signals that commitment to others.

There's an additional reason why your learning place is crucial to your most effective performance. Psychologists now know that learning is *state specific* in some important respects. This simply means that our learning is connected to the specific state and situation we are in when we do it. For example, students who learn a subject and also take the final exam *in the same room* generally do and feel better than if they learn it in one place and are tested in a new, alien environment. Apparently the visual, auditory, and other cues in the environment are associated with the learning, which becomes easier to recall when those cues are present.

Creative space . . . is the sum total of what nurtures, supports, inspires, and reinforces our creativity.

NED HERRMANN

171

Be thine own palace,
or the world's thy jail.

JOHN DONNE

An even more commonplace experience is going into your kitchen to do two or three things and finding that you forgot one of them on the way. If you're concerned enough to try to remember the forgotten item, you probably instinctively go back to the room where you thought of the three things and find that being there enables you to recall it.

This principle is applied in several ways in what follows. I'll discuss how color, sound, and graphics can all contribute to your productivity and learning effectiveness. You will learn how to harness these factors for your learning by *creating* the state-specific cues that work for you.

YOUR PERSONAL VISION

Start by simply identifying some of the elements that make up your ideal learning environment. First, recall one specific instance of feeling impressed by someone's workspace or office. What gave the room you're thinking of its distinctive qualities of both comfort and energy? When I ask my students this question, these are the qualities they usually recall in such rooms. How many apply in the case you've thought of?

- *Decor*—including light, color, and sound as well as evocative and intriguing pictures, photos, charts, sayings, objects, or plants.
- *Furniture*—the right chair, desk, shelves, work tables, and lamps.
- *Tools*—exactly what's needed, right at hand, nicely designed (computers, typewriters, pens, and so on).
- *Resources*—depending on what kind of office or workroom you want, the resources may range from a comprehensive and current dictionary (for wordsmiths) to the equipment of, say, a photographer's studio and darkroom.

Continue by doing a visualization of your ideal learning place in the following exercise. This visualization will be your base-line image. At the end of this chapter, after exploring some of the resources you might not be aware of, you will have a chance to revise that initial image, enriching it with new details that can make it work for you.

◆ ◆ ◆ ◆

Visualizing Your Learning Place

Make notes in your learning log or on a separate sheet of paper in response to the following questions:

1. Where would you like your learning place to be located? (In your home? If so, where? As part of the place you work?)
2. How large would you like it to be?
3. What kind of acoustics would you like? (Quiet or with some sound, and if the latter, what kind? Acoustically private or open to sound from the surroundings?)
4. What kind of lighting and color scheme would you like? (Strong or subdued? Lamps or diffuse lights? Natural or artificial?)
5. What kind of decor would you want? What kind of color scheme, floor covering, decorations, or art?
6. What kind of equipment would you want? (Typewriter or computer, drawing table or photography tools, etc.?)
7. What kind of furniture would you want? (What style of chair, desk or work table, bookcase or tool cabinet, etc.?)

Now, on another piece of paper, do a rough sketch of how all this would look. Don't worry about any lack you feel in drawing or designing ability—this is merely for your own reference later, at the end of this chapter.

◆ ◆ ◆ ◆

We can begin to experience fulfillment as soon as we choose to create environments permitting us to do so.

BOB SAMPLES

TUNING YOUR LEARNING ENVIRONMENT

It is time to explore some options and resources you may not have thought of. As you read, keep handy your notes on your ideal study, but jot down any thoughts you have for changes as you learn more about what questions you might ask and what possibilities are available.

You can start with decor, under which I include, as my students usually do, the use of light, sound, and decoration.

SOUND

For decades, teachers have been telling students that they can't learn well with the radio or TV on, yet many successful students have gone right ahead and done so. Now, psychologists are catching up with the kids' awareness of what works for them.

According to Professor Rita Dunn, one of the leading authorities on learners' preferences, "teachers and counselors frequently project their own preferences for sound or quiet onto students during learning, assuming that if *they* require the absence of sound to concentrate, the same condition must hold for everyone." She cites studies suggesting that "inherited differences in nervous system functioning require that extroverted individuals learn in a stimulating environment, while introverted persons prefer a quiet, calm environment with few distractions." Another study found that when sixth-grade students were matched with their "preferred acoustic environments" (with the presence or absence of sound), these students scored significantly higher in reading achievements and evidenced more positive attitudes toward school than did students who were mismatched.

Comfortable learning area off living room.

So you should feel free to suit your own stylistic preference in your learning place. Fortunately, you can do this even if you do not have acoustical privacy. If you prefer sound but want to avoid bothering others in your acoustical space, there are headphones such as those used with Walkmans. If, on the other hand, you prefer quiet but your learning place does not provide acoustical privacy, simple earplugs can very effectively muffle external noise to a degree to which you can easily disregard the residue.

Still another aspect of sound in your learning place relates to state-specific learning. You can actually *use* specific sounds, such as music, to cue your learning and creativity. Here is how Liza Cowan of the New York Training Institute for Neuro-Linguistic Programming does it.

> When I'm writing an article or working on a design I always listen to music. I will listen to several tapes before I find one that has just the right sound to accompany me for the specific work I'm doing. Once I've found it, I like to stick with it. I find as I go along that if I switch tapes I lose the mood and momentum; so I listen to the same tape over and over again. If I have to leave the work-in-progress for any length of time, which I frequently do, I find that when I put that tape back in

Full room study with filing area and wall shelves.

*And life is color and warmth
and light
And a striving evermore
for these.*

JULIAN GRENFELL

the machine, I re-access the state of creativity for that particular piece I'm working on. I have had people ask me how I can stand to listen to the same music over and over again. It seems boring to them. But I'm not really listening consciously. I'm feeding my unconscious mind, my creative part, keeping it on track.

There is even more evidence that sound can improve your learning. A Bulgarian doctor and educator, Giorgio Lozanov, was a pioneer developer of techniques for accelerated learning. In one study, Lozanov worked with students who were learning a foreign language. He discovered that if he played Baroque music in the background while they studied, the students were able to learn more vocabulary words than they could in a silent room. The background music seemed to significantly enhance their learning skills.

Whether or not you have been raised to believe that learning requires silence, feel free to experiment with sound as part of your Peak Learning environment. Try several different kinds of sounds for different learning projects and see if any of them allow you to feel more relaxed and focused on the subject you are learning. Remember, the basis of Peak Learning is discovering how *you* learn best.

LIGHT

One of the simplest exercises I use in my workshops is simply to sit a student down in front of a book and ask him or her to read a page. Then, before asking the student to repeat the performance with the next page, I replace the 60-watt bulb near the chair with a 90-watt bulb. "That's wonderful," the student invariably exclaims. Particularly as we get older and our vision becomes a little less sharp, simply increasing the wattage in our reading lamps can be a blessing.

But there's a broader aspect to the question of light and learning. Psychologists have discovered that many people suffer seasonal depressions when the natural light of the sun wanes, in the winter. This depression can be successfully treated merely by increasing bright, white light in your environment. Think back to any seasonal differences in your learning behavior. Do you generally find, for example, that you rack up a rash of reading over the summer, even during the times you're *not* on vacation and just as busy as during the winter? Or that your ambitious September learning plans, inspired by school openings, freeze up by early January? You may be unconsciously disinclined to read or engage in other learning activities in the lower lighting levels of winter.

If any of the examples rings a bell, you can use a number of different approaches to improve your learning environment. Try to take advantage of natural light by moving your desk or reading chair beside a window or by replacing your usual light bulbs with stronger ones. You might also consider full-spectrum lighting that reproduces all the wavelengths found in natural sunlight.

COLOR

The influence of color in our lives has recently been discussed in books, courses, and workshops around the country. The uses of color are being explored by psychologists in areas ranging from healing to personal success. For example, if you've visited a hospital recently you'll likely have noticed that bright colors are now widely used to improve morale and promote recuperation. You can even hire a color consultant to tell you which colors are best for you. They usually suggest different colors for different seasons of the year and, if you're female, which colors to use in your makeup. This know-how can be applied to learning as well, although some of the ways will surprise you.

First, you can choose a color scheme for your learning place that pleases you. More important, though, you can select colors that actually trigger the state of feeling in which you like to learn.

For example, here are some powerful feeling states that many of my students like for their learning. Each is associated with the kinds of colors that seem to reinforce that feeling, according to the Nippon Color and Design Research Institute.

♦ *Energetic*—orange–white, yellow–green, green–purple, gray–red, blue–orange:

Color helps determine whether people feel their surroundings are cramped or spacious, and how hot or cool the room feels. For a sense of excitement, cheer, and relief from boredom, use warm colors. Reds, oranges, yellows, and browns increase heart rate and respiration. . . . If you want to create a calmer, more serene, and restful environment use cool colors. Blues, greens, and grays slow down body responses.

PAUL AND SARAH
EDWARDS

177

A man should keep for himself a little back shop, all his own, quite unadulterated, in which he establishes his true freedom and chief place of seclusion and solitude.

MICHEL DE MONTAIGNE

"There is a lot of energy in colors such as these, and they transmit that energy to whatever they are applied to."

♦ *Dynamic*—red–orange, orange–blue, black–yellow, red–black, black–orange:
"Brilliant, energetic colors such as these suggest vitality, health, aggressiveness, humor, and youth."

♦ *Fresh*—yellow–green, blue–gray, blue–white, green–light green, green–white:
"Use these color combinations to brighten and give a cool and refreshing look."

Needless to say, you can express your color preferences in many parts of your learning place: the walls, rug, furniture, and accoutrements. Just imagine for a moment the difference between a study space in which the palette is red, black, and white (perhaps with a white formica desk top, black filing cabinets, and a red chair and desk accessories) and the same set-up in lavender and brown: a wooden desk, lavender chair, and light brown rug. Obviously color schemes like these suggest different styles of learning and thinking, since each of these two palettes would put you in different frames of mind for learning.

Colors can also be used to make the very *materials* of learning better organized and more stimulating. You can color-code your four or five major interests by using one color for each. Thus your red folders, notebook, and even pens can identify one major area of interest, whereas blue or yellow or green supplies can signal another. Such a system speeds up locating materials on each project—particularly when you're grabbing for the right folders as you run out to a meeting.

But far more significant is the psychological impact, yet another manifestation of state-specific learning. The unique *color* of each project energizes you for working on it. The color triggers feeling states and recollections about what you've been learning in that area. Recall the discussion of Edward de Bono's six thinking hats in Chapter Seven. Color serves to activate a different part of the brain for each hat in order to help you think differently.

Some notable thinkers of the past and present have used

colors this way: students of philosophy are familiar with the philosopher Wittgenstein's notebooks known by their colors; students of literature will recall Doris Lessing's *Golden Notebook;* and psychologists are familiar with Carl Jung's *Red Book,* in which he transcribed his inner learnings after his break with Sigmund Freud.

GRAPHICS AND DISPLAY

Your learning place should welcome you and stimulate you with vivid reminders of your interests and passions. You can inspire yourself by displaying photos, drawings, and other visuals about the people, places, and events in your field, or by posting mind maps of what you're learning and key words that have emerged from your study, or even mounting affirmations about your learning or key quotes from people you admire.

The great French essayist Montaigne created one of the first "ivory towers" as his personal learning space (he actually constructed a tower on his property, which he reserved for reading, thinking, and writing). He decorated its beams and columns with maxims and adages from the writers who had meant the most to him. There were fifty-seven quotes in all, such as this one from the Latin writer Lucian: "Preserve measure, observe the limit, and follow nature."

Informal sun room converted to a learning area.

179

Professor Robert McClintock comments:

Fifty-seven sayings upon the wall, upon the *study* wall. [Montaigne] sustained himself in a life of continuous self-education. The sobering sentences that surrounded Montaigne as he worked helped direct and sustain his formation of self; they reinforced a regimen of self-culture, speaking to him sagely as he cut his quill, shelved a book, stoked his stove, or gazed in silent introspection. Such sayings . . . set forth the ends and means of study, of meditation, inquiry, and self-formation.

FURNITURE

Most of us have a limited imagination when it comes to the kinds of furnishings now available from contemporary designers. If you haven't looked at fine furniture design recently, seek out the nearest outlet for it at office-supply and home-furnishing stores. You will find that your imagination will be stimulated by the many novel ways in which designers are using new materials, colors, and shapes to combine comfort and efficiency. And sometimes you'll be pleasantly startled by how some great old designs can be revived to good effect.

For example, several decades ago designers rebelled against the old-fashioned roll-top desk and introduced the contemporary ideal of the clean-as-a-whistle slab of wood, for-

Roll-top desk in living room.

mica, or glass. Recently, the most avant-garde designers realized that the old roll-top was actually an aid to learning. By leaving your materials as they are when stopping work and simply closing the top, when opening it when you return, you gain a wealth of cues about where you were and what to do next. Cleaning up by sweeping everything into a file folder or an in-basket, on the other hand, breaks up the patterns in which you've organized what you were doing and may necessitate a lot of time spent finding where you left off.

All I want is a room somewhere, far away from the cold night air, with one enormous chair. Oh, wouldn't it be loverly!

LERNER AND LOEWE

COPING WITH ENVIRONMENTAL PROBLEMS

All of us run into obstacles when we're learning. For some they may be interruptions, in person or by the omnipresent telephone; for others they may be noise, visual distractions, or even irritations within one's own body due to posture.

The best way to deal with such problems is to treat them as one-time mistakes that provide the impetus to take corrective action. To treat them this way, simply identify whatever it is that is interfering with your learning on a given occasion and consider how you can alleviate the problem. There's almost always a practical way. Eighty percent of the problems raised by participants in my seminars involve one of these five, for which I suggest the following solutions.

- *Background noise.* Earplugs may do the trick.
- *Visual distractions.* A simple screen may work.
- *Bodily discomfort.* Consider your posture, your chair, and the height of your chair and desk or work table.
- *Interruptions by phone.* Try having an answering machine take messages or screen calls.
- *Interruptions by people in your environment.* Let them know what simple signals will indicate that you're at work and that you would prefer not to be disturbed.

REVISING YOUR VISION

After covering the information about environmental effects and resources that improve learning, many of my workshop students rethink their plans for a personal learning space. To stimulate your own imagination further, I'd like to share four examples of what they came up with, ranging from the simplest to the most ambitious.

The first plan was drawn up by Marge Raymond, a purchasing agent and poet living in Lincoln, Nebraska.

> I don't have the luxury of extra space to claim for myself. So I knew my place wasn't going to be ideal, right away. But you said we should start, so I did, and it paid off. Just making the following small improvements made a big difference in my learning and my self-image.
>
> I was working with severe limits on the two things you need most to do this right: space and cash.
>
> I looked at desk surfaces that you can push up flush with the wall and latch closed when not in use, the old door-stretched-over-two-filing-cabinets trick, and making the dining-room table double as a desk. I did the manual work myself, including scraping, plastering, and painting the walls.
>
> It's quite a feeling to have worked successfully within the constraints to create the best possible solution for myself. To me, this personal place symbolizes that I'm now doing my personal learning. After all those years of using my mind for others in their space, I'm doing my work, for myself, in mine.

Here is a plan created by Jane Coos, a computer programmer and amateur stand-up comic who is studying for a B.S. in business administration at Pace University in New York City.

> Some of my happiest hours were spent in the library carrels at the Smith College library when I was a student. So after going through the two visualizations, I realized that replicating that would suit me just fine. It would evoke the warm, supportive, secure yet intellectually venturesome feelings I usually had when studying or doing research as a student. So I bought a carrel in lovely blond wood (nicer than the ones at Smith, I noticed when I returned recently). Since the walls of my apartment are a little thin, I also use earplugs when nec-

A place for everything, and everything in its place.

SAMUEL SMILES

essary. The sides of the carrel are covered with corkboard and serve as a bulletin board with a changing selection of sayings, pictures, and other visual stimulations. I have a wonderful cactus which sits on top, and reminds me of how much you can do with each little bit.

Albert Bosker teaches and works with environmental activists in Racine, Wisconsin. He describes how he planned his new workspace.

The look I was after was the one I'd seen several times at Wingspread, the Frank Lloyd Wright house hereabouts, built for the Johnson Wax family and now a conference center. From the first time I visited that building I had that feeling that "this place *works*—I could learn, create, and solve problems here." Maybe that's why they turned it into a conference center in the first place, actually. Anyway, what I did was choose that Wright-type wood decor. In fact, I bought some beautiful photos of Wingspread, and an architectural drawing, and used them as my decorations. I also have several wonderful quotes by Wright up on the wall, because he's an idol of mine, such as "Early in life I had to choose between honest arrogance and hypocritical humility. I chose honest arrogance and have seen no occasion to change."

My key inspirational books on the environment are right at hand, but the reference materials are tucked away in files to keep that clean-desk look that makes me feel everything's under control, and I can focus on the topic I want to put under the mental microscope. I don't think it would suit others, but for me the space and what I've made of it is perfect. Whenever I sit down at my desk there, I feel a little bit of Wright's spirit inform what I'm reading, studying, writing, or planning.

Andrew Payton, a retail store manager and amateur astronomer from Modesta, California, describes his work environment.

My learning place is built around my computer, because most of my learning is through communications, nationwide and occasionally international, via modem and telecommunications. For that reason the space has to be insulated from the outdoors, and rather antiseptic. Naturally, I've got storage bins for print-out paper, and bookcases built the right

On the threshold [of my study] I slip off my day's clothes with their mud and dirt, put on my robes, and enter, decently accoutered, the ancient courts of men of old, where I am welcomed kindly and fed on fare which is mine alone . . . and for two hours I forget all my cares.

NICCOLO MACHIAVELLI

size to hold my manuals. The color scheme suggests the computer age—it's beige and gray. But I like it that way. *Colorless* might be the word other people would use, but for me it's both restful and exhilarating to enter my little cocoon. I've found fellow-enthusiasts for the topics of major interest to me right now—lunar transient phenomena (that just means shifting light on the moon's surface, which can be very revealing about the lunar landscape), and an amateur astronomer named Kinnebrook (who was fired from the Greenwich Observatory in 1796 in a disagreement with his boss).

What makes this style of learning perfect for me is that I'm a night owl. Now, instead of searching around for the late-night movie on TV, I can spend an hour or two inputting my contribution to ongoing dialogues with others via modem. Then, the next day, at their convenience, my co-learners access my work on their computers and respond. The next night, there'll be two or three comments, references, thoughts, criticisms, or whatever, in my computer's in-basket. I find that the half-dozen people in each of these little networks can come up with the relevant data I need on virtually any topic within these fields. For me, that's a much more agreeable way to learn than poring through books at the library, or even searching on-line data bases, to find what I'm looking for.

Now, with the example of these four students fresh in your mind, it's your turn again. You had a chance earlier in this chapter to do a base-line visualization and plan for your learning place. Now that you've learned about other ideas and possibilities, you might want to reconsider your plan. This time, you will bring to the following exercise an enlarged sense of the possibilities.

◆ ◆ ◆ ◆

Your Ideal Learning Place—Not-So-Instant Replay

Visualize once more your optimum learning environment. Given some of the suggestions you have just read about, and engaging all of your senses, what additions or subtractions would you now make to the "room of your own"? How would you alter its decor, furniture, location, equipment, supplies, lighting, and color? How would you further enhance your study?

Think back to what you learned about your personal learning style and read the profile of yourself as a learner that you wrote at the end of Chapter Five. Does it suggest anything about how you might design your best place and conditions for learning?

The revised list of questions that follows is designed to draw on what you've just learned about your ideal learning environment. Note your response to each question on a separate sheet of paper.

1. Describe the location and size of your ideal learning space.
2. What type of acoustical environment do you prefer for learning? What kind of sounds, if any, do you feel might stimulate your best learning?
3. From the previous discussion, what color combinations do you think will enhance your comfort and ability to learn?
4. Describe the type of lighting and furniture that would most assist you in achieving your learning goals.
5. What kinds of decorations—pictures, mottos, mementos, objects, or whatever—will inspire your best learning?
6. What kind of equipment will you need—from an easel to a computer—to support and implement your learning projects? How can those tools best be arranged in the space described in your answer to question 1 to make them easily accessible when you need them?

◆ ◆ ◆ ◆

Every idea is a source of life and light which animates and illuminates the words, facts, examples, and emotions that are dead—or deadly— and dark without them. Not to engage in this pursuit of ideas is to live like ants instead of like men.

MORTIMER J. ADLER

Now, what can you *do* with what you've learned—and dreamed—about your ideal learning place?

FIRST LEARNING PROJECT: YOUR PERSONAL LEARNING SPACE

As an initial example of a learning project, this chapter can provide the basis for a project on this very subject. It will guide your further inquiries over the next few weeks as you drop into stationery and furniture stores; browse in bookstores and libraries for books on interior design, personal organization, and study systems; and talk with people you admire about *their* learning places (visiting them if you can). The result will be a design for your personal learning space that is congenial, inspiring, and practical.

Here's a sample outline for such a project. It is only one example of how you might organize your learning. Feel free to change this in any way to make it more in tune with your own personal learning style.

Purpose. To design a desirable and practical learning environment for myself.

Rationale. I've decided to take my learning seriously enough to do it as effectively and enjoyably as possible—and that includes the physical aspects.

Prior knowledge and experience. I've had some good and bad experiences with learning environments in the past, which I'll re-examine for leads to what works for me.

Environment. That's what this is all about!

Style. I'll approach this using what I've learned about my learning style (head for the nearest store with up-to-date furniture, equipment, and supplies; read up on interior design at the library; begin sketching alternative arrangements and showing them to friends who are sensitive to design. . . .)

Resources. In addition to the ones just mentioned under *Style: stores* that sell especially attractive furniture or supplies for my field (stationery store, art-supply store, etc.), art galleries and print shops, and computer outlets; *books and magazines* on interior and industrial design, available at the library; *interior designers* among my network of friends, acquaintances, and professional colleagues.

Results

1. A listing of the essential furniture, equipment, resources, and supplies for my learning space.

2. A layout plan for their placement.
3. An evaluation of items 1 and 2 above by someone knowledgeable in the interior-design field.

This chapter has discussed a number of the environmental factors that can help to make your learning easier, more enjoyable, and more productive. You've witnessed how color, light, and sound can combine to stimulate a state in which you can learn and remember better. You have also seen that designing your own personal learning space can be tremendously rewarding, a way to show yourself that you take your own learning seriously.

At this point, perhaps you are beginning to catch a glimpse of a pattern of habits that can encourage lifelong learning and improve the quality of your life. In Chapter Nine, "Setting Up Your Own Learning Projects," you'll see how to tie everything you've learned together and establish your personal "Research and Development Department."

IX

Setting Up Your Own Learning Projects

You have come a long way on the road to Peak Learning. One vital step remains: tying all the techniques and tools together into a workable system for lifelong learning. In this final chapter, you will do precisely that.

I'm going to offer first a graphic example of how two of my students have experimented with different types of learning methods. Both had useful experiences, but the differences in how they got them will provide a valuable illustration of the importance of self-directed learning. To clarify that lesson, I will introduce a model of personal learning drawn from the corporate world—the idea of a "Research and Development Department" for personal learning. Then, I'll get right down to some practical tips on planning your own learning projects. (You might want to dig out your learning project plan for an improved learning environment that you developed in Chapter Eight.) I will cover how to go about selecting the goals for your projects, choosing the right resources, and evaluating your results.

A human being should be able to change a diaper, plan an invasion, butcher a hog, conn a ship, design a building, write a sonnet, balance accounts, build a wall, set a bone, comfort the dying, take orders, give orders, cooperate, act alone, solve equations, analyze a new problem, pitch manure, program a computer, cook a tasty meal, fight efficiently, die gallantly. Specialization is for insects.

ROBERT A. HEINLEIN

AN EXPERIMENT WITH
LEARNING METHODS

*Two roads diverged in
a wood . . .*

ROBERT FROST

Two or three times a year I conduct an experiment that reveals the benefits and advantages of Peak Learning. The reason I can do this experiment only occasionally is that it requires an unusual situation: a pair of participants in a workshop who are each about to embark on learning the *same* subject, one by conventional instruction and the other using the methods you are learning in this book. By having each of them keep a log of their experiences, I get a vivid picture of what it's like to learn via these two routes.

At the time of this writing, the most recent occasion occurred about four months ago at a workshop in Kansas City, Kansas. Two comparable participants, Rob Patterson and Ruth LaCosta, were both about to engage on learning the same subject but in very different ways. Moreover, the subject they had in common is one of interest to virtually everyone: midcareer change. Both Rob and Ruth wanted to learn how to assess whether or not they should change their career paths and, if so, how.

Fortunately for my experiment, Rob decided to enroll in a course entitled "Mid-Life Career Assessment," since he would get it tuition-free on his campus as a faculty member. Ruth decided to use the methods you are learning.

I asked them both to keep logs of their experiences. Exactly three months later (when both Rob's course and Ruth's time frame were completed), I interviewed them both by phone after having reviewed their logs. The result was the following comparison of their experiences. I've selected representative entries from their much longer chronologies, but these entries were the most telling about the quality of their learning. Keep alert for three things as you read this fast-forward version of several months' learning by these two career-changers.

1. Who's experiencing more *high learning* and who seems mired in *slow learning*?
2. Who seems to be having more fun?
3. Who seems to be learning more that will be useful?

ROB—TAKING A COURSE

September 16
Enrolled by phone. Class meets Mondays 6–7:40 P.M. for the next 8 weeks. No special feelings at this time, other than a slight *chill* at getting the computer-generated registration receipt—seems a little alienating for a course in this sensitive area . . .

September 23
Stopped by bookstore and bought the two books for the course: *Career Development Workbook* and *How to Get Control of Your Time and Your Life.* The first looks interesting, but I'm a little put off by the hectoring tone in the other Lakein—just not my style. But having these new books is exhilarating, and I'm eagerly awaiting the start of the course.

September 30
First class session was last night. Instructor had us introduce ourselves and tell why we'd come. Several of the people around the room sounded interesting. Got overview of the course. Most of the stuff sounds useful, though there's going to be a couple of weeks on time management I don't think I need.

October 12
The course is picking up steam. In fact, it's so interesting that I really regret having to wait a week between classes. Seems to me we'd make a lot more prog-

RUTH—DOING IT HERSELF

September 14
Browsed through the shelf at the library on career change and found *Starting Over,* which looked intriguing. While at the library, also checked out catalogs of nearby colleges for courses, making copies of the catalog descriptions (the instructors might be useful to talk with). Feeling a little daunted by the "embarrassment of riches" in terms of how I might tackle this vast subject . . .

September 18
Two things happen when I mention this learning project to friends: *I* get more excited by it, and usually they mention some book or workshop or article they've just read that I didn't know about. So compared to a week ago, I'm more excited, and have numerous leads to resources.

September 29
This morning my goals for this project finally fell into shape. The long list of possible outcomes which I'd made from my reading and conversations winnowed down to three, and they seem important and manageable. Decided to postpone aptitude testing for now—I'm pretty sure my top priorities are in areas where I know my strengths. But I need to learn a lot more about opportunities.

October 6
I've discovered that I don't get

191

ROB—TAKING A COURSE

ress right now, as a group, if we could meet two or three times a week and really build on the momentum we're developing.

October 14
Not much to report. Had to miss last night's class (emergency faculty committee meeting about the dispute over parking privileges). Hated to skip the session—this is stuff I can really use—on how to interview people in other fields of interest. Actually, this is a topic on which I'd really like to focus—but there's only time for one session on it in the course. Then we have to move on to time management.

October 20
It was good to get back to class. Just wish we could dig deeper into information-finding techniques about fields I'm interested in knowing more about. I think that's the main thing I should be focusing on at this point. But this session was the first of a couple on time management, and it confirmed my sense that I don't really need this particular skill, though I can see that many other people in the class *do*, so it's certainly a justifiable part of the course. But sitting there while they go through it, hoping there may be some nuggets I can use, is slow going.

RUTH—DOING IT HERSELF

much by *reading* about this subject—I really need the immediate application to my situation and job-search strategies. So the main resources I'll be using will be: videotape series (3 tapes) on job search; structured interview with two job counselors; and a couple of hours on the SIGI computer-based system at the library. But scheduling appointments and carving out time to get to the library presents problems, so I've revised my schedule, tacking on two weeks to the deadline.

October 26
I'm on a run or something! Last night I watched one of the videotapes on job searching, and this morning woke up early with about a dozen ideas, which I mind-mapped before coffee! Realized this was that *flow* we talked about in the workshop, and that I should go with it, so I cancelled a loose lunch date, postponed the shopping I was going to do after work, and put in probably six hours on and off during the day. Result: I've got my second goal done!

November 11
Goal 3—writing six letters to "hiring people" in three different fields—is done. The letters went out this morning. This completes the project. But of course I can't relax: I've got to

ROB—TAKING A COURSE

November 14

The course has been a success for me—I certainly have gotten value for my money. But I don't think there's more to be gained in the three remaining sessions. Maybe it's time for me to continue on my own, setting some goals as we did in the workshop, and following up on some of the leads I've gotten in the classes. That way, I can go on from here at my own pace, poking into the topics I really need, and doing it where and when it's most convenient.

November 29

Finished the write-up for Gross. It was interesting to look back and realize how excited I was about this subject when I signed up for the course. I think the main problem was the lack of *fit* between my needs and style and what the course covered, how it was taught, and the books used. Sometimes the fit was just fine, and I learned a lot and enjoyed it tremendously. But at other times it went too slowly, or got off the track that was of keenest interest to me, or was too "discussiony" when I wanted more facts and techniques. Overall it was a good experience with a fine instructor and some interesting fellow students. But it feels good now to have the freedom to go further in my own directions.

RUTH—DOING IT HERSELF

look over my notes for Ron Gross, and write up that damn chronology! What a pain! Why did I ever agree to do it?

December 4

OK, I admit it: looking over my notes was of some value, as Ron said it would be. I was struck by three things that made this a good experience for me. First, I was flexible, changing my strategies when things bogged down. Second, I was resourceful and lucky in finding good resources to use. Third, I simply enjoyed the feeling of having the process under my control, so that I could step up the pace when I wanted, rest back on the oars at other times, and generally "go with the flow."

Tell me, I'll forget. Show me, I may remember. But involve me and I'll understand.

CHINESE PROVERB

What were your reactions to these dual chronologies? Take a moment to glance back at the three questions I posed before presenting them, and formulate your own responses before reading my interpretation.

My own impression is that Rob found himself mired in *low learning* at certain points ("sitting there while they go through it, hoping there may be some nuggets I can use"). Ruth, despite the initial frustrations of freedom ("an embarrassment of riches") entered the "flow" of learning once she had settled on her goals ("I'm on a run or something").

Rob clearly gained many benefits from the course. But he would have been helped even more if he hadn't suffered the glitch in his schedule ("emergency faculty meeting") and the too-long space between sessions just when he was getting really excited ("we'd make a lot more progress if we could meet twice a week").

Ruth, on the other hand, seems to have the advantage of being able to revise her schedule to fit her circumstances and fresh opportunities ("decided to postpone aptitude testing for now," "tacking on two weeks to the deadline," "cancelled a loose lunchdate").

It's hard to tell who got more out of the experience. Both Rob and Ruth appear to have considered it worthwhile, but my sense is that Ruth had more fun. Rob believes that his benefits were limited by the ways in which the class didn't fit with his changing circumstances, his style, and his individual priorities within the subject. Ruth attributes her feeling of success to her flexibility, resourcefulness, and "luck."

I have conducted this experiment nineteen times over the past seven years, and the results are remarkably consistent. In seventeen of the experiments, the do-it-yourself approach proved more satisfying, beneficial, and enjoyable. In over half the cases, the learner going the conventional route had a *more* negative experience than Rob did. There were four principal reasons for these poor outcomes.

1. The course did not address the learner's priority interests within the subject.
2. The style of teaching or the instructor's personality did not suit the learner.

3. The pace of the course was too fast or too slow.
4. The learner's participation was interrupted by some change in life-circumstance what precluded attendance or proved distracting.

Overall, then, this experiment has consistently confirmed my conviction of the superiority of the do-it-yourself approach. The contrast between Rob's and Ruth's experience is typical. You, too, will make your learning more flexible and powerful by taking control of the process.

SETTING UP YOUR PERSONAL RESEARCH AND DEVELOPMENT DIVISION

One interesting way to think about learning as part of your life is to picture yourself setting up your own personal *research and development division.* This little sector of your life is devoted to creating, through trial and error, the *next you.*

All successful businesses and other organizations these days must have a Research and Development Division—an R & D unit. Its job is to experiment: to develop the new ideas, products, and services that the organization will be offering in the future. No company or organization can afford to assume that it will continue indefinitely producing its current line. In a world of future shock, the future belongs to those who anticipate it, prepare for it, and even invent it. Unless an organization devotes some small portion of its current profits in R & D, it will find itself moribund the day after tomorrow.

Each of us needs to think of ourselves in this way, too. We need to invest a certain amount of our current resources—our time, our funds, and our energy and commitment—in developing our knowledge and skills. We need our own inner "skunk-works"—to borrow the striking if homely term used by Peters and Waterman in their *Pursuit of Excellence*—a time and a place to cultivate our own capacities and power, which are the products and services we offer to the world.

The purpose of this unit of your mental organization is to experiment with the interests, enthusiasms, skills, knowledge, and understanding that most attract you. It is an area of freedom in which you can play, taking risks that would be too scary to take in the more settled portions of your life.

Here is how I like to think of how such an area can be carved out of one's current program of activities.

Skunkworks refers to a small, high-powered organization working on a special project in a secluded facility . . . [and] is based on the idea that certain special work requires unique people working in ways that are legitimate, but that differ so much from the ongoing culture of the business that they cannot be contained within it.

NED HERRMANN

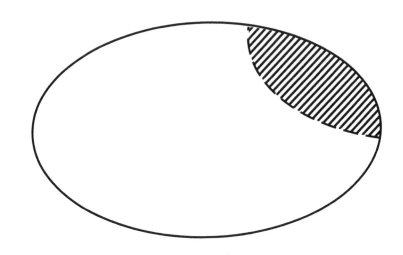

The shaded area is a portion of your time—perhaps 5 percent, or eight hours a week—devoted to your personal R & D. In this 5 percent of your life, you can run risks. Unlike at your job or in your personal relationships, you can pursue your most fanciful impulses, explore things that have no possible practical use, and entertain ideas that are out of step with what everyone "knows" is true. You can go down blind alleys without anyone else ever knowing you entered them and stumble without having to explain why. Or, if you tell everyone you know what you're up to, you will likely stumble onto some intriguing connections via networking.

You also will without fail find the seeds of the next you. What this means is that the "R & D" area is the best place to acquire the new knowledge, skills, and understanding that you want and need—and that will redefine who you are and what you do.

Here is how your skunk-works lead naturally to your next, expanded self.

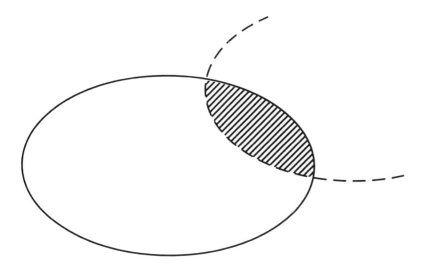

I've seen this happen a hundred times. Nearly every day we receive one or two letters from participants in recent—or not-so-recent—workshops who basically say one of two things: "It worked. I got so turned on once I started really following my interest in my chosen area that I just kept going on the momentum. I couldn't have guessed where it would end up, but you'll never guess what's happened . . ." or "Once I realized what I needed to learn to get what I wanted, I became energized in a new way. And once I knew how I learn best, I could make the process even more comfortable—in fact, quite enjoyable. And the results have been even more than I'd anticipated. You'll never guess what's happened. . . ." They are right—I never *can* guess!

I propose that you think of your Peak Learning activities as your personal R & D unit. A certain proportion of your time and energy should be devoted to acquiring new "product lines" of your own—knowledge, skills, and understanding. In that R & D area you can afford to take risks and explore areas that may not work out or in which you make some initial mistakes. But some of those probes will pay off, and those will form the basis of the new improved you—the person you want to become.

197

*Iron rusts from disuse,
stagnant water loses is purity,
and in cold weather becomes
frozen; even so does inaction
sap the vigors of the mind.*

LEONARDO DA VINCI

Viewed in this way, your personal R & D department will quite naturally use Peak Learning techniques. You will plan learning projects that derive from your goals, objectives, and concerns. You will conduct and manage these projects guided by your own most important questions about the subject, issue, or problem—not by an academic syllabus.

Your resources for learning can embrace the array of materials and services displayed in The Invisible University (see Chapter Eleven), including personal consultants, conferences, special-interest groups, computer databases, and simulations.

Finally, your learning will be monitored by you, as you reflect on and apply what you are learning, rather than by a test. The benefits are reflected in your heightened skills, wider knowledge, and deeper understanding. You know you have learned because your new knowledge moves you measurably closer to your goals. Peak Learning used for this purpose isn't education for its own sake or to satisfy some institutional requirement; it's education for practical utility, to help you succeed.

This is the Peak Learning approach to "learning your living." Significantly, it is the approach you would experience in the most innovative training programs available today for executives on the fast track. For example, The Corporate University has served executives from major companies including McDonnell Douglas, Atlantic Richfield, and Honeywell. It enables these future leaders to plan a self-development program to lead them where they want to go in their organization. The techniques and strategies that you are learning in this book are the ones these top executives master.

"You need to begin your preparation for major leadership responsibilities *now*," says Corporate University founder Lincoln Norton. "You can't wait until six months before you take on a big new job. Learning takes time, and it often has to happen at the *right* time. Your knowledge and skills must grow at a natural pace—not be force-fed in a hothouse, high-pressure environment. Start now, and you'll have the chance to let your knowledge 'season' as you apply new learning to new situations, month after month. Then, when opportunity comes, you will be ready."

PLANNING YOUR LEARNING PROJECTS

To implement your personal R & D, you will need to be able to make an effective learning project plan. An example of such a plan was presented in Chapter Eight, and you might want to refer to it during the following sections. Three key issues will be covered in this section.

Learning by self-directed inquiry is a perpetually self-empowering activity.

CHARLES D. HAYES

- ◆ How to select your learning goals
- ◆ How to choose the best learning resources
- ◆ How to evaluate the results of your learning

HOW TO SELECT YOUR LEARNING GOALS

When you take a course, you are accepting the goals predetermined by the instructor. Those goals are based on a general conception of what all the students should learn. Like any such generalization, it is not likely to apply precisely to *any* individual student in the class. Each student will have personal priorities for what information or skills should be included in the course and which of those should be emphasized. Even in a class on a subject as seemingly cut-and-dried as a foreign language, the businessman who will be conducting negotiations in Germany will need a different emphasis in vocabulary, idiom, and depth compared to the prospective tourist.

Moreover, when most of us take courses we don't even ask what the goals of the instructor are. If goals are indicated in the course description, we don't tend to look at them closely or compare them with our own objectives. We tend to project onto the enticing course description our own inchoate fantasies about what the course will do for us. That's a primary reason for the vague feeling of mismatch we usually have as we go through a course and sense that what we are learning isn't quite what we had in mind.

The first advantage of self-directed learning is that you set your own goals. When you plan and conduct your own learning, you define—and *refine* as you go along—the areas to be covered, in what depth, and with what slant.

199

The strongest principle of growth lies in human choice.

GEORGE ELIOT

Setting your own goals may seem to be a bit of a bother at first, but you will quickly find that the rewards come fast and are substantial. By really looking at what you want from a learning experience, you will be assured of getting results *and* you will enjoy yourself more along the way. The following are a couple of typical examples of how peak learners set their own goals.

Ruth Lewin, a middle-management executive in the toy industry, based in Chicago, had been bothered by her lack of an MBA. It wasn't that the degree was required for advancement; Ruth's worth in this highly competitive business was well recognized. "But I just wondered exactly what people learned in those programs—whether I had missed something essential that I didn't know existed." For a year-and-a-half Ruth weighed enrolling in such a program. But after the workshop, she decided instead to take a four-session "MBA in a Nutshell" course, just to get a birds-eye view of the contents and style of the program. She had a chance to examine three typical textbooks used in the key courses during her own course. As a result, Ruth realized that there were fewer than six topics covered in the standard MBA program about which she didn't already know and would like to know. Furthermore, she could readily see how she could learn about four of them quite adequately on her own. The fifth was offered as a separate course, and when last heard from Ruth was on the lookout for a way to learn the sixth. Instead of buying the standard MBA package, 40 percent of which she didn't need and 35 percent of which she didn't want, Ruth had identified the specific objectives and found her own best ways of achieving them.

Ned Herrmann, whose brain-dominance ideas were discussed in the chapter on learning styles, didn't start learning about the brain in a psychology class. Rather, he undertook a project: to put on a symposium on creativity at the public library in his community. "To prepare for the program panel," he recalls, "I began poking around the Stamford Public Library and, within an hour, experienced one of those wonderful moments each of us has during our lives when we feel suddenly illuminated by instant understanding. What I found in the library were contemporary reports describing historic breakthroughs in our understanding of the human brain. . . . Suddenly, here was a scientific explanation . . . of my own duality, a key not only to the mystery of my own makeup and behavior, but to that of others as well." Of course, Herrmann extended his "instant understanding" with months, indeed years, of further reading, research, and experimentation. But the important point is that he continued to pursue the subject in his own way, based on his developing needs and interests. He, too, was succeeding by selecting his own learning objectives.

The same basic principle applies to the most ambitious intellectual projects. Here, for example, is another learner's recollection of his project. Eric Dodds defined his learning objective out of a personal experience.

If a little knowledge is dangerous, where is the man who has so much as to be out of danger?

T. H. HUXLEY

> Some years ago I was in the British Museum looking at the Parthenon sculptures when a young man came up to me and said with a worried air, "I know it's an awful thing to confess, but this Greek stuff doesn't move me one bit." I said that was very interesting: could he define at all the reasons for his lack of response? He reflected for a minute or two. Then he said, "Well, it's all so terribly rational, if you know what I mean." I thought I did know. The young man was only saying what has been said more articulately by Roger Fry and others. To a generation whose sensibilities have been trained on African and Aztec art, and on the work of such men as Modigliani and Henry Moore, the art of the Greeks, and Greek culture in general, is apt to appear lacking in the awareness of mystery and in the ability to penetrate to the deeper, less conscious levels of human experience.
>
> This fragment of conversation stuck in my head and set me thinking. Were the Greeks in fact quite so blind to the importance of nonrational factors in man's experience and behavior as is commonly assumed both by their apologists and by their critics?

Eric's project took ten years and resulted in the book *The Greeks and the Irrational,* a milestone study in classical literature.

To formulate learning goals for your project, respond to whichever of the following categories apply. As an example, I've quoted the answer that Ruth came up with for her learning project on midcareer assessment.

Give us the tools, and we will finish the job.

WINSTON CHURCHILL

1. *What knowledge do I want to acquire?* What facts, concepts, terms, data, etc., do I seek?

   To list six good sources of counseling and job-finding help in this community. (*resources*)

   To discuss the important factors to consider in assessing the desirability and possibility of changing one's career. (*concepts*)

2. What do I want to *understand?* How do I want to be able to interpret the facts and data? How do I want to apply terms and principles? What reasoning and creative thinking do I want to do?

   To understand how midcareer assessment relates to my particular stage of life in other respects (marriage, children's ages, etc.).

3. What *skills* do I want to master? What specific know-how and how-to do I need?

   To use the SIGI computer-based career development system and the Occupational Categories handbook.

4. What *attitudes* do I want to develop? What new feelings, convictions, values, or sensitivities do I want to cultivate?

   To develop a positive and resourceful commitment to looking critically at my current situation and developing alternatives.

5. What *behavioral* changes do I want to implement? Which habits do I want to make or break?

   (*Not applicable.*)

HOW TO CHOOSE THE BEST LEARNING RESOURCES

In the next chapter you will become aware of the riches of "The Invisible University," the treasure house of resources for your learning. For any particular project, you will be choosing *which* resources you want to use. At that point you will want to come back to this section. For now, you may want to scan it quickly just to get an idea of the simple process involved.

Have you ever signed up for a class or workshop and discovered within the first hour that it wasn't exactly right for you?

(Rob, you'll recall, had a minor disappointment of this kind.) Or, worse, that for one or another reason it was *really* wrong? Have you ever read a third or half of a book on a new subject only to discover, when you mentioned it to someone in the field, that it had been superceded by a later treatment of the same subject? Some other examples will likely come to mind. Dull lectures? Inept seminars? An unhelpful videotape? An impractical computer program? The wrong expert or consultant?

Avoiding disappointments like these is what choosing resources is all about. Put more positively, it's about getting the best results from your learning.

Choosing resources smartly assures you that the materials or opportunities you are using are the best possible ones for you. Rather than just accepting the first or second thing you find available, you're taking the time to find the best.

The choice I'm talking about can be as simple as which of three books to pull off the library shelf and check out, or as consequential as which of two year-long certificate programs to enroll in. Choosing smartly applies equally to selecting a videotape course on improving your golf score and to sizing up a prospective mentor.

The principle for choosing resources is called the Five Percent Upfront principle.

Take 5 percent of the time you will be spending using the resource, to evaluate it in terms of your goals, style, and circumstances.

Remember Rob and Ruth? Rob's course took a total of some forty hours (it met once a week for two hours over fourteen weeks and required time for travel, homework, and writing a paper). Ruth spent just about the same time on her project. The planning of her project took about two hours—about 5 percent of the total time, including intermittent planning sessions to make midcourse corrections in her learning trajectory, resources, and schedule. But she clearly felt that her experience was successful and gratifying.

Based on Rob's and Ruth's experiences, it seems as though a "front-end" investment is well worthwhile. This conclusion is amply confirmed by adult-education research. Researchers agree on the value of time devoted at the *start* to planning,

Learning is more efficient if guided by a process structure (e.g., learning plan) than by a content structure (e.g., course outline).

MALCOLM KNOWLES

Forewarned, forearmed; to be prepared is half the victory.

CERVANTES

motivation, and the adjusting of the environment and resources to the individual learners. Adult-education experts advocate this practice even *in classes and courses.* When you sign up for a class or course, the instructor should, according to the best advice of the experts, devote the first few hours of class time *not* to starting to teach you the subject but to assuring that his or her curriculum, methods, setting, resources, and style are really apt for the particular students.

You can feel confident that the time you spend on planning your learning will be more than returned as you proceed with your project. Yet how do you do it?

Consider the simplest problem first: choosing the right book from among several you've found in the library on your subject. Ordinarily you might just glance over the three or four volumes and pick the one that looks the most attractive and inviting. You suppose you'll be able to decide whether it's exactly on target for you once you get home and start reading it. There is nothing wrong with this approach if you're not particularly concerned about your time and with satisfying your need with more despatch. If, however, you want to make a more informed choice, one that will make the most of the time you have and assure a rewarding experience when you open that book at home, follow the Five Percent Upfront principle.

Suppose you intend to spend eight hours using this book if it proves to be the right one. A little mental arithmetic yields the fact that 5 percent of that time is about twenty-five minutes. So instead of making your choice on the basis of surface attractiveness, you can take that extra half-hour upfront to choose more smartly among the three or four books.

To do that, you can call up a dozen of the leading experts in our field to advise you. They'll tell you how authoritative the book is, whether the author has a slanted point of view, what aspects of the subject are covered, how the book relates to other literature in the field, whether there are any major mistakes or omissions, and anything else you need to know to make your choice. You can locate these experts simply by going over to the computerized book-review digest in your field (the librarian will help you find it and show you how to use it). Within ten minutes you will have before you on the screen the thoughtful appraisals of leading experts who examined each of the books you are considering.

These reviews, in full or digested, will place the book in its context within the field. They will indicate how the author is regarded by his or her peers and will review the contents of the book from several points of view, enabling you to form a composite picture in your mind of what you're likely to get from your reading. They will indicate any major flaws or prejudices that you should be aware of. Now go back and apply the techniques of Chapter Six for pro-active reading.

Half an hour later you'll be ready to check out your choice. But you've gotten more than a book: you've chosen the best among several books for meeting your goals. You've sharpened your enthusiasm and interest in reading it and gotten an appraisal of the author and his or her point of view. Finally, you've become more familiar with how some of the leading experts in your field think about key topics covered.

In short, by investing Five Percent Upfront in choosing more smartly, you've greatly enhanced your learning and enjoyment during the other 95 percent of the time you will be spending with your book. And you've probably already saved the half-hour you've invested, by not risking wasting time on the wrong book.

Consider a more complex example. You are sitting at your desk and have just opened a brochure for a two-day workshop or seminar that looks enticing. The subject is just what you need. It could help your organization and boost your career at the same time. Or perhaps it's an opportunity to enrich yourself by exposure to an exciting new set of ideas or techniques.

However, the brochure is a little vague, and you haven't heard of the sponsor or the presenters. Furthermore, the attendance fee is high. How much time should you take to make the right decision?

The sessions run from 10 A.M. to 4 P.M., or six hours a day, to which you must add a couple of hours for transportation to and from the campus over the two days, for a total of fourteen hours. Five percent of that is about forty-five minutes. Is it worth spending forty-five minutes up front to make sure your weekend results in successful learning?

William Draves, director of the Learning Resources Network, the national organization that works for the improvement of adult learning, offers the following guidelines for evaluating your time spent in up-front preparation.

Refund policy. Look at the stated refund policy in the brochure. If the seminar is guaranteed, that is a positive sign. If the policy does not give refunds or is not stated, beware.

Stated outcomes. Look beyond the headlines and the fancy words to find out what the behavioral outcomes will be after you attend the seminar. What will you know? What will you be able to do? If the brochure is vague on this count, beware.

Teacher biography. What are the qualifications of the presenter? Are these qualifications based upon experience, which is highly valued today, or merely on academic credentials or an association with an organization, which may not indicate firsthand knowledge?

Content outline. What are the actual components of the seminar? How much attention is devoted to the topics you want to learn? The sum of the seminar is made up of the parts. How excited are you about each of these parts?

Calling the instructor. Call the sponsor if you are in doubt about whether the seminar will be helpful to you. Not every seminar is right for everyone. A good presenter will delineate who should attend and what you can expect to get out of the experience. If the sponsor will not provide a work number for the presenter, beware.

References. Ask the sponsoring organization for the names and phone numbers of two to four past participants. Yes, these past participants will invariably be enthusiastic about the seminar, but you can still ask them questions that will supply important information, such as about what kinds of people attended the seminar and what the participants liked least about it. If the sponsor refuses to provide references, beware.

Evaluations. A good seminar will be evaluated by the participants every time it is given. If you are in the same city as the sponsor, you can request to look at past evaluations. Even if they are not available, or you are miles from the sponsor, you can request a copy of the evaluation form. Just looking at this form can give you important information about what the seminar covers and what aspects the sponsor thinks are important.

Ask your colleagues. It is a small world. If, as some contend, you can locate an unknown person across the country in as few as six phone calls, surely you must know someone who knows someone who has had an experience with this seminar provider. Ask around.

Call the sponsor. Ask the person who answers the phone, as well as the person you get transferred to, "Is this seminar right for me?" Describe your situation and your objectives and ask for an honest opinion. Whether the response is honest or not, you will still get an adequate impression of how well the sponsor understands the seminar and its benefits.

Don't judge the seminar by the sponsor's reputation. While there are fly-by-night seminar providers without a solid track record, even reputable institutions can offer poor-quality seminars. And almost every kind of provider, whether it be for-profit, nonprofit, educational, an association, or a university, will offer an activity sometime that will not be up to par. Do not judge a seminar solely by the sponsor. Do not assume a sponsor offers all quality seminars if your past experience has been good or all poor seminars if your experience has been disappointing. Most seminar providers have good intentions and want to produce useful seminars.

As you can see, there's a particular *way* to evaluate any resource for learning. From these above two examples you will find it easy to see what questions to ask and what criteria to use for virtually any kind of opportunity. Once you commit yourself to spending that 5 percent up front on evaluation, rather than just settling for the first thing that comes along, the process will be apparent.

HOW TO EVALUATE THE RESULTS OF YOUR LEARNING

You can easily provide evidence—for yourself as well as for others—of how much and how well you've learned. In fact, the process is much more interesting when your learning is self-directed. The secret is that in this kind of learning, in which you are constantly *active*, the *process is the product.*

In the conventional classroom situation, learning, evaluation, and application are separate, like three separate boxes. First you're supposed to learn, via a process planned and administered by the teacher. Then, after you've learned, you are tested—according to an instrument and criteria of the teacher's. Finally, it is hoped, you *use* what you've learned.

But in the kind of learning you are now going to do, these three elements are combined. You will have defined the goals and results of your learning in action terms, and many of those actions will occur during the process of learning itself. For example, you'll recall that a difference between Ruth and Rob is that Ruth seemed to be *doing* career assessment and career change, not just learning *about* it. She had defined her goals and results to include such actions as letters actually sent out to prospective employers. Rob, in a conventional classroom situation, was learning *about* such techniques, with the expectation that he would put them into practice *after* the course was over.

John Holt, the late educational reformer, described this typical pattern of learning by doing in one of his midlife learning projects.

> Not many years ago I began to play the cello. I love the instrument, spend many hours a day playing it, work hard at it, and mean someday to play it well. Most people would say that what I am doing is "learning to play the cello." Our language gives us no other words to say it. But these words carry into our minds the strange idea that there exist two very different processes: (1) learning to play the cello; and (2) playing the cello. They imply that I will do the first until I have completed it, at which point I will stop the first process and begin the second; in short, that I will go on "learning to play" until I "have learned to play," and that then I will begin "to play."
>
> Of course, this is nonsense. There are not two processes, but one. We learn to do something by doing it. There is no other way. When we first do something, we probably will not do it well. But if we keep on doing it, have good models to follow and helpful advice if and when we feel we need it, and always do it as well as we can, we will do it better. In time, we may do it very well. This process never ends.

Holt found this experience so significant that he wrote an entire book, *Instead of Education,* arguing that it should and could become the model for all of education. The subtitle of Holt's book is "Ways to Help People Do Things Better." He believed that we could learn everything that we want and need to know if we had the right kind of help and resources to do things better. Your capacity to do things better—whether those things are discussing *Macbeth* after seeing a performance, reading a corporate financial report, or suturing a wound as a member of a first-aid team—is your evidence of learning.

Even colleges realize this and are moving away from conventional testing and grading. They know that if learning is geared to answering examination questions, the student has to come up with a right answer only once, and that this can result in a rate of forgetting that is astonishing and dispiriting. Colleges are rapidly shifting in the direction of competency-based credentialing, in which the award of a diploma is based not on simply piling up course credits but on demonstrating competence to do specific things.

Just consider how we find out in everyday life whether someone has certain skills, knowledge, or ability. We ask questions like "Can you do this? How well? Who can tell me how to perform in a given situation? Can you follow what I'm doing or talking about? Do you have a license to do this? How much money did you make in this field? Can I see what you've produced? What have you published? What do people in the field say about your work? How do you rank yourself among others whose work you admire?"

You can measure your learning by standards growing out of the learning itself. Sometimes the measure will be a tangible product, such as a salable tomato, a usable road, a smoothly running office, or a well-received book. Other times it will be less tangible but equally important, such as a new awareness of options in everyday life, a sense of community, or a capacity to enrich one's life. On still other occasions it will be a change wrought in other people's lives: a child awakened to learning, for example, or a parent emboldened to challenge school authorities.

Accomplishments, capabilities, social effects, strengthened sensitivities and convictions—in such consequences is learning properly measured. Appraising such outcomes is, in a way, more difficult than taking a test at the end of a course and getting

Today's organization is dominated by uncertainty and intense competition. During such times organizations need people who can do more than answer questions. They need people who can ask the right questions. When competition increases, competence becomes critical.

CHARLES D. HAYES

209

a grade, but the rewards are worth the challenge. Here, for example, is how Lynn Hinkle, a commercial artist from Minneapolis, handles the problem.

I've learned a lot about different aspects of commercial art, but haven't had formal training in a vocational program. What I have been doing and intend to continue doing for credentials is four-fold.

1. Maintain a complete portfolio of material I have produced.
2. Describe the particular tasks I undertook for production of the material, like copy writing, graphic design, key-line, and paste-up.
3. Compare the speed at which I was able to perform these particular tasks that require methodical care with others that can be done more quickly.
4. List either coworkers or employees who can verify my portfolio and description of my abilities.

If I continue to specify and document my work experience in this manner, I will probably be able to provide as accurate a description of my skills as a commercial artist as someone who can specify the content of certification from a commercial art training program. Although I'm reluctant to speak for anyone else, this knowledge can help me to:

1. Remind myself of my limitations if I decide to work independently.
2. Develop a program to learn from or teach the people I work with.
3. Negotiate with a boss if I decide to work for someone else.

Lynn's listing of specific skills is right in line with what employers are increasingly looking for. Sophisticated career counselors are now advising their clients to forget about the conventional résumé. They advocate just this kind of analysis of one's "skill clusters" to present to prospective employers. As the college degree continues to lose its value as a guarantee of competence, more and more jobs are opening up to people who can show what they know and what they can do.

Describing yourself in understandable terms—your life-work, your image of yourself, your priorities, what you would like people to think you do, what you do, and what you would like to do next—is a telling slice of reality and aspiration. . . . We should all have a personal curriculum vitae or résumé that attempts to describe who we really are and not who we are trying to pretend to be (the motivation behind most conventional résumés).

RICHARD SAUL WURMAN

210

Note too that in keeping careful track of what she has actually done and produced, Lynn is also making herself aware of what she might want to learn next. I like this kind of appraisal, which feeds back into the learning process. To my mind, one of the most important reasons for evaluating one's learning is to become alert to how one learns, in order to increase the ease and effectiveness of the process.

Whatever you can do or dream you can, begin it. Boldness has genius, power, and magic in it.

GOETHE

USING A LEARNING PROJECT PLAN

By now, I hope it is clear that planning your projects in advance can pay off in a big way. The following list is designed to make explicit the relationship between the material that has been covered in each chapter and the learning project plan. Specifically, your plan will enable you to do the following ten things.

1. *Choose your own goals.* Clarify them as you start learning; refine or change them as you proceed. Thus you create your own custom-tailored curriculum. As your perspective broadens, you can add new areas that catch your interest. Or, if you get entranced by a narrow topic, you can put your other goals on hold while you dig deeply into it.

2. *Marshal your full energy and enthusiasm.* You will readily enter the flow state by engaging your subject at the right level of challenge and in the right style for you.

3. *Take full advantage of your prior knowledge, experience, and attitudes about your subject.* Start out from your unique point of leverage and confidence.

4. *Fine-tune your environment* so that you learn in the best place, at the best times, under the best conditions for you and for this particular subject.

5. *Use your own style.* As you "feel" your way into the subject and become aware of the ways available to learn it, you can match learning opportunities and resources with your own style.

211

Most important of all, we Americans as individuals seem to be developing a fresh hunger for experience, for growth, for personal cultivation. Men and women of all ages today feel the urge to seek more in life—to shape a larger self. That quest I call lifelong learning.

RON GROSS

6. *Benefit from a wide range of resources and opportunities.* You can draw from a wide range of people, organizations, media, and situations. From each of them you can take the element that's of most interest to you. Your local library may be the source of a videotape and books; a college may yield an interview with an expert or practitioner; an institute or conference can provide opportunities for contacts and mentors.

7. *Control your time.* You can slow down, speed up, or otherwise adapt your schedule to your changing life circumstances.

8. *Use innovative learning techniques* to process what you're learning in active, personal ways.

9. *Benefit from change, luck, and intuition.* Whenever you plunge into a subject, skill, or issue, you will find that suddenly information, contacts, and insights begin to appear. "The gods give thread for the web begun," says master networker Lief Smith of Denver's Open Network. When you are in charge of your own learning you are well positioned to take full advantage of such occurrences.

10. *Determine what results you want from your learning.* Measure them in the ways most congenial and productive for you.

ON YOUR OWN

This chapter has tied together nearly all the strands of the Peak Learning approach. The next chapter, "The Invisible University," is an up-to-date summary of resources available, but it is not the last word.

As peak learners, you now know that there will always be more to learn and more ways to learn it. You recognize your own personal learning style and are capable of developing a learning project plan to make the best possible match between your style and what you want to learn. You have a learning log where you can keep track of everything from your main learning projects to casual notes for future learning, and you have an assortment of tools and techniques that will help you learn anything you choose.

I hope you've also discovered, over the course of this book, that learning need not be the painful drudgery it once was in school. Rather, I hope you share with me the conviction that learning is a vital part of a healthy life. It is a combination of a mental exercise and a constant joy of discovery that makes life richer and more fulfilling. Learning is time invested in yourself, in the growth and development of your own unique experience.

The next steps are up to you.

X

L(earning) Your Living: Self-Development for Career Success

If you were worth $170 million, would you feel that you had reached the point where you didn't have to worry any more about learning?

Marc Andreessen, the inventor of Netscape, found himself in that position. The software program he invented had changed the world for computer users when it appeared in 1995. The day of the IPO (Initial Public Offering) of stock in his company, he watched shares soar from $7 to $36. "I saw the stock price and went 'Eeek'!" he recalls. By December 5th, the stock had reached an all-time high of $85.50, and Andreessen's shares were worth over $170 million.

But by the fall of 1997, Microsoft struck back with its competing product, Explorer 4.0. Netscape's stock tumbled, and by January 1998 Andreessen had to report an $88 million quarterly loss, and fire 150 people. Such is life in this tumultuous field— and in many other fields these days.

Andreessen was now involved in a life-and-death struggle to save his company. And his chief tool was . . . learning.

Business Week's cover story on the crisis was titled, significantly, "The *Education* of Marc Andreessen."

What did Andreessen have to learn?

He had to learn the same things we all have to learn throughout our careers:

- Attitude
- Skills
- Knowledge

Attitude. Andreessen had to overcome the psychological trauma triggered by his company's reversal of fortune. "At one point, he was so discouraged he could barely drag himself out of bed before noon," reported *Business Week.* He had to *learn* how to reignite his enthusiasm and confidence. (The cultivation of this kind of "Emotional Intelligence" is now considered more important for your success in your career, and in your life, than your IQ or your professional skills—which is why it has been stressed so much in the early chapters of this book.)

Skills. Andreessen had to make the transition from inventor to manager. In his particular situation, this translated into spending less time with his engineering cronies, and much more with his mentor in management, Netscape CEO James Barksdale. But most people's careers involve a similar need to shift at a critical point, from focusing on the technical aspects of your job, to becoming more adept at teamwork, leadership, and management of major parts of the business. Whether you're a salesperson becoming a sales manager, an editor becoming a publisher, or teacher becoming an assistant principal, you will need to navigate these waters. You will master the strategies for learning from others in your workplace, in this chapter.

Knowledge. Andreessen also had a lot of learning to do in terms of knowledge. Despite being a pioneer in his field, he still had to "acquire as much knowledge as he can as fast as he can," reported *Business Week.* (Andreessen used techniques covered below.)

So even after making $170 million before he was twenty-five, Marc Andreessen still needed to learn new skills, attitudes, and knowledge.

Your success in your career, too, depends on your capacity to learn and grow. I call this principle L(earning) Your Living— or, for short:

L(earning)

THE LAWS OF L(EARNING)

Every study of the new American workplace confirms this pair of iron laws for career success today:

1. *The more you learn, the more you earn.* Gaining the right skills, knowledge, and attitude pays off in advancement.

2. *The more you earn, the more you need to learn.* The more you advance in your career, the more your jobs will require you to make use of up-to-date information and more complex skills.

No matter where you are in your career—entry level or senior management—continued learning will enable you to earn more, advance faster, and get more gratification out of your work. No matter how top-grade was your formal education, you cannot rely on it to propel your career after graduation.

Take Harvard MBAs, for example. John Kotter studied the job histories and personal autobiographies of Harvard MBAs from the last twenty years. These are men and women who are currently entering the upper ranks of management in our major corporations, or making their mark as entrepreneurs.

Kotter, who is Professor of Leadership at Harvard, has scrutinized the career patterns of these top MBAs. They are certainly among the best-prepared to cope with a changing work environment.

We might think that these Harvard graduates, who have literally received "the best education money can buy," could simply use what they learned at the university to achieve success in their careers.

Not so!

Comparing those who were clearly successful with those whose careers had foundered or stagnated, Kotter made a startling discovery.

If you are not being educated in your job today, you may be out of a job tomorrow.

STAN DAVIS AND
JIM BOTKIN

Those who reported that they had *learned* from a wide range of experiences were consistently in the top half of their classes in earnings and achievement.

"What is so interesting about these people," Professor Kotter writes, "is their ability to turn turbulence in their business environments into something useful. New competition, raiders, reorganizations, and the like become (for them) not just destructive, but an important source of growth. Because they look honestly at their successes and failure, they learn and grow."

Such learning was not confined to these people's *careers,* by the way. Professor Kotter notes that many of them whose careers seemed untroubled actually had to contend with grievous personal and family problems: illness, death, divorce, etc. Among those individuals, too, the capacity to learn, cope, and move on differentiated those who overcame their trials, from those who foundered.

Professor Kotter has even calculated the *amount* of advantage you will gain from continual learning—and the cost to your career if you neglect it. Even a slight edge in growth will pay off big time, as your career proceeds.

Let's take a hypothetical manager, Alice, who's truly proactive about learning continually, both in the classroom and from her experiences in her career. Compare her to another manager, Bob, who just does his job satisfactorily, but doesn't make the effort to continue to grow. What difference will show up over the long haul?

On the basis of his studies, Professor Kotter calculates that if Alice is just 5% more effective in her continual learning than Bob is, she will end up three times as competent by the time they are both being considered for the move into top management.

THE THREE MAJOR STRATEGIES
FOR L(EARNING)

How do you build learning into your own job, occupation, profession, and career?

You need to begin thinking about your present job—and

the next one—in terms of *learning*. There are three steps to doing this:

1. *Choosing* your job, and your specific assignments, with a view to how much you can learn from them.
2. *Infusing* your work, on a daily basis, with learning and growth. (Infuse means to fill, steep or soak, and, metaphorically, to imbue and inspire.)
3. *Using* what you are learning, to advance in your career.

You are going to find this gratifying, because you will be learning what *you* need and want to know, to become what *you* want to become. Each day on your way home from work, you'll have a gratifying feeling that you have learned at least one interesting and valuable lesson which enhances your skill, knowledge, or attitude.

This is especially important when you're just starting out in a career, because you're likely to have lots of tasks that are routine and uninteresting. It is essential to find ways to enliven this "apprenticeship" period with the exhilaration of learning.

As you move forward in your career, this process will become even more sharply focused. I know one young medical professional who clipped out of a professional journal the ad for the ideal job she wanted to have in five years, then highlighted the specific experiences and kinds of expertise and credentials asked for, and used that as her overall learning program! (She got the job she wanted in three and a half years!)

In this kind of career-driven learning, the key question becomes: "Where do I want to go in my career and my life—and what do I have to *learn* to do *that?!*"

In this chapter, I'm going to discuss this in terms of *a job-holder within an organization,* since the rest of this book provides the tools and strategies for the *individual working independently* (see such sections covering personal R & D on pp. 195–98, your learning project plan on pp. 211–12, the comparison of the learning logs of two individuals studying career change on pp. 191–93, etc.). However, if you are self-employed or an entrepreneur, you will find plenty in this chapter that you can use for your own growth, or within your own organization, whatever its

Burn this into your brain: You must become a learner.

PRICE PRITCHETT

size—especially the strategies in the section on "Infusing" your daily work with learning.

Doing this kind of learning as a regular part of your daily work has a number of exhilarating and profitable benefits:

- ♦ It gives you a feeling of control, despite the turmoil in your job. It helps you deal with the stress of constant change and challenge.
- ♦ It gives you the sense of continual growth, rather than just keeping your head above water.
- ♦ It makes you a valued employee, team member, boss, or consultant. You will find that those around you are energized by your continual development.

Employers are seeking this kind of employee. In fact, awards for Peak Learning in Business and Industry, inspired by the principles and practices in this book, have begun to be provided to outstanding organizations throughout the country. The most recent awardees, as of this writing, have been top firms ranging from BHP Copper to the Hughes Knowledge Center Southwest.

Choosing *the right job and assignments*. The smartest careerists find ways to choose their jobs and assignments with a view to what they will be learning.

For example, John Fiorello, a financial executive who lost his job when his firm merged with a larger one, discovered that the jobs he wanted most required "SEC experience"—working with the Securities and Exchange Commission (his former employer was a privately-held company which did not issue stock).

"So I chose a position that would give me precisely this experience," he reports. "After two and a half years at that job, I landed just the position I'd sought—because I now had the requisite knowledge, skills, and understanding for dealing with the stock market."

This is just as important on the entry level. Deborah Angnent started her career five years ago with a medium-sized publishing firm as a receptionist. She knew this wasn't the job she wanted, but it was what she could get, and she was determined to do a first-rate job.

But she also started looking around from Day 1 for the job opening that would let her learn her real interest, copy editing, working on an editorial team, and eventually becoming an editor.

"I turned down several openings in sales and accounting, because those were not the places I thought I'd learn what I needed to know to become an editor," she recalls. Today, Debbie is second in command of the juvenile books department, and well-launched on a gratifying and well-paying career.

To follow the lead of these savvy career-builders, you need to answer three questions:

1. What do I need to know, and be able to do, to succeed in the position I want most?
2. In what job or assignments can I master that knowledge and competence?
3. How can I use training and educational opportunities of the organization to broaden and strengthen my skills? (See section below on checking with your training department).

Infusing *your work with learning.* I have chosen the word "infuse" to describe this process, because its root meaning is "to pour into." Your learning for your career is not going to be something you add on to your other job tasks. It is going to permeate everything you do at work.

Learning isn't something you do occasionally, at an occasional workshop or seminar. It doesn't wait until you attend an annual professional conference in your field, or enroll for a certificate or degree program.

Rather, learning is simply an aspect of your day-to-day work. Every day, you can and should find exciting opportunities to learn something new. Every initiative or project, if you approach it correctly (and debrief it creatively), will yield new knowledge and sharpened skills. Every evening on the way home from work, you should be able to answer the question: "What did I do today that was important and meaningful for my career?"

THE WHEEL OF L(EARNING)

The basic model for L(earning) is the Wheel.

It's so important that, when I lecture on it to conference audiences, I actually use a physical wheel.

Of course, I get a funny look at the airport when I arrive at the gate with my neon-red plastic hoop that stands as tall as I do. At the hotel, the bellman pretends not to notice it, as he hangs the hoop on his cart. When I'm being introduced to speak, and the hoop is conspicuously resting next to me at the speaker's table, my host seems to feel the need to stress my academic credentials a little more than usual. . . .

But it's worth it. The giant red hoop helps me explain why the Wheel is the best model for learning at work. By revolving it one-quarter turn at a time, I dramatize the four-step cycle which keeps our brains active. When we say about someone at work, "You can practically see the wheels turning in her head all the time," this is the wheel we're talking about!

Real learning is always about answering a question or solving a problem.

CHARLES HANDY

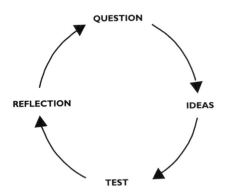

Every time you confront a problematical situation at work, start the wheel turning.

"What's the *question*, problem, or issue here?"

"What old, or new, *ideas* might work?"

"Let's try this one, as a *test*."

"What can we *learn* from reflecting on the results?"

Question: Why are too many widgets being rejected for defects?

Idea: Workers are careless in putting the material through the machine. If they are reminded to be responsible, their performance will improve. "They really oughta wanna."

Test: Each worker is reminded every Monday morning that he or she should be more careful in processing the materials.

Reflection: That didn't reduce the number of rejected items. What's a better way to encourage workers to perform as we'd like them to?

Charles Handy explains why the Wheel is the perfect symbol of this process in *The Age of Unreason* (Harvard Business School Press).

I describe it as a wheel to emphasize that it is meant to go round and round. One set of questions, duly answered and tested and reflected upon, leads on to another. Step off The Wheel and you ossify, becoming a bore to others. One has only to look at little children to see that wheel turning furiously. Why, we must wonder, does it slow down for most of us as we grow older?

You can learn a lot about your own executive style by using the Wheel. After wielding it for a week at work, ask yourself where *you* feel most comfortable on the Wheel.

Do you get the most gratification out of formulating the *questions* and problems? Thinking things through to come up with the *ideas?* Getting things done in the *testing* phase? Or *reflecting* on how to do it better next time? Your preference will tell you a lot about the kind of work you thrive on, and how you can make your maximum contribution to any team.

This Wheel of L(earning) is basic to the most progressive management philosophies. It grows out of the work of John Dewey, Kurt Lewin, and Jean Piaget, as synthesized by David Kolb and Walter Shewhart. The two best discussions of it in current management literature are in Charles Handy's *The Age of Unreason* and in *The Fifth Discipline Fieldbook* by Peter Senge and Associates.

For adults, the first option is consider is always self-managed learning.

WILLIAM CHARLAND

223

AFTER ACTION REPORTS

A key technique for keeping the Wheel of L(earning) turning is conducting "After Action Reports" at the end of every major piece of work. Here's a brief description:

> When your annual meeting is over, before you pack up all the unused brochures and settle your account with the catering manager, sit down in a quiet corner and make two lists: (1) everything you did right, and (2) everything you did wrong. Then put it in the file for next year's convention.
>
> The military calls this an after-action report, and it's one bit of military red tape that is worthwhile and should be adopted by any organization of any size. Such a report should be made on any significant activity that is going to recur in the future, whether it's a meeting, a corporate acquisition, or a backpack trip. Memory is treacherous, and a year from now you will have forgotten the valuable lessons you learned this time around.
>
> Your brief written record of what happened and why, including recommendations for how to do it better and more quickly next time, can save a lot of time and energy.

It's important to do the steps in the order suggested by the writer and management consultant Edwin Bliss in *Getting Things Done* (Bantam).

Most people tend to focus immediately, and often exclusively, on what went wrong. That's important for L(earning), of course. But from the standpoint of morale, it's crucial that you begin with a review of the things that went *right!*

Always begin by giving yourself as many well-deserved pats on the back as you can. (To kick this off, just recall Woody Allen's dictum: "Ninety percent of success in life is just showing up.")

What you *do* with your After Action Reports is also very important. First, consider with whom you could share it—either by sending a copy, or by using it as a "talking sheet" in a discussion about the project, to that you present the results, and learnings, most effectively.

Second, you need to be sure to file it, in paper form or digitally, so that you are sure to be reminded of it, and benefit from it, the next time a comparable problem or challenge comes up.

THE "HEY JOE" SCHOOL

"Hey, Joe, how do you launch Power Point?"

"Oh, it's no problem. Let me show you."

"Thanks, Joe."

Questions and responses like this are a major but unrecognized source of L(earning).

Studies by the Department of Labor have revealed that about 70 percent of the training in American business and industry is "informal." That means it doesn't happen through classroom instruction or even organized self-directed learning. It happens one worker or manager or professional to another, in the "Hey, Joe" School, as Eliot Masie has dubbed it.

At its higher reaches the "Hey, Joe" School becomes deep, sustained, and profound, and we call it *mentoring*—the kind of thing that Marc Andreessen was doing with his top-level colleague James Barksdale. But it also happens everywhere and all the time, in healthy "learning organizations."

At some companies, workers and managers share so much in the "Hey Joe" School, even over breakfast and lunch, that the firms have set up one corner of their cafeteria with the tools and supplies to support the process: colored markers, a flip chart or whiteboard, paper tablecloths that can be used to sketch out ideas.

The "Hey Joe" School isn't confined to your own organization. Many managers I know say that their single best source of new information about their field is . . . *vendors!* Vendors know their products and services, and those of their competitors, better than you do—especially when you are exploring a new field or trying to solve a novel problem. Of course, they'll push their line. But by getting multiple viewpoints for several vendors, including how each of them sees their competitors as falling short, you'll become keenly aware of the key issues, criteria, and pitfalls in the field.

LEARNING CIRCLES

"Learning Circles" are the next step up from the "Hey Joe" School. They are simply groups of people talking together, out-

An old friend of mind happened upon a novel way of learning Spanish, and it was the fastest I've ever seen. She met a Latin lover on Friday night—and I swear she was speaking Spanish by Monday morning.

MARILYN VOS SAVANT

side the formal structure of the organization, in ways that result in continual improvement and personal growth.

In the most successful enterprises, you find them in every nook and cranny.

Wander the corridors at Microsoft, Memorial Sloan-Kettering, GE, or Sprint—peer into offices, cubicles, and conference rooms—and you'll find these kinds of conversations everywhere. For example, during a two-day consultancy at a leading firm in the burgeoning long-distance reselling industry, I discovered:

- a noontime "brown bag" lunch at which workers learn more about their new equipment than they did in their training class.
- a high-energy, *ad hoc* discussion of a just-out journal article, trade survey, etc.
- a first-thing-in-the-morning "creative huddle" to anticipate what was going to hit the fan during the day, and plan to stay ahead of the curve.
- an on-line forum, chat room, e-mail list, and collaborative work group.
- a regular Friday afternoon conclave over sherry in the CEO's office, to review the week's accomplishments.

My daughter, Elizabeth Cohn, created and conducts a Learning Circle for doctors at the large hospital at which she works. Once a month, the docs convene at 6:45 a.m. for a one-hour "Journal Club." They've all read several selected articles from top publications in the field including the *Journal of the American Medical Association (JAMA)* by cutting-edge theorists or practitioners. They discuss, criticize, and apply these up-to-date findings to their own work. And they earn credits in continuing medical education from the AMA—testifying to the validity and effectiveness of this kind of professional education.

These groups are the ground floor of a learning organization. If you've got this sort of thing going in your shop, you've created a solid foundation on which to build.

Learning circles have a built-in dynamic of growth. Once started, they develop their own momentum and direction.

People begin to "select their own society": colleagues who stimulate one another's thinking. More people are attracted, or start their own groups. Together, they gravitate to topics that are interesting and productive for them. They share information and resources that loft the talk.

This model for learning can transcend the individual workplace. Here's how Bob Guns used it when he was writing his book, *The Faster Learning Organization:*

When I realized how much reading I had to do, I was overwhelmed. One Sunday, however, I had an idea. On Monday morning I started phoning various executives I knew around town. I told them I wanted to share an exciting proposal:

I have to do a lot of reading in order to write my book, and I need help. What if you read one assigned book a month over the next five months and summarized your reading in three clear, substantiated points that relate to creating faster learning organizations?

The executives waited to find out what was in it for them. So I continued:

What if ten other people do the same thing? And they fax their summaries to you at the end of the month. And you fax your summaries to them. So for every book you read and summarize, you get ten other summaries. Is that worthwhile?

Moreover, what if those who are willing and able got together once a month to share findings? Wouldn't that be fun?

And what if I arranged for all of us to share our ideas about how to create faster learning organizations using an electronic bulletin board? Wouldn't that be even more fun?

Twenty-four hours later, the FLO Reading Network had been created. I got the help I needed, and the networkers learned and enjoyed the experience. Faster learning is facilitated by an exciting, joyful environment. Faster learners continually look for opportunities to have fun in learning and to share that fun.

Learning Circles can also become a major mode of continuing education throughout a profession or industry. I proposed such a program when I keynoted at the annual convention for the Association of Professional Directors (of the nation's major

The most successful corporation of the 1990s will be something called a learning organization.

FORTUNE MAGAZINE

*Once you stop learning,
you're dead.*

GEORGE POWELL

YMCAs). The challenge was eagerly accepted by executive director Jim Stooke, who got a remarkable response from his members. Stooke and his association's leaders launched the Learning Circles program, to encourage their members to create groups committed to learning together. An initial announcement drew eight hundred inquiries! Stooke put it simply but warmly: "Friends getting together to share in mutually chosen learning experiences is the heart and soul of this program."

How do these Learning Circles work in practice? Each five-member group is self-selected and self-governing. They get a "starter kit" with guidelines and resources ranging from lapel pins to an audio tape.

Together, the members of each Circle choose learning projects based on their needs and interests.

Among typical activities are:

- ◆ discussing sections of Tom Peters's new book that are highly relevant to the local situation.
- ◆ attending a seminar on using the Internet, as a team, and working together on implementation.
- ◆ focusing on three future trends in the community that impact on all members.

The starter kit provides each group with exciting materials ranging from lapel pins and information cards to promote the group, to an audio tape and guidebook on Peak Learning, learning logs, and "Great Ideas" pads.

"The possibilities of what can happen to our profession by having hundreds of colleagues learning together in informal settings throughout the country boggles the mind!" Stooke says.

LISTENING WITH THE GOLDEN EAR

As I was writing this section, Phil Condit got a new job—and he insists that one of his chief qualifications was his big ears. And they *are* large—they're sometimes the first thing people notice when they meet him. So he capitalizes on them to stress the importance of listening in his line of work.

"The most important management rule in my organization is to be a good listener," Phil explains. That's probably true in your organization, too—only people may not recognize it.

Condit has gone so far as to establish an award, the "Golden Ears," for fellow employees who used their listening skills to make improvements.

What kind of job is it that requires, above all, such really big "ears"?

Phil Condit is the chief executive heading up the $13.3 billion merger of McDonnell-Douglas and Boeing, involving 200,000 employees.

Almost every major organization today is talking the talk about becoming a learning organization. I like to cite Phil Condit to suggest that a practical way to start is to start listening to each other.

Whatever your job or position, it pays to upgrade your listening. Read a good book on the subject, readily available in any business or professional library. One of my favorites is *Effective Listening: Hearing What People Say and Making It Work for You*, by Kevin Murphy (Bantam).

Begin to use your listening skills strategically, not just tactically. Go even further than merely picking up a random idea here and there. Good listening can enable you to find out what's really going on in your organization—why high-flown goals aren't being achieved, and where new opportunities lie hidden.

"Once every couple of weeks," advises Tom Peters, "have an hour-long discussion with some first-line person. Think of yourself as a consultant called in on a nitty-gritty systems improvement assignment. Track down, in great detail, the nature of one or two critical tasks the person performs—precisely what's done, why it doesn't get done faster, and so on. This little listening device, repeated regularly, will unfailingly yield strategic insights."

USING NEW TECHNOLOGY
INCLUDING THE COMPUTER

In Chapter Nine I guided you through the learning opportunities opened up by your computer and related technologies. So here I merely want to note that this should be a prime resource for your continual self-education on the job.

Many of the kinds of learning covered in this chapter can be facilitated or enriched by technology. Learning Circles, for example, can spark their discussions with a videotape. Listening skills can be upgraded using instruction on a CD-ROM. The stimulation and information needed to keep the Wheel of Learning turning can come from computer-based sources.

"Kanbrain" is the catchy term invented by Lewis Perleman to sum up the potentialities of using technology to augment your on-the-job learning. It comes from the Japanese *kanban*—the just-in-time inventory system in which the part needed in the manufacturing process is delivered to where you want it, when you want it. "Kanbrain" applies this concept to learning: its ideal is to put the total base of corporate knowledge and expertise at the disposal of each employee, just-in-time, on-demand, anytime, anywhere.

While this ideal is visionary at this point, it is happening in bits and pieces throughout American business. Dinty Moore, whom you met in Chapter Nine, reports, "As a college teacher, I hear over and over again from former students, that the magic bullet for job success is fast becoming . . . web-based searching. I keep hearing about former students who leapfrogged their way onto important projects, or up the corporate ladder, simply because they knew where to find strategic information."

Using your L(earning) to advance your career. Now that we've explored how you can *Choose* your job and assignments for their growth opportunities, and then *Infuse* your work with learning every day, let's look at how to *Use* what you have learned to advance your career. I have covered the major strategies for documenting what you have learned in the section on *How to Evaluate the Results of Your Learning,* in the chapter on Setting Up Your Own Learning Projects.

Here, I'd like to suggest some additional ways you can use your learning to advance your career. Of course, you may not need or be able to document all of your learning, day-to-day, in the "Hey, Joe" School and Learning Circles, for example. What's important is your own recognition that you are "on the grow," day in and day out, in those important ways. Here, I'm talking about noting and recording, more formally, your learnings from major projects, inquiries, or experiences such as:

- conducting a major project
- attending a workshop, seminar, or conference
- participating in a highly significant meeting or trip
- completing an extended self-study project or program

INCLUDE YOUR LEARNING IN YOUR "PERMANENT RECORD"

You want to make your significant learning a permanent part of your job history. By doing that, you will assure that you

- get full recognition and credit for it, when it's time for promotion;
- have it readily at hand for updating your resume by reminding yourself of how your capabilities have grown and deepened; and
- can use it to boost your morale when you hit a rough patch on the job, and want to remind yourself of how far you've come, and how you've used L(earning) in the past to move forward.

The first thing to do is to start "capturing" your learning by using your learning log (see p. 13), and a cumulative set of your learning project plans (see pp. 211–12). (If you haven't started using these strategies yet, this is an important additional incentive.)

Using this documentation as your source, make sure that your learning projects get reflected in your personnel file kept by your supervisor or in the training office in your organization. If that's not appropriate, maintain your own dossier, and list major items on your resume.

You should never be at a loss to answer the question: *"What are the three most important things you have learned this month?"* Many people have trouble answering it because they are trapped in the assumption that learning only happens when they are sitting in a classroom, being taught. Your commitment to the principles of Peak Learning should make it easy to overcome this fixation.

TEACH WHAT YOU HAVE LEARNED

Teaching others what you have learned not only nails down what you've learned in own mind—it also contributes to your organization, and hones your skills in planning, writing, and communicating. "It's the single most important thing you can do to multiply the impact and value of your learning," says Linda Meyer, founder-director of the famed Meyer Learning Center in Denver.

This is one of my favorite ways to learn and grow. When I began work on this update of *Peak Learning*, I immediately scheduled myself to teach workshops and seminars on the major new topics featured in this book: L(earning) Your Living, and Peak Learning in Cyberspace. I arranged for every kind of teaching I could do, from adult education courses in my community, to workshops and seminars in organizations, to presentations at conferences and conventions. As a professional speaker, using what I have learned by teaching it to others is central to my work.

But you don't have to mount a full-scale class or course. If it's appropriate, you can divide up your subject into bite-sized chunks, and invite people to discuss them at a "brown-bag lunch." (See section on Learning Circles in this chapter.)

Your teaching doesn't even have to be face-to-face. If it's appropriate, write a cogent memo sharing useful techniques and strategies. This not only shares what you've learned, but yields a document to go into your dossier as a permanent record.

REPORT THE "RETURN ON INVESTMENT" FOR YOUR L(EARNING)

This is the key term which sophisticated managers use to talk about the business results of learning. They are looking for a *dollar amount* for the *value* to the organization, of what you have learned. "How much money has your new knowledge or skill saved, or made, for us?"

Once you start thinking about it, it is not so difficult to calculate such a figure—and it shows your supervisors that you are thinking in down-to-earth, dollars-and-cents business terms.

Sometimes you can directly measure how much faster, better, or more cheaply you are getting something done for the company. Have you used what you have been learning to do something more handily? To avoid costly mistakes? To make better decisions? To improve morale? To save time or expense? To provide customers, outside and within the company, with improved service?

Put a dollar value on what that's worth. If it's not amenable to direct measurement, you can develop such a figure by simply *asking* your supervisor, or your clients, or your customers, what the improvement has been worth to them.

Here's a simple formula for calculating what I call DAVALEL: the Dollar Amount of the Value Added by Learning as Estimated by the Learner.

Learn or die.

DOROTHY CANFIELD
FISHER

A. What *percentage of your total working time* do you spend on tasks in which you can use what you have learned?

(15% . . . 40% . . . 60% . . . 85% . . . or what?)

B. *How much of an increase in productivity* or profitability do you estimate you will experience, by using what you have learned?

(15% . . . 40% . . . 60% . . . 85% . . . or what?)

A = _____   B = _____
(transcribe figures from above)

To compute your estimated dollar value added by this learning:

A × (Your Annual Salary) × B = $_____
Dollar Value Added

Source: John Noonan, *Elevators: How to Move Training Up from the Basement* (Twain Publishers, Wheaton, IL, 1985).

If you would like to learn more about using your L(earning) to advance your career, the best book on it is Charles Hayes's *Proving You're Qualified* (Autodidactic Press, P.O. Box 872749, Wasilla, AK, 99687). Hayes provides both inspiration and guidance on parlaying your new skills into advancement. "An enlightened perspective will keep you a step ahead of the game while helping to change the rules," he writes. "Each day thousands of experienced, competent people in America are denied job opportunities and well-deserved promotions because of a lack of formal credentials. Often the credential requirements are arbitrary, having nothing whatever to do with the job in question. The result is that organizations lose added value and the individuals involved lose money, prestige, and fulfillment."

STEP OUT TO STEP UP: PLANNING YOUR CONTINUING PROFESSIONAL EDUCATION

We have focused so far on L(earning) in your present job by

1. *Choosing* a job—and specific assignments—that offer opportunities to learn.
2. *Infusing* learning into your job every day, and over the longer haul.
3. *Using* what you have learned for advancement.

At certain points, however, you will want and need to go "outside" for some special, "formal" learning opportunities, such as:

- ♦ a half-day workshop on-site.
- ♦ a three-day seminar downtown.
- ♦ a week-long conference in your field in another city.
- ♦ a three-week executive retreat at a university-based graduate school.

Here are the ways to assure that you take advantage of such opportunities in your work situation.

VISIT YOUR TRAINING DEPARTMENT

Start by taking the initiative within your organization. After getting the OK from your supervisor, visit the training department. Go to the highest appropriate person or their designee (training director, chief learning officer, HR director, etc.), and discuss your interest and commitment to self-development.

I know of no case in which an employee has not been well-received when they did this. The training department in most organizations is staffed with people who believe deeply in the value of continual learning. But they usually face deep-seated resistance among many workers and managers. The most pervasive resistance is the tyranny of the urgent: "The people in our department have so much work to do every day, they can't take time for a workshop or seminar." (As a management consultant I immediately recognize that as a symptom of defective management, of course. Such managers do not see the value of investing the time needed to "sharpen the saw" to increase productivity and profitability.)

One of the practical results of this resistance is the *under-utilization* of the talents, resources, funding, and opportunities that training departments have put in place. Hence, they are almost always delighted to see employees who are keen to take advantage of what they have to offer.

Here's a suggested agenda for working with your training department:

First, obtain and review the written materials in the employee manual, your employment contract, or the appropriate documents. The best companies these days have written commitments to a minimum amount of education and training

Then, after this preparation, seek answers or further information about the following:

♦ ♦ ♦ ♦

What is the organization's *commitment* to
continual learning for employees in your situation?

What does the organization's mission statement, personnel policies, and training practices say about your learning?

What we know today will be obsolete tomorrow. If we stop learning we stagnate.

DOROTHY BILLINGTON

Does the organization designate that a certain minimal hours or days per year should be devoted to training and education?

Is training and education part of your job description?

Is it evaluated and planned for as part of your regular performance appraisal?

Who decides what training opportunities are appropriate for you?

Is the training that is available to you geared to your overall professional development, or focused on "Just in Time" skills to solve problems as they emerge?

What are the specific upcoming *opportunities* (over the next year) for workshops, seminars, distance learning programs, self-directed programs, or other opportunities and resources you might use?

Pre-booking yourself is the key strategy here.

Decide well in advance on the most attractive opportunities coming along over the next twelve months, and commit yourself to them. Put them on your calendar, discuss them with your supervisor, begin background reading if appropriate. Then, protect that time—use your commitment and your pre-scheduling to resist, sidestep, and decline assignments that would interfere—to the degree possible. Of course, a major crisis or change in your job circumstances might override your commitment. But having one in place can greatly add to your strength.

If you don't do this, it's likely that the "tyranny of the urgent" will make it all too easy not to attend.

What resources are in place that you can use for your *self-directed learning?*

Explore the resources of the organization's training library, including print (books, journals, newsletters) as well as AV and computer-based resources.

Computer-based learning provides important opportunities here, too, as explored in the chapter on Peak Learning in Cyberspace.

What support does the organization offer for *formal educational opportunities?*

Find out the policies regarding tuition reimbursement, released time, recognition, and reward for formal learning you may wish to do at a college, technical school, or other educational institution. If the arrangements you wish to make don't quite fit the organization's usual policies, ask about bending the rules a bit. I've yet to meet a training director who wasn't more than willing to accommodate a reasonable request from an employee eager to learn.

How should you structure and *document your learning* to receive the appropriate support, recognition, and support?

We can no longer shortchange our brains and impoverish our spirits.

JEAN HOUSTON

Many organizations have established forms for planning and documenting your learning, and showing how it relates to your job responsibilities and forwards the organization's goals and objectives. They are usually titled Individual Development Plan, or a comparable title. By using these forms, you assure that your learning fits the requirements for support and recognition.

◆ ◆ ◆ ◆

You should also take full advantage of the adult and continuing education offered in your community. Get on the list to receive the semi-annual catalogs from your area colleges and universities, plus any non-academic institutions like growth centers, institutes, or schools. Please see the entry in the chapter on the Invisible University, "Continuing Education: Creating Your Own Curriculum."

THE $17.00-AN-HOUR LEARNER

At the start of this chapter, you met "The $170 Million Dollar Learner"—Marc Andreesson, who discovered how much he still had to learn.

I'd like to conclude by introducing you to a $17-an-hour learner—an employee at the other end of the spectrum from Andreessen. She is Delores Franklin, who was earning $17 an hour when I met her several years ago. Delores, like Andreessen, recognized that L(earning) was essential to her success—and used it to jump-start her career. What she accomplished shows how these techniques can serve anyone, in any position, at any time in their career.

I was working as a consultant with a medium-sized firm (two thousand employees) in the computer industry. My assignment was to enhance the profitability of a work-team of seventy-five people.

Delores was the newcomer to the team, and this was her second job out of high school. She did not go to college, but she was bright and ambitious.

Consultants are supposed to be neutral and objective, and to focus on the "biggest bang for the buck" opportunities in any assignment. But I like to find the Delores in any group I'm working with, and give him or her special attention. Sometimes, you can make a crucial difference in an individual's life.

Delores caught my attention because of a little anecdote told me by the head of her unit, when I was interviewing all the managers about their challenges and opportunities. "I asked her to find a pile of monthly reports which I needed to review," said the manager. "I didn't think to give her a deadline, but I guess she could see I was a little frantic. Twenty minutes later, she came in with the reports—three-hole punched and inserted into a binder with section-divisions for each month, labeled with a Day-Glo sticker on the spine. This made them much easier to use, and assured that they wouldn't be lost in the shuffle again."

I suspected that I had a winner on my hands!

Sure enough, when I stopped into Delores's cubicle, she said almost immediately: "I'd like to take advantage of the fact that I'm new here—and the fact that they've got this project going with you right now."

"Delores," I answered, "if you're willing to ask questions, take chances, and seize your opportunities, we can really jump-start your career."

Here's what Delores did, with a little help from me and her colleagues, over the next six months. You'll recognize virtually everything here as being among the techniques you have been mastering.

- ◆ I acquainted Delores with the principles and strategies in this chapter to heighten her awareness of the need for L(earning), and the opportunities and strategies available. Delores was particularly impressed by Professor

Kotter's calculations about the dire consequences of failing to continue learning, because she had many friends who were already mired in dead-end jobs.

- ◆ We reviewed, with Delores 's supervisor, her possible next job in the company, her performance appraisal, and the best next things for her to learn to prepare herself for promotion. (The supervisor was delighted at Delores's initiative.)

- ◆ I helped Delores choose a self-study business book from the training library, to read and use on her own. I told her that no one would check up on what she learned— this was not like school. If she found useful things she could use, that was fine. If not, no one but she would ever know.

  (Delores picked *Managing Upward: Strategies for Succeeding with Your Boss,* by Hathaway and Schubert, one of the excellent "50-Minute Books" published by Crisp. As you'll see below, she found it quite useful.)

- ◆ We discussed Delores's assignments to find ways she could do more, do a more diverse range of things, and learn about the rest of the division.

- ◆ We explored which manager would be willing to serve as Delores's informal "mentor" for occasional talks about her progress, or problems.

- ◆ We ascertained what Delores could and should expect from the training department—courses she could take, materials she could use—and choosing an upcoming workshop being brought on-site, on "Managing Multiple Priorities."

Every day, Delores asked a few well-thought-through questions about the goals of the division, what everyone did, why things were done the way they were done, and how she could help. She cultivated a "Golden Ear"—although she was doing lots of talking, the buzz in the office was: "That Delores—what a *listener!*"

Delores looked at each of her assignments in terms of the Wheel of L(earning), and did After Action Reports on the way home each evening. She thought about ways to get her tasks done faster, better, cheaper. (In one case she realized that a

$160 tool would double her speed at one job, and therefore pay for itself in one month. She presented a proposal to purchase it and got approval.)

Within two weeks, a couple of the managers realized that explaining what they did and why they did it, and learning from Delores what the other managers had said, was really useful. It turned out (it always does) that there was a lot of ignorance and misunderstanding about who was doing what, and why—and a crippling lack of useful communication.

So a two-hour meeting was set up, to formalize the process. The agenda: each manager explaining what and why they did what they did, and fielding questions. Delores and I referred to it as a Learning Circle—but to her co-workers, it was known as Delores's Roundtable.

At her next performance appraisal, Delores was highly commended for her initiative, energy, and self-development; she received a promotion to department associate, and the maximum raise for which she was eligible.

As my work at the company drew to a close, I did an exit interview with Delores. "This was a great break for me," she said. "I really feel I'm on my way in this company."

"Delores, it's *you* who did all of this," I replied. "You started the process, you rose to every challenge, you took the chance of speaking out and asking 'dumb' questions, you read and used the book, you made it all work. Congratulations!"

Of course, this process didn't stop here. Delores's major initiative for the next year was to get approval to attend the annual professional conference in her field. Usually, this was a privilege accorded to more senior employees. But after ascertaining from her supervisor that there was no hard-and-fast rule against someone at her level attending, she took the initiative again. She used the techniques and strategies on profiting from conferences (see the entry on Conferences in the "The Invisible University") to design a plan which demonstrated how much value and profit the company would derive from her attendance. It was approved!

Now, four years later, Delores is a manager herself. And she promises me she is keeping her eye peeled for the next Delores!

The best web sites for up-to-date information on the topics in this chapter are:

American Society for Training and Development:
www.ASTD.org

Your organization's training director uses this site to keep up to date on how to encourage, facilitate, and reward your learning—so you should, too.

Lifelong Universe:
www.lifelong.com

This source of individualized interactive distance learning includes my own web site, and the opportunity to subscribe to my weekly "Dose of Gross" mailing list.

XI

The Invisible University: Learning Resources from A to Z

Fellow learners, it's my pleasure to welcome you to the Invisible University.

Please don't look around for the usual ivy-covered buildings and rolling greensward. Here at IU we've *really* gone back to basics. We're what universities were before the ivy had centuries to grow: *People learning together.*

We have no central quad, since our approach is to be *everywhere.* If you want to see our learners pursuing their studies, just punch up some bulletin boards on your computer terminal, drop into your local library, or visit one of your neighborhood clubs, associations, public-interest groups, specialized bookstores, political clubhouses, arts centers, or other places where people gather to talk, create, share, help, argue, advocate, or otherwise use their minds.

If there are any Americans with an education sufficient for useful criticism and constructive proposals, one fact about them will be sure: they will be self-educated.

PHILIP WYLIE

243

*Discovery . . . is in
its essence a matter of
rearranging or transforming
evidence in such a way that
one is enabled to go beyond
[it] to new insights.*

JEROME BRUNER

Although we're invisible, we are actually the biggest learning enterprise in the nation. We have the most students—approximately 70 percent of the adult population who, research shows, do substantial amounts of learning in their lives, 80 percent of it on their own.

We're especially proud of our unparalleled tradition of excellence. We have been enrolling the wisest people in every generation since before Oxford and Cambridge were founded.

Another point of pride is the *diversity* of our student body. Anyone can get in. (Some people have objected to this feature, however, on the same basis on which Groucho Marx once declined an invitation to join a snobbish club: "I don't think I'd want to be associated with any club that would let *me* in.")

The Invisible University, in short, is another way of looking at America: as an emerging learning society. But to us in the IU, a learning society doesn't mean that everyone goes back to *school.* Rather, it's a society in which learning and growth are integral parts of everyone's daily life—whether or not they are currently enrolled in a class.

But enough about us. Let's talk about *you.* Actually, the U in our name also signifies *you*! You are at the center of the Invisible University—*you*, not a catalog of courses, programs, and requirements; not a tenured faculty; not even a campus on which you must reside.

In this university, *you* define the educational goals. You select your teachers from the field you're interested in, rather than from one institution's employees. You surround yourself with fellow learners to enliven your pursuit of knowledge. You marshal and access the materials and resources you need. And you decide how, and how much, you study each subject.

Of course, there are certain requirements. In fact, the IU is in the forefront of the current movement toward more unity and coherence in the curriculum. We have a "national curriculum" in which virtually all Americans are regularly enrolled. But its content, unlike the core curriculum at other institutions, is changing constantly, to assure relevance.

Where and how do you start? How do you identify your learning goals? By looking at your life and asking: "What new things do I want to know or understand, what do I want to be-

things do I want to know or understand, what do I want to become, or be able to do, next month? A year from now? Five
years from today? What do I have to learn to do that?"

Once you've set some learning goals, you can really begin
enjoying the Invisible University. Its resources comprise a
wealth of ways to learn that are available for the first time in
our era.

First and foremost is the rich array of offerings in adult and
continuing education now available in every community, offered by colleges and universities, public school systems, and
libraries. But the IU encompasses much more.

You have at your fingertips, via telephone, computer, or
correspondence, grander resources than could be com-
manded by Alexander the Great, Napoleon, or, indeed, by
learners as late as Buckminster Fuller twenty years ago. If
you're not yet plugged in at home, your local library is your
gateway to databases, information sources, and materials. It
puts the world's wisdom, know-how, and knowledge at your
command.

If you prefer high-*touch* to high-*tech*, you can pursue your
studies in the IU via apprenticeship, tutorial, mentoring, work-
study, correspondence, travel, or reading. Many IUers have
become adept professionals by learning at conventions, by
apprenticeship, or by networking.

We learners in the IU follow a myriad of paths. You might
invite renowned scholars to join you on your drive to and from
work every day (via audiotapes), then enjoy relaxed reading in
the evening. Or you may prefer to plunge into a conference of
four thousand people on the subject you're studying, then network like crazy, and follow up by phone and fax. Or you could
access computerized materials and join the chatter via E-mail,
or combine correspondence study with a small local group of
enthusiasts in the back of a specialized bookstore.

You can start wherever you like, with whatever materials
appeal to you, and proceed at your own pace. You can mean-
der, savor, enjoy, plumb depths, leapfrog, backtrack, review, or
change course on short notice. You determine your level of
effort and measure yourself against standards you set or
choose.

*Today a society of and
for intelligence can be
consciously and humanly
planned. This is not a
theory; it is a reality that
transforms. . . . In
possession of more developed
minds, people will be able to
find within themselves the
elements needed to build
a new society.*

LUIS MACHADO

Your learning here in the IU will be lifelong and worldwide, though intensely personal. And you won't have to come to any further meetings. *This* is your commencement—a true beginning, not a capstone as at most universities.

ADVERTISING: WINDOW ON SOCIETY

Because there's no escape from inundation by advertising messages, why not make the most of them? You can learn to read ads for insights into our culture, even into yourself. By taking an active, critical stance, you'll enchance your awareness of what makes us all tick.

People who complain that there's no good news fail to realize, as Marshall McLuhan pointed out, that the *good* news is called advertising. In ads you can see what people want, which needs are being expressed, created, and fulfilled by products and services. Keeping this in mind, you can use the constant stream of ads to stimulate your reflections about what people seek and what appeals to them. What kind of society is revealed by your reading of advertising? How and why do the appeals in ads affect *you*?

Advertising is also the best laboratory for studying the art of persuasion from the master practitioners of our time. For this purpose, I invented the ad game for my kids (see Chapter Seven, pages 161–162). The result was that we made the ads more interesting, created for ourselves the basic categories of propaganda, and used our minds in a critical and creative way.

Access: *The Mechanical Bride*, by Marshall McLuhan, is the classic text for discerning the hidden messages and impact in ads. It's all the more useful now that the particular ads it reproduces are obsolete—their appeals and implications are easier to see with hindsight than those of ads today that appeal to current interests, which we can be blind to recognizing.

BOOKSTORES: GOURMET FOOD FOR THOUGHT

The library is your supermarket for learning. But when you're pursuing a topic in depth and with passion, there's an even better place to explore your field: bookstores specializing in your

A book of verses underneath the bough, a jug of wine, a loaf of bread—and thou.

EDWARD FITZGERALD

246

subject. Whether you visit them in person or via catalog or correspondence, you will find not merely books but people who share your interests and have taken the trouble to select materials from a wide variety of areas for their relevance to your topic.

Consider just one example: the philosophy of libertarianism. (I could just as well have chosen psychoanalysis, occult spirituality, astronomy, or home repair.) You will not readily find a course on libertarianism at most colleges and universities. Even if you go to a fine public or research library, you'll have a hard time assembling or even identifying the books you might want.

For example, works by Ludwig von Mises and F. A. Hayek, bastions of the Austrian School, are classified under "economics," with newcomers Milton Friedman and Murray Rothbard, yet social critics like Ayn Rand and Nathaniel Branden are in quite a different Dewey-decimal classification. And activist individualists like A. S. Neill, the creator of Summerhill, and teacher/author John Holt are somewhere under "education." Investigators of the psychology of individuality and social coercion, like Thomas Szasz, are elsewhere. And you wouldn't want to miss such *sui generis* types as H. L. Mencken, Albert J. Knock, or Robert Nozick.

So where can you go for an overview of the thinkers and writers germane to your interest? Laissez Faire Books in New York City issues a catalog that isn't merely a listing of works in this area, but a lively, engaging introduction to the field. Such bookstores also serve as clearinghouses, bulletin boards, message centers, contact points, and networking nodes. You can usually get reasonable questions answered by phone or at least get a referral to the right person or organization, and you can request a catalog by postcard.

The point isn't merely the information: it's the *esprit*, the style, the energy, the glimpse of a community of thinkers and enthusiasts that welcome newcomers. Whatever your field of interest—games or game fish, sports or torts, Marx or the Marx Brothers—you can find specialized bookstores, if not in your community than elsewhere in the country, which can both fuel and fan your enthusiasm.

If humanity is to pass safely through its present crisis on earth, it will be because a majority of individuals are now doing their own thinking. This [Peak Learning] project has pioneered in improving the climate for such thinking in the United States.

R. BUCKMINSTER FULLER

CASSETTES: VOICES OF WISDOM

There's a world of learning and enjoyment on the humble little audiotape cassette. It enables you to listen to the greatest thinkers of all time, to leading experts of today, and to novels, poems, and plays.

The advantages of this medium for learning are well expressed in this list by one of the leading producers of such materials, the Nightingale-Conant Corporation.

1. You don't have to keep up with the class. If there are lessons you want to dwell on, you can replay them as often as you want.

2. You're not held back by the class. You can zip through lessons that are easy for you, even though others may find them hard.

3. You can take "class" at any time you want. If 5:00 A.M. is your best time to study, go for it. And you don't have to miss lessons because of illness or schedule conflicts.

4. You can take "class" any place you can bring your tape recorder. Nothing—not vacations, business trips, or even blizzards—can interfere with your learning.

5. You can review your lessons anytime, anywhere, and as often as you want. You should, of course, listen to each lesson at least once wth absolutely no distraction. But you can review them while showering, driving, jogging, or doing chores *with the original teacher*, not just from notes or a textbook.

Consider one learner's experience in using the cassette curriculum. When O. B. Hardison drove to Ontario, Canada from his home in Washington, D.C., he listened to David Howarth's *1066: The Year of the Conquest*, about the Norman invasion of England. He was so absorbed in the book he was hearing that he slowed down for the last half-hour so that he could reach the end of the tape. On the way back, he listened to Bruce Catton's *The Civil War*. Since then, Hardison has listened to full-length works on the battle of Waterloo and, for relaxation, to Jane Austen's *Sense and Sensibility*.

The cassette curriculum is great, you might think, especially for someone who probably doesn't have much time to read during a regular working life. But Hardison is professor of English at Georgetown University. He gets paid to read books.

The cassette curriculum is a blessing for filling dull times with intellectual stimulation. Depending on your tastes, you can find a cassette company that provides your fare. You can listen to such great thinkers as Jefferson, Marx, Thoreau, Machiavelli, Hobbes, and de Tocqueville; if you prefer more contemporary thinkers, tapes with the works of Buckminster Fuller, Margaret Mead, Carl Rogers, Carlos Castaneda, S. I. Hayakawa, Michael DeBakey, Alan Watts, Robert Lowell, and Linus Pauling are available.

For this kind of use, I recommend that you consider getting a tape player on which you can adjust the speed from normal up to twice the original pace. This will enable you to review factual material faster and more enjoyably, because your mind prefers to absorb such material faster than the normal speaking voice. One reason lectures are usually boring is that your mind prefers to listen at 250 to 300 words per minute, but the normal speaking voice goes at only 100 to 150. Speed listening overcomes that problem, making listening more enjoyable. The best variable-speed machine permits you to adjust the pitch, restoring the sound waves to their original shapes so that you avoid "chipmunk" tone characteristic of accelerated playback.

Another accoutrement you might consider for private-time listening is a mask-phone, an eye covering that blocks out light but has places for two mini-speakers positioned over each ear. This eliminates distractions from outside light and sound, creating a relaxed, concentrated environment. Naturally, this is particularly good for motivational, literacy, musical, or language learning.

Using tape cassettes adds a powerful dimension to your learning, quite aside from their convenience. For most of us the human voice is an appealing, memorable way to take in new information and ideas. Moreover, fine prose, whether fiction or nonfiction, gains resonance from being well read, and interview or panel-discussion tapes add drama to the play of ideas. In short, there's a distinctive quality to learning via audiocassettes that you should experience directly in order to discover whether this medium is for you.

Access: *The Audio Book Rental Catalog* is issued annually by Talking Tapes, 60 West Littleton Boulevard, Suite 102, Littleton, Colorado 80120. It lists over 2,000 titles. Specialized tapes may be available in your field; ask at your library. For example, the Behavioral Sciences Tape Rental Service offers over 500 tapes in its area.

CONTINUING EDUCATION: CREATING YOUR OWN CURRICULUM

Twenty years ago I would not have suggested that your local college and university could be part of your Invisible University. Back in those days, students were routinely "stapled, spindled, and mutilated" by the academic bureaucracy. Adults with their own learning agendas were especially trammeled. *Your* learning needs weren't a major concern on the campus. Rather, the colleges and universities had *their* system in place—entrance exams, departments, majors, minors, and distinct freshman, sophomore, junior, and senior levels. You were required to fit into that system. If, as a divorced mother with two kids and a forty-hour work week, you couldn't manage the same schedule as your classmates, too bad.

Now, however, the situation has changed dramatically. Virtually every college and university in the country issues a listing or even a whole catalog of continuing education courses and programs designed with you—the adult learner—in mind. Using these offerings, you can select and actually put together your own ideal curriculum.

You'll find marvelous courses on a wide range of subjects. Often the faculty is drawn from the ranks of highly successful business, community, and intellectual leaders in your community. The costs are much lower than for credit courses.

Moreover, on any major campus you'll find a constant flow of fascinating activities that never appear in the course catalog,

The adult learner of the future will be highly competent in deciding what to learn and planning and arranging his own learning. He will successfully diagnose and solve almost any problem or difficulty that arises. He will obtain appropriate help competently and quickly, but only when necessary.

ALLEN TOUGH

250

from interest groups and guest lecturers to clubs, films, concerts, conferences, and exhibits. Some of these ad hoc opportunities may be more to your interest than any course, and they are usually free. Call the public-information office on campus and get on its mailing list for a calendar of events open to the public. Obviously, the campus is also a prime place to find others if you want to start a group, club, or other activity.

If you are interested in cumulative coursework leading to a degree, there's additional good news. Hundreds of colleges have reorganized to become "adult-friendly," in the words of Peter Smith, former Lieutenant Governor of Vermont and author of *Your Hidden Credentials*.

These adult-friendly colleges offer you opportunities to complete the class work required for a degree at convenient times—evenings, weekends, or summers—and in your own community rather than on campus.

Some programs allow you to develop a personal plan of study through independent reading and fieldwork related to your occupation, which will earn you a diploma. Often you can obtain credits for prior learning, whether in a classroom or on your own. If you don't want to leave home, you can take courses via television or through a combination of televised instruction, correspondence study, and other media. You also can earn a degree solely by examination.

If you want or need formal learning for credits or a degree, you don't need to feel that your circumstances are an obstacle. You can overcome problems of time, distance, and money by choosing the program that best suits you from this burgeoning marketplace of institutions that want to serve you.

Access: For a complete, up-to-date overview of such opportunities to continue your education on your own terms, consult *Who Offers Part-Time Degree Programs?*, a compendium published by Peterson's Guides, in Princeton, New Jersey.

CONFERENCES: LEARNING IN THE COLLEGE OF BRIGADOON

Conference-going has become a routine part of life for many professionals. The motivations behind meeting mania are mixed, and some have little to do with learning. You may go to get away from home, to visit an appealing city, to make contacts or find a new job, or simply to have adventures of various sorts.

However, you may feel you don't *learn* as much as you'd like from these conferences. "I sit in sessions wondering if it's better on the other side of the movable wall," confesses an appliance wholesaler. "I always want to figure out how to find and meet the *names*," confides the vice-president of a major women's organization. "The laughter always sounds louder at the next banquet table," says a lawyer with General Motors in Detroit.

In fact, you *can* learn a lot at conferences. But first you need to begin to think of them in a different way: as a special kind of college within your Invisible University. Every time you attend a conference, you're joining a "College of Brigadoon." Like the town in that classic musical, the conference springs to life for only a few exciting days in a hotel's seminar rooms and banquet halls, and then disappears.

From your point of view as a learner, a good conference brings together the best people in the field. This is your faculty, usually a better, more up-to-date one than any single campus offers as permanent faculty.

Second, conferences draw an array of the best learning aids in your field: exhibits and exhibitors. They are like the college's library, but a library of books and authors plus all kinds of learning gear in other forms, including equipment, technology, and aids for effective thought and practice.

Third, the best conferences define the state-of-the-art curriculum in your field. They present the theorists and practitioners who have recently emerged as the most significant, usually ten years or so before their impact has been integrated into the campus curriculum.

Finally, the student body, your fellow participants, may be the most significant players in your field. And they are, hopefully, brought together for effective networking.

Faculty, resources, curriculum, and fellow learners—these are the elements of this ad hoc college. But being ad hoc, it must be used then and there, before the conference vanishes. If you've ever walked through the hotel corridors and meeting rooms two hours after a major conference has ended, you had a keen sense of transience. Yesterday these rooms were filled with the heady life of a world theory and practice; today, they are lifeless facilities. The conference lives on only in the minds of the participants who made the most of it.

You can be one of them. Here are the half-dozen keys to learning more from your next conference—and every one after that.

Technique 1: Get the Program Beforehand. The time to read the menu is while you're still outside the restaurant. If your first sight of the program is when you open your participant's kit, you're already behind.

Simply call the conference organizers two weeks before to get the detailed program. If it's not ready, they'll be embarrassed enough to send you a photocopy of the proof, especially when you mention that you may write something on their conference for your organization's newsletter.

Technique 2: Plan on the Plane. When the stewardess has stopped demonstrating the safety instructions and the pilot has stopped telling you what fun it is to fly a wide-belly through the friendly skies, it's time to get out the conference program. Start by circling those sessions you *must* attend in person, either because they're vital to your interests or just plain fun. Then check those sessions that are of secondary but compelling interest but may be no fun.

Put a star by those individuals you'd most like to meet. Make a schedule of periods of free time during the conference, including meals—especially those breakfasts and lunches during which there are no conference activities—as well as major breaks between late-afternoon and dinner sessions and late evenings. These are your opportunities to find the people you want to meet.

Technique 3: What's a Winner Like You Doing at a Conference Like This? The familiar 80–20 principle applies to conferences:

80 percent of the benefits will come from 20 percent of the people. How do you navigate in a sea of badges to find the one in five who's most worth meeting? Start by reaching for the stars. Someone spends part of the conference with the notables. It can be you, if you just get to them before everyone else does.

The best method is to write them a brief note on your professional letterhead. (Hopefully, you brought some on the plane.) Explain your interest and invite them to their choice of one or two appointments, either at the coffee shop or one of the meals. You can leave such notes for three or four people right after you arrive, filling in your room number. As a result, you may have some very rewarding conversations.

Technique 4: Skip Speeches. Despite popular opinion, you will save time by skipping plenary sessions at which major speakers read a prepared text, except when the speaker is a dramatic or witty platform performer. Ordinary speeches that merely convey information are, in my opinion, an obsolete mode of communication. Modeled on the lectures in a medieval university, such presentations were rendered technologically obsolete by the invention of the printing press, although no one seems to have noticed.

Moreover, speeches are psychologically fatiguing. Because our minds move three times faster than the spoken word, and because we are accustomed to taking in information at the accelerated rate and multisensory complexity of television, oral speeches are almost inevitably boring. Sitting through them can sap your energy for later sessions when you will want to be at your peak.

Each speaker's prepared text will be available before or after the speech in the conference press room. You can read it in ten minutes, mark the important points, and reread it when you like, all in less time than it would take to sit through the talk.

Technique 5: Overcome Panel Envy. Panel envy is, of course, that distinctive unease that arises when you've been listening too long to other people pontificating on a subject you know just as much about. If a session is worth going to, it's worth stretching yourself to formulate a creative response when it's time for questions or discussion. Committing yourself to coming up with a really good contribution is the best way to get the most out of the session. It also brings you to the attention of the people assembled, which never hurts.

Technique 6: Homeward Bound—To Reap the Benefits. On the plane home you can gain the full advantages of the conference. In two hours you can distill the best new ideas, information, and contacts you have obtained, draft your follow-up letters, and prepare reports to others. The result: a happy landing—and no time needed for debriefing when you get to your desk the next morning.

Access: A listing of all the major conferences in any field you're interested in—professional or avocational—can be found in the appropriate trade or special-interest magazine. For tips on getting the most out of attending conferences, see *Getting Results Through Learning*, Patricia McLagan, McLagan & Associates, Rosedale Towers, 1700 West Highway 36, St. Paul, Minnesota 55113.

CORRESPONDENCE COURSES: TUTORS IN YOUR MAILBOX

"The Poetry of Yeats" from the University of California and FORTRAN from the University of Chicago have been among my students' most treasured studies. Both were correspondence courses taught by senior professors and leading experts on these subjects. These students felt they learned better from them, and enjoyed the process more, than they did from most of their college courses.

Other learners regularly turn to this mode from time to time when it matches their needs. Sometimes they combine it with other resources. While taking a correspondence course in general semantics, for instance, one student borrowed a series of film lectures by S. I. Hayakawa, the master interpreter of this system of thought, from the public library.

The range of offerings is immense. A partial list of subjects

255

The adult should recognize that there is no limit to acquired knowledge nor significant decrease in the ability to learn. The process of learning for an adult can be likened to weight lifters exercising muscles under regular programs. The maintenance of present knowledge requires review and the constant addition of new information through reading and exposure to learning through university programs, adults schools or community groups. When you associate with other "students," it helps your motivation to keep "exercising your mind."

RUTH AND ART WINTER

currently offered contains hundreds of items starting with Academic Degrees, Accounting, and Advertising and ending with Writing, Yacht and Small Craft Design, and Zoology.

If you don't already have a college degree and you want one, you can apply academic courses that you take by correspondence toward a degree. Many adult-friendly colleges will count up to thirty credit hours of home-study work toward a B.A. This kind of learning has been shown to be as effective as classroom study. It's widely recognized by employers, licensing boards, the V.A. and military, and unions.

You also can explore alternative careers via these courses. "Many courses provide complete vocational training," says Bill Fowler, long-time director of the National Home Study Council and acknowledged guru in the field. "Others prepare you for upgrading in your present job, without losing experience or seniority. You don't have to give up your job, leave home or lose income. You learn as you earn. The school comes to you. The emphasis is on learning what you need to know. Instructional materials from accredited schools are up-to-date, clearly written, and easy to understand."

Knowing in advance what correspondence study is like can help you decide whether it's for you. You'll start with a booklet of twenty or twenty-five lessons and assignments plus a textbook you can either buy locally or order from the school. Each lesson usually includes some assigned reading in the text and/or notes in the syllabus. There is also a short test or essay keyed to each of the readings, which, when completed, is sent to the instructor. Within ten days it comes back marked with marginal notations and perhaps a note from the instructor. Before the last lesson, you arrange to take an examination, which is sent to some local school or college contact, clergyman, or librarian

Increasingly today, correspondence courses   ss some of the other media of the Invisible University. Many courses come with audio and video cassettes, slides and filmstrips, and hands-on kits for technical skills. Often, you will be provided with a toll-free telephone number to encourage talking with the instructor or an advisor at school.

All of this technology places home study, which many people regard as a bit old-fashioned, right at the forefront of some of the boldest futurist thinking about education. *Distance learning* is the catch phrase for using communications technology to make top-quality learning available everywhere. Educators throughout the world are moving in this direction. I've discovered a lot of admiration abroad for American efforts in home study while visiting such pioneering projects in this field as Britain's Open University and Israel's Everyman's University.

Above all, the intimacy of home study makes it attractive. Think of it this way: if you were learning about Peak Learning via a correspondence course, at this point you'd have the chance to write me a letter about your reactions to this material and promptly get one back from me.

Access: The best source for selecting a correspondence course keyed to your interests is Peterson's *Independent Study Catalog,* published for the National University Continuing Education Association, a nonprofit group. It lists more than 12,000 high school, college, graduate, and noncredit courses.

ELDERHOSTEL

We now know that the human brain does *not* "die back" when you reach fifty, sixty, seventy, or even eighty. Rather, the iron law of the healthy older brain seems to be "use it or lose it." Constant mental stimulation, enjoyment, and growth can keep us keen throughout our lives.

The Elderhostel program is the world leader in the burgeoning field of learning in the later years. It's a non-profit organization which provides high quality, affordable educational opportunities throughout the world. You can find courses in their heft catalog of over 100 pages, in Cicero and computers, politics to poetry—in places from Maine to Wales.

As I write this entry, I've just booked my next Elderhostel adventure: to Sicily next March, to study the origins of Roman and Greek civilization.

Access: Elderhostel, 75 Federal Street, Boston, MA, 02110-1941, or you can consult the catalog at any public library.

ENVIRONMENT: AWARENESS EQUALS LEARNING

It's been said that if fish could think, they'd be the last creatures to discover water. So it is with our physical environment, the water in which we swim. It's always there, yet we rarely really see it. Opening your eyes to your physical surroundings makes your everyday life more interesting and rewarding.

Start with whatever aspect of your environment has always intrigued you, big or small. For example, really look at the style and materials of the houses in your neighborhood, or consider how your city got laid out. (The streets of Boston, for example, followed the paths that herds of cows had worn into the grazing pasture.) Virtually any city has a pocket guide to its architecture and history.

You can start as small and mundane as you like. Herbert Kohl, a teacher and writer, became intrigued by the graffiti he saw on walls around him. He really took a fresh look at it, talked with other people, and produced a whole book on the topic, *Golden Boy as Anthony Cool.*

The man-made environment is constantly available for study. Right now you are probably reading these words in an almost wholly designed environment, from the chair in which you are sitting to the building in which you are located. Look around—almost everything you see was originally an idea in someone's mind.

Access: Your enjoyment, comfort, and efficiency will be greatly enhanced by becoming conversant with modern industrial design through books such as Ralph Caplan's *By Design,* Henry Dreyfuss's classic *Designing for People,* or Vincent Papanek's *Designing for the Real World.* After reading any of them, you will never see your everyday world in quite the same way again.

GREAT GOOD PLACES:
"HANGOUTS" AS COMMUNITY LEARNING CENTERS

"And they're always glad you came . . . You want to go where everybody knows your name." The theme song from the TV series "Cheers" evokes a kind of place that's hard to find these days. But it is coming back, and it is the locus of the kind of learning that fomented the American Revolution in colonial taverns.

Sociologist Ray Oldenburg gave such places a name in his wonderful treatise *The Great Good Place: Cafes, Coffee Shops, Com-*

munity Centers, Beauty Parlors, General Stores, Bars, Hangouts, and How They Get You Through the Day (Paragon House, 1990).

"The course of urban growth has been hostile to informal public life," writes Oldenburg. "What America needs is not more television, exercise and psychotherapy but a 'third place' that will nourish the kinds of relationships and the diversity of human contact that are the essence of sociability uncontaminated by status, special purposes or goals."

The Great Good Place shows how informal gathering places are essential to the vitality of a city and its people. The author illustrates how the grass roots of democracy are weaker and our individual lives less rich as these places become more scarce and the diversity of human contact diminishes.

Oldenburg offers a variety of cultural and historical examples of "third places," from German beer gardens to Parisian cafes to Japanese teahouses. His book will show you how to find your own, local great good place—or even suggest how to create one!

LEARNING STORES

Retail stores built around learning, knowledge and the mind, have appeared in major cities over the past five years. The Store of Knowledge, in mid-Manhattan, exemplifies his new genre of retailers. Often these stores are sponsored by major museums, public libraries, or local public television stations. The products they sell include books, games, puzzles, posters, and computer software such as CD-ROM and programs with an emphasis on using your mind. These are wonderful sources of inspiration and practical help in enlivening your learning, and your that of your children.

LETTERS: BACK TO THE FUTURE

Think of two or three of your intellectual heroes or heroines, masters of learning whom you most admire. Chances are, their *letters* were a key part of their learning lives.

The decline of the personal letter is one of the losses to learning in our time. Fortunately, it's coming back strong, thanks in large measure to Stephen Sikora, founder, publisher, and editor of *The Letter Exchange* in Albany, California. "I was looking far and near for people to write to," Sikora notes, explaining the origins of his venture. "I tried placing classified ads in national magazines and also slipped brief notes into periodicals at the local library, asking other readers of the article at hand to get in touch with me. Reading by itself simply wasn't enough. I craved feedback, the stimulus of interaction with another mind."

Sikora's search for like-minded correspondents led him in 1982 to publish his own magazine devoted to matching up letter writers who share general or specific interests. Five years later, he had three thousand subscribers. "From yachts to Yeats, from daily life to Dharma Bums, someone somewhere wants to write a letter about it."

Published three times a year, *The Letter Exchange* consists of subscribers' personal ads arranged in such categories as literature, history, seniors, travel, and contemporary issues. The ads carry no addresses; each one is identified only by a code number. Through a free forwarding service (and with the help of his eighty-six-year-old mother), Sikora forwards all initial responses to the ads. Correspondents usually write to one another directly once this initial contact has been made.

Sikora has invented the notion of *ghost letters*—correspondence between historical, literary, or imaginary characters. A Canadian woman in her sixties had two special interests: ancient Rome and Native American Indians of the Southwest. She placed this ad in the ghost Letters section: "Navaho woman of the 1890s seeks exchange of views with Roman soldier." Among several responses came one from "Flavius the Centurion"—a young college student in Tennessee, actually—who reported on his military adventures in Britannia and other outposts of the Roman Empire. Throughout the following year, "Willowleaf" responded in kind. "I ransacked my local library," the woman told Sikora, "digging up everything I could find about Navaho, Hopi, and Zuni life to send to my Roman soldier. And I realized only afterward how much knowledge I had gained through these lighthearted exchanges."

Through another special section of ads, for amateur magazines, correspondents circulate informal newsletters and round robins among a small number of writers. Topics range from dreams and journal writing to travel, television, and Sherlock Holmes. *Postal Possibilities,* a periodical for brainstorming by mail, grew out of one of these; a review of current murder mysteries and thrillers emerged from another; and a newsletter for single-parent mothers evolved from a third.

Sikora concludes: "We're exploring as many alternatives as possible to what has become an impasse in the life of the mind. Literacy and learning cannot thrive when only a few professionals do the writing while thousands, or hundreds of thousands, of the rest of us only read. Letter-writing redresses this imbalance, placing the power of the pen in our own hands."

Just one last word on letter-writing: you can write to me or to the author of any exciting book in whatever field you're currently interested in. If you really don't think you'd want to mail the letter, write an imaginary one. You'll benefit from the exercise anyway, and by the time you finish you may be surprised how you feel about it. If you write care of the publisher, your letter will be forwarded. Or, with a modest amount of sleuthing, you can get an author's address through an agent. Use this exercise to take a fresh look at the writer's work and how you feel about it.

Access: For more information send a business-sized stamped, self-addressed envelope to Sikora at The Letter Exchange, P.O. Box 6218-LL, Albany, California 94706.

Learning to me means infinite curiosity on any subject, and never accepting final answers until we have explored every possibility that there is no more to know.

MARVA COLLINS

LIBRARIES: BOOKS AND BEYOND

Nowadays libraries have even more to offer than ever before. They can often serve learners in unexpected and useful ways that most people haven't heard of and only a handful know how to gain access to. Such aid and comfort is available for the asking.

Central to the library, of course, is its book collection, which may have special strengths in your field of interest. The card catalog will give you an overall picture of what the library has and will steer you to the right section of the open shelves for the subject at hand. The books on the shelves will in turn, through their bibliographies, suggest other books. By comparing bibliographies on any subject, you are likely to find an easy way to identify the best (or at least the most highly regarded and the most often quoted) works in your field. Books that turn up frequently in bibliographies usually are worth paying attention to.

If you can't find what you're looking for, it doesn't necessarily mean that the library doesn't have it. Ask a librarian for help. By observing what the librarian does—what library tools are used—and by asking questions, you will learn new ways to use the library more effectively.

Most libraries have open-shelf magazine and newspaper racks. If your interest is in language, there are usually foreign periodicals. There are also hundreds of special-interest magazines about such subjects as photography, stereo equipment, and automobiles, to name only a few. Ask for a directory of publications to see if you have completely surveyed the field.

In addition to a wide range of music selections, the library's record collection may well contain foreign-language recordings, recordings of plays, radio documentaries, and poetry readings. Are other media available? Many libraries now routinely circulate films and slides. Some even lend or rent projectors and check out tape cassettes. The library may be able to get access on your behalf to larger audiovisual storehouses in the public schools or colleges.

Check the reference department. There are some excellent reference books for learners: directories of organizations by type *(Encyclopedia of Associations, Directory of Research Centers);* vocational information *(Resources: Recommendations for Adult Career Resources Supplement);* and standard reference works, such as yearbooks or guides within your special area of interest *(The Yearbook of Education).*

See if the library has a bulletin or calendar of events listing lectures, discussion groups (on great books, current affairs, or other topics), workshops, films, concerts, and so on. If you have young children, find out about story hours or preschool activities. These can provide babysitting services that help your children to learn while you pursue your learning program.

Try to evaluate the professional staff when you use the library. As in all organizations, there is usually a wide range of competence among the employees. If you are inadequately served by one librarian, don't give up; try others. Build up a good working relationship wit those who are most helpful and most familiar with the library collection. The librarian is a key to the resources of the library; if you locate a skilled librarian who cares, your use of the library will be a pleasure.

If the library does not have the material you are looking for—a book, a magazine, or perhaps a phonograph record—interlibrary loans may be possible. Libraries in small communities often can, and do, borrow from state or large municipal libraries. In large cities interlibrary loans between branches are common and frequent.

Does your library have a learner's advisory service? This innovation may not yet be available, but asking for it might help speed its arrival. Briefly, the learner's adviser is a librarian who will be your personal learning consultant; he or she has been specially trained to help you articulate your needs and goals, plan a learning program, select and obtain materials, and solve problems in the learning process as they arise. Usually the smartest, most personable, and most committed librarians have involved themselves in the program. If there is a learner's adviser, introduce yourself. You will acquire an invaluable consultant for your learning.

Databases are computerized indexes of journal and report literature in specific subject areas. Database searches save learners time by doing in minutes what would otherwise require days. These searches can provide you with a list of documents tailored to your individual needs, often including abstracts or summaries of the articles listed. They may be broadened to encompass general areas or narrowed by specifying publication date, language, geographic area, and so forth.

Database indexes are often more comprehensive than printed indexes; they usually are updated before the latter, and the computer can search for terms and information sources too current to appear in printed indexes. Computer logic can be used to combine related aspects of a problem such as driving and alcoholism in order to generate a custom-tailored index, which is impossible with printed indexes. Some databases contain nonbibliographic information, such as the texts of legal cases, statistical data, and reports of research in progress.

Database searches often are accompanied by document delivery systems, through which the full texts of the articles, re-

ports, or other documents cited in the search are provided to
the user. This service is especially valuable for people who cannot easily obtain the actual documents, perhaps because they
live far from or do not have ready access to the available
sources. Document delivery systems enable these people to
call, write, telex, or cable their requests and to receive their materials quickly and easily.

Some public libraries offer database searches free of
charge to the general public, but you may have to inquire specifically about them, since librarians sometimes are reluctant
to volunteer information about costly services that might be
abused. The New York State Library, for example, makes a limited number of free searches available to public library systems
throughout the state, which in turn pass them on to individual
public libraries for use by their patrons.

*Access: Computer-Readable Data Bases: A Directory and Source-
book,* by Martha Williams, American Society for Information
Science. Includes names and producers of over 700 databases
worldwide.

LUCK: THE BONUS AND BENEFIT OF LEARNING

We've all had the experience of learning a new word and then
finding that it pops up in conversation at least once or twice
during the next few days. That commonplace experience
points to the connection between your learning and being
lucky. The more you are involved in learning, the luckier
you're going to get. That's because luck is actually *caused* by the
very same things you do when you learn in the way you've
learned in this book: by following your own interests, using a
wide variety of resources, and structuring your learning to fit
your style.

Consider what is now known about luck. We are beginning
to understand a little bit about this mysterious phenomenon
that means so much in our lives.

"Chances can be on our side," declares a noted scientist, Dr.
James Austin, "if we but stir up our energies, stay receptive
to random opportunity, and continually provoke it by individuality in our hobbies, attitudes, and our approach to life." I've

found this to be strikingly true, and I've seen how easily people can learn to tap this resource.

Drawing from Dr. Austin's work and that of other pioneers in this field such as Edward de Bono and Max Gunther, we can identify five kinds of luck. Each of them is more likely to happen when you are learning.

Luck One is blind luck, dumb luck, such as the luck involved in drawing four aces in a poker game or winning the lottery. The only thing you can do here is to be in the game. As my state's lottery commercials put it, to *win* it you've got to be *in* it.

So go where the stuff of your field *is*, whatever your game is. (And I hope you'll pick a better game than the lottery!) For you, this might mean going to the right library, circle of acquaintances, occupation, or TV program. But get in the game you want to be in; as Judy Collins says, "the muse does not visit an empty studio."

Luck Two consists of the "happy accidents" that occur when you are just going about your business. We often use the enchanting word *serendipity* for this kind of luck. Such luck likes a moving target. "Get going, and the chances are you will stumble on something," urged the prolific inventor Charles Kettering. "I've never heard of anyone stumbling on something while sitting down."

Luck Two happens when you are learning—being curious, nosy, inquisitive. You activate this kind of luck, for example, when you announce at a networking meeting that you are seeking some situation, person, or resource and it turns out that, "as luck would have it," there's someone in the group who can help. You've put your need "in motion" instead of just sitting there with it.

Luck Three requires even more of you than just being in the right place and being in motion. Here, the happy event is something quiet or disguised, which you might miss if you weren't sagacious (the quaint word, meaning "shrewd," used in the original definition of *serendipity* by Horace Walpole in the eighteenth century). In this case, the good luck occurs only because you are alert and smart enough to discern its significance.

The best advice on attracting Luck Three is Pasteur's "Dans

Selective reading habits are taking hold as Americans read more magazines and newspapers to gain information of significance or personal value to them.

LENA WILLIAMS

265

les champs de l'observation, le hazard ne favorise que les esprits preparés" (Chance favors only the prepared mind). When Fleming "stumbled" on the accident that revealed how penicillin kills bacteria, he had been honing his mind in this area for thirty years.

Dr. Austin identifies the fourth form of good luck in his bright little book *Chase, Chance and Creativity*. Luck Four occurs when you are doing something that is characteristically, perhaps uniquely, *you*. This may sound arcane, but what's being described is the savvy strategy suggested to career-changes by the most sophisticated career counselors. They advise clients that one of the surest routes to the top in any field is to identify their *unique* style or slant and go where it leads. That's when the lucky break is most likely to come. Mythologist Joseph Campbell's advice to his students is apt here: "Follow your bliss."

Luck Five is sparked by intuition. Here, a little voice from within goads you to do something you wouldn't otherwise do, and the result is a remarkable piece of good fortune. Obviously, this plumbs even deeper in your inner resources, tapping senses of which we are only dimly aware. Yet it, too, can be cultivated.

To sum up these five ways to get luck: (1) be there, (2) be active, (3) be prepared, (4) be yourself, and (5) be intuitive.

You'll already have noted that these five categories overlap and intertwine. In any important piece of learning you are very likely to find traces of each kind, in varying proportions. But my students and clients find this conceptual model a useful one in identifying specific things they can do to spark more good luck in their lives.

Access: The Luck Factor, by Max Gunther, Macmillan, 1977.

MAGAZINES AND NEWSPAPERS: WORLDS IN A GLIMPSE

For a refreshing glimpse of another world of skills, knowledge, and style, nothing beats an hour with a magazine in a field you know nothing about. So once a month, browse through the magazine rack at your local library, where you'll find the latest issues of magazines on a wide range of topics, from drag racing and chess to foreign affairs and costume design. Dip into one that catches your fancy. (See Chapter Four, page 71, for a list of a few recommendations).

You will suddenly find yourself in a strange but friendly world of fresh enthusiasms, people, and issues. The goings-on and ads will provide easy entrée into the field. Unlike picking up a survey or textbook in the field, reading a magazine lets you hear real people talking about issues, and there'll be plenty of upcoming events you can take in if you get hooked.

Another powerful way to use specialized magazines is to flip through a pile of the last year's issues and find the review of the major events of the year. Most specialized magazines publish such lists in their December or January issue. Often it will be in the form of a full-fledged article commenting on the ten or twelve major events in the field. There's no better way to gain an instant introduction to where a field is *right now* than reading such a review of the past year. You won't understand much of the lingo or recognize many of the names, but you'll get an excellent overall feel for what's going on—the major issues, developments, and people.

On a more regular basis, you can get much more out of reading the newspaper every day. Start by really *using* what you read. Read with a pen and, if possible, a pair of scissors in hand. Mark, clip, and tear—not just for yourself, but for friends. The right clipping for the right person is the most attractive no-cost present you can give. When you find something absorbing but lack the time to read it well, don't try to skim it on the run. Clip and save it for the weekend.

Your newspaper may offer a handbook on getting the most out of it. Most major papers do.

Once a week, focus on some part of the paper. Use the newspaper to explore new areas. If, say, you routinely skip sports, business, or the arts or science section, make a point of really giving it your attention. This will open a door to some intriguing developments, and I guarantee you will find a use for what you learn within forty-eight hours (see the preceding section on luck).

Switch papers once every three months (with the seasons, to change the climate *inside* your head). Read a different one for a week or just add it to your regular papers if you're addicted. You'll find it startling to be reminded of how the world looks to the reader of your local brash tabloid if you're accustomed to high-class fare. The columnists and Op-Ed writers of a highly conservative paper will wake you up fast if your favorite newspaper is middle-of-the-road or liberal. Treat yourself to another view of the world at least once a month, and ask yourself whether there are any kinds of news or points of view there that you need to consider.

MUSEUMS: HOW TO USE THEM

My friend David Carr has written a one-page pamphlet on how to use a museum. It's brightened my visits, so with his permission I'm sharing his advice. Here are five basic ideas for learning in any museum.

Think about what you see and what you find to be especially interesting.

Decide what attracts you most and spend time observing it.

Document what you find, with notes, sketches, or photographs.

Communicate about your favorite parts of the museum with someone you know.

Pursue your interest after you leave the museum. A clear plan for learning also gives you something to think about after the visit. Did I see everything I wanted to see? Were my questions answered? In fact, some of your most valuable museum learning can occur *after* you have left the museum itself. When you start to set an agenda for museum learning, you may be starting a long-term pursuit—it may even follow you home!

You will find museums (like libraries) to be good places for learning because they let you become deeply involved in your subject, concentrating and thinking about it as much as you want.

Use the museum with a plan in mind. You may think of it as an agenda, a theme, or a path to follow during your time in the museum. The plan may change, but it is useful to have at least one idea or topic in mind when you walk through the door. It can be a simple idea: "I want to look at masks." Or general: "What can I find out about tropical fish here?" Or more specific: "How do animals adapt in order to survive?"

Each of these agendas or questions uses specific words: *masks, tropical fish, animals, adapt, survive.* Words like these give you a focus to start your learning. Unless you already have some relevant expertise, it is a good idea to keep your question somewhat limited at first. There will be plenty of time for complexity later.

Write your plan or question down, before you go to the museum, even if you are not absolutely sure of the right words or ideas.

Your plan should always be flexible, so you can change it when something more important or more pertinent attracts your attention. This doesn't mean that you must abandon your original plan. Once it is written down, you can always come back to it, or follow it when other important interests are satisfied. *You* are the only person to decide what interests you most.

Your best questions or plans will follow your own special interest, so ask questions you may know something about. Think of questions as special invitations to learn—invitations you extend to yourself.

Access: For Professor Carr's complete pamphlet and/or to share your museum learning experiences, write to Carr at the Graduate School of Education, Rutgers University, 10 Seminary Place, New Brunswick, New Jersey 08903, enclosing a self-addressed stamped envelope to facilitate his responding.

PEOPLE: NETWORKING FOR KNOWLEDGE

You are surrounded by literally hundreds of people with knowledge, skills, interests, and contacts that could be highly valuable to you—if only you could gain access to them. "Mastering these hidden resources all around you can enhance your enjoyment and productivity immensely," says Robert Lewis, founder and CEO of Network Builders International in Atlanta.

Lewis has earned the right to make this claim. He has spent fifteen years creating networking directories for local businesses, neighborhood churches, clubs, and associations. His methods have worked in schools, colleges, libraries, condominiums, and retirement villages.

"We've discovered—and proven—that there are hidden resources in every organization," Lewis says. "When we go into a company or association to delve for them, we find that more than 90 percent of the participants are willing to share what they know. This yields a wealth of know-how for others to tap."

It turns out that people *like* to share their knowledge, skills, and contacts, and when given the chance to do so, their self-esteem soars. Organizational morale is buoyed. Everyone feels a greater sense of mutual support and encouragement and a new respect for the full range of talents and interests of others. "Eighty percent of the energy and talent within people in any organization is buried on the second pages of the résumés in the Personnel Department's file cabinets, never to be used," asserts Lewis.

Here are a few of the ways that my students have used such hidden resources in their organizations. One woman realized she needed to take a workshop on time management. Three workshops were readily available in her community, so she did not know which to choose. She easily found someone who'd taken each course.

Another person had just finished the best-seller *In Search of Excellence* and was eager to talk about it with someone else in the company. He found four people who had read it in the last year.

A third student wanted to put together an ad hoc task force to do something about pollution in her community. She identified a half-dozen people interested and knowledgeable about the subject, who joined her in researching the situation and planning a campaign.

Lewis suggests how you can go about finding who knows what in your organization. First, he says, define the specific purpose of your networking exercise. What kinds of information, understanding, talent, insight, or help are you looking for? Next, create a simple questionnaire that elicits, in less than a half-hour, the topics on which people in your organization are willing to be used as resources. People's names and numbers can then be listed under such categories as:

Professional skills (accounting, art exhibiting . . .)

Products/Services/Industries (airlines, auto repair . . .)

Contacts (attorneys, builders . . .)

Discussions—job and professional (assertiveness, budgets . . .)

Professional growth (acquisitions, benefits information . . .)

Academic experience/Certification (architecture, boating . . .)

Other categories might include favorite magazines, recently read books, classes and academic programs, travel experiences or plans, hobbies, physical fitness, and support groups.

This information, collected and properly processed, yields the primary product: your own network directory. "Once such a network directory is in the hands of everyone in the organization, there's an immediate and sustained upsurge in communication," Lewis claims. "Faced with a problem, anyone can reach a person within the organization who can offer personal advice or information. Soon you will find people pairing up to swap knowledge in related fields, ongoing groups forming, and problem-oriented task forces marshaling in-hour expertise with sharp efficiency. On personal interests, too, employees will look increasingly within the organization, forging links that transcend bureaucratic categories."

This kind of network also can operate as a community service, run by an independent agency or an enterprising public library. The Learning Connection in Nassau County, New York has a community-wide version of the networking directory. It matches people who want to learn with people who want to teach. "The Learning Connection was launched seven years ago and it's thriving, particularly now that we're computerized," says Dorothy Puryear of the Nassau Library System. "Our idea was that any community contains a vast untapped reservoir of talent. Our computer can now track hundreds of courses, subjects, and up to 5,000 teachers, each of whom may teach up to 10 different topics. And it can crank out the names of the teachers of a given subject within a specific Zip Code area, and therefore is accessible to a given learner." Look for the learning exchange in your area—or start one.

Learning from tutors, masters, and mentors presents a wide range of possibilities. For most of Western history, this

271

was the way the elite was taught, and it is still prevalent. When a six-figure executive needs to learn something important, he or she usually doesn't sign up for a class. Instead, the executive has an assistant find out who the leading local expert on the subject is and hires that person to come in and work with him or her—not as a *tutor*, of course, but as a *consultant*. Scientists apprentice themselves in the laboratories of senior scientists, and artists do the same.

Learning through daily contact with the mind of a master can be a crucial experience. Such instruction is, obviously, tailored to the individual learner—in this case, you. The tutor can adjust the pace, the topics, and even the style of learning.

You can explore this possibility by linking up through a learning exchange, but you also can take direct action if an exchange is unavailable or doesn't produce a tutor. You can even *advertise*. This works for virtually any subject, topic, issue, or skill. Once you put the word out, you will discover that some of the most interesting people in your community are eager to share their knowledge and skills.

TEACHING: SHARING YOUR LEARNING

An old adage says, "Teach what you need to learn." In our era of high educational attainments and specialized expertise, we each have something important to teach others. Just as everyone can learn, everyone can teach.

The advantages are many. Teaching will increase and extend your command of your subject. Professional teachers confess that they never learned as much about a subject, in all their years of study, as in the first time they taught it to freshmen.

Whether it's tutoring one person or lecturing to a hundred, teaching will prompt you to take a fresh overview of your subject. It will impel you to think through the basics and prod you to be sure your knowledge is up to date. Moreover, your students will likely stimulate your thinking.

Fortunately, opportunities to teach are mushrooming. The explosion in continuing education has generated a demand for teachers at all levels and in every kind of institution. Not only colleges but also churches, YMCAs and YWCAs, parks, public-school adult programs, voluntary associations, and

If you are in a teaching/coaching role, or in any sense a facilitator of learning processes, always bear in mind that your own thinking style probably dominates your approach to teaching, perhaps much more strongly than you may realize. We tend to teach in the same way we like to learn.

This advice on teaching extends to the entire process of human communication. The more clearly you understand your own thinking style, and the better you appreciate the other person's thinking style, the more effectively you can get your message into that person's mind. In this sense, the Golden Rule does not strictly apply: instead of doing to others as you would like to be done unto, you must do unto them as they would like to be done unto.

KARL ALBRECHT

272

many other agencies need teachers. Generally, neither a teaching certificate nor an advanced degree is required.

If you want an eye-opening perspective on how varied and intriguing such courses can be, send for the catalog of the New School for Social Research (66 West 12th Street, New York, New York 10011) or New York University's School of Continuing Education (Washington Square, New York, New York 10003). These are two of the most ambitious such catalogs in the country. If you've never seen them, you will be amazed at the range of offerings.

To arrange to teach a course, you'll need to think through three items and then prepare a course proposal as outlined below. First, think about how your subject can be made interesting and useful to other people. How does it relate to *their* interests? What are the themes that are featured when it's written about in popular books or in general newspapers and magazines? You might draft a story for your local paper on the topic. This will also prove useful later, for promotion of your course.

Second, consider what's most worth learning, and therefore worth teaching, about your subject and how you can best convey it to a group or an individual. Then brainstorm how you can contact people and groups who would be interested in learning about the subject. Here is the form in which to make a course proposal.

1. *Course title.* Offer three alternatives if you can. For example:
   Introduction to Personal Time Management
   Time Management for Businesspersons
   How to Get Control of Your Time

2. *Course description.* Write it up just as you would like to see it run in the catalog of the program or institution to which you are proposing it, in their style and format.

3. *Course instructor.* Summarize your qualifications to teach the course, including your study and experience with the subject, evidence of expertise, and teaching experience.

4. *Course outline.* Session-by-session goals and topics.

5. *Course materials.* Books and any other materials or aids (such as AV) you would use.

6. *Competing courses.* List other courses in your area that might compete with this one.

7. *Time and place.* Indicate your preferred day and time for the offering, plus location if the sponsoring institution has a number of teaching sites.

Beyond the benefits of teaching for your own learning, it's the best possible way to meet others interested in your field, people who are eager to share your enthusiasm and fuel yours and likely to become colleagues and friends.

Access: How to Teach Adults, by William Draves, is available from LERN, P.O. Box 1425, Manhattan, Kansas 66502.

TELEPHONING: TAPPING THE EXPERTS

The faculty members of your Invisible University are the leading experts in your fields of interest. In this section you'll learn how to (1) identify them, (2) reach them, (3) talk with them, and (4) use what you learn.

If going to the leading experts sounds bold, it's because most of us have been led to believe that knowledge is to be found first, foremost, and finally *in print*. However, the best reference librarians know better. Learning directly from the experts is important to you for several reasons: it's more fun than just reading; it brings your learning to life, connecting it with voices, personalities, and feelings; and there's nothing like a conversation with someone in love with your subject to add to your excitement.

Moreover, this kind of back-and-forth conversation gets your mind much more active. You can ask questions and respond to new information. When something's confusing, you can get clarification in a way that you can't with a book or an article. And you can politely channel the conversation into your areas of keenest interest, tailoring your learning to personal needs.

Identifying the experts in any field is fairly easy. Your initial list of leading experts will be authors of the best books in the field; editors and chief writers for the leading magazines, newspapers, and journals; and experts cited most prominently in those books and periodicals.

To those you may wish to add public-relations professionals, whose role it is to supply information to the public and the media; federal government personnel, whose job it is to monitor the field; staff members of associations in the field who, like government officials, have as part of their responsibilities responding to requests for information; and *horses' mouths*—individuals who actually *do* what you want to learn about.

Reaching these people is not as difficult as you might think. Telephoning rather than writing the experts is normally the best way to make contact. It's quicker, and you can ask questions and have a dialogue. The "guru of getting through" is Bob Berkman, who devised his expert-tapping techniques during five years at McGraw-Hill as a researcher and subsequently taught the subject at New York's Learning Annex. Here's his handy checklist from the book *Finding It Fast.*

1. Prepare for your talk with the expert beforehand. Do some reading on the subject, make a list of questions, and think how best to probe each source's area of expertise.
2. Decide if you will tape-record your conversation or take notes.
3. Don't contact the leading expert first. Instead, talk to someone who is not too technical and is accustomed to explaining concepts to nonexperts. One such source could be a journalist.
4. Get the secretary interested in your project. Talk to the expert's assistant. Call a related office. Be patient and keep plugging.
5. Don't be too quick to accept an "I can't help you" or "I don't know" response to your request to talk to an expert. If necessary, call and try again some other time.

Once you have your expert's ear, you may wonder how to conduct the interview. First, explain the history of your research in a way that shows the expert that you've done your homework and are reasonably knowledgeable about the field. Then, explain your purpose in terms of your ultimate objective—don't lead up to it with tidbit questions. The expert may know of a much faster, easier route to what you need to know if he or she knows what you're up to. A long lead-up may just be irritating and unproductive.

Indicate early on that you understand the expert's concern with getting proper credit. Work into the conversation such terms as "I'll want to quote you on that" or "I'll be citing your book."

Finally, ask for further contacts and references at the end of your interview, so that you know the next steps to take if you realize there are still loose ends. Drop your informant a thank-you note, not only to be courteous but to provide your name and address in case an afterthought or new development prompts the person to want to get back to you.

You can *use what you've learned* in many ways. Bob Berkman offers another handy checklist on "wrapping it up" in a way that nails down your new knowledge, puts it in permanent form for later use, and documents it in case you want recognition from others or academic credit:

- ◆ You'll know it's time to conclude your talk with the expert when you can predict the answers to your questions and when you're putting out a lot of energy but not receiving much new information.
- ◆ Before you consider your project complete, ask one of the experts to review your work for accuracy. This is a critical step in the process.
- ◆ Organize the information you've collected by subject rather than by source. This will make it easy to arrange your final work.
- ◆ When deciding what is worth including in your final report, select information that's relevant and reliable.
- ◆ Make conclusions whenever appropriate.
- ◆ Always remember to be fair. Search for opposing views; be complete and honest.

Once you have mastered these simple techniques, you will find that tapping experts by phone is one of your most efficient—and enjoyable—ways to learn. As far as efficiency goes, you get just the information you need, and it's up-to-the-minute. You get something equally valuable in terms of enjoyment: the upsurge in your own energy level that comes from talking with someone who's highly charged and enthusiastic about your subject.

TELEVISION: CULTIVATING THE VAST WASTELAND

The chief problem in learning from TV is that the programs lack structure. There might be a talk show today, a documentary tonight, and a panel discussion this weekend. Although each may be compelling, they don't add up to a complete learning experience, unless you do the adding. That's why active learning is needed to provide your own framework and meet your own needs.

There are ways to get more out of the time you spend watching TV without being glued to public television documentaries. You can add delight, stimulation, and depth to your viewing.

"Most people will make plans, and go to trouble and expense when they buy a book or reserve a seat in a theater," notes TV broadcast journalist Eric Sevareid. "But they will not study the week's offerings of music, drama or serious documentation in the radio-and TV-program pages of their newspaper and then schedule themselves to be present (or tape). They want to come home, eat dinner, twist the dial, and find something agreeable, ready, and accommodating to their schedule."

It's easy to take greater control of your viewing. First, use your interests to guide your choice of shows, and consider a far wider range of programs than usual. Sample some completely unfamiliar fare. Jolt yourself out of your ordinary viewing: listen to your first opera, see what an expert on the male mystique has to say, or visit the imaginative world of J. R. R. Tolkien or Charles Schulz, whichever is less familiar to you. A dozen such forays into *terra incognita* during the next three months will very likely open up at least one new realm that you will find fascinating.

The second step is to follow up. Use other resources: books, audio and videocassettes on the same subject of the programs you viewed, and conversations with knowledgeable people.

This adds up to becoming an *active* viewer—active before switching the set on; active during viewing, by being alert, probing, asking yourself questions, and making notes of important points; and active afterward by doing something with what you've seen.

Taking creative control of your television viewing in these ways can add an entirely new dimension to your learning life. For example, Fred Brussat, the nation's leading advocate of such an approach, suggests creating your own "Theater of Life." "Simply by selecting from available videotapes, you can explore the 'seasons of your life', on your own, with friends or family, in ways you will never forget. Gifted film-makers have created films dealing with the different seasons of life— childhood, adolescence, young adulthood, middle age, and old age. Their titles suggest this: *Old Enough, Puberty Blues, An Unmarried Woman, Starting Over, Summer Wishes, Winter Dreams, The Electric Grandmother.* Watching such films, thinking about them and discussing them with others, we find ourselves reviewing our own lives, or looking ahead, more perceptively. The subject of the film isn't just what happens on the screen— it's what has happened and will happen in your life."

Access: You're going to want to know well in advance what's in the pipeline over the next few months. Also, you may want some help in framing a learning project around shows that are directly in line with your interests. Such advance information about television offerings, films to come, and other such resources is available in Brussat's newsletter, "Living Room Learning," from Cultural Information Service, P.O. Box 786, Madison Square Station, New York, New York 10159.

The best single source of information about videocassettes is the *Video Source Book,* available for reference at your public library or for purchase from the National Video Clearinghouse, Inc., 100 Lafayette Drive, Syosset, New York 11791. Of course, you should also consider joining your local public television station, to support its work in giving you wider viewing choices.

ZOOS: LEARNING FROM ANIMALS

For hundreds of thousands of years human beings learned from animals. Just think of the way the American Indians associated themselves and their tribes with animals and their characteristics of the folk wisdom embodied in Aesop's fables or the pervasive metaphor of the *human barnyard*. Both emotionally and intellectually, the animal kingdom provides us with constant and powerful images of human behavior.

Yet most of us are out of contact with this realm of being. We hardly ever come into contact with animals, and thereby we miss much stimulation toward understanding ourselves and our situations. We also miss a lot of fun.

Visit your local zoo occasionally. Watch the animals and think about how they behave and what this reveals about the hidden springs of human action. Note how territoriality, curiosity, self-expression, and other basic motives drive animals behavior—and our own.

♦   ♦   ♦   ♦

Keys to Success: A Supplementary Reader

Taken from: *Keys to Success: How to Achieve Your Goals,* Second Edition, by Carol
Carter, Joyce Bishop, and Sarah Lyman Kravits

Keys to Success Reader, by Joyce Bishop, Mary Jane Bradbury, and
Julie Wheeler

I

Critical and Creative Thinking

Tapping the Power of Your Mind

In this chapter you will explore answers to the following questions:

- What is critical thinking?
- How does your mind work?
- How does critical thinking help you solve problems and make decisions?
- How do you construct an effective argument?
- How do you establish truth?
- Why shift your perspective?
- Why plan strategically?
- How can you develop your creativity?

Thinking It Through

Check those statements that apply to you right now:

- ❑ I'm not quite sure what "critical thinking" means.
- ❑ I am usually happy with how I've solved a problem.

Taken from: *Keys to Success: How to Achieve Your Goals,* Second Edition, by Carol Carter, Joyce Bishop, and Sarah Lyman Kravits

❑ When I have to make a decision, I often have a hard time making up my mind.

❑ Plan for next year? I can hardly get past next week.

❑ I'm not sure I often take the time to question the validity of my opinions.

❑ I find it hard to convince anyone that my argument makes sense.

❑ I think my perspective is generally on target.

❑ I consider myself to be a creative person.

Your mind's powers show in everything you do, from the smallest chores (comparing prices on cereals at the grocery store) to the most complex situations (figuring out how to earn money after being laid off). Your mind is able to process, store, and create with the facts and ideas it encounters. Critical and creative thinking are what enable those skills to come alive.

Understanding how your mind works, both its simple actions and more involved thinking processes, is the first step toward critical thinking. When you have that understanding, you can perform the essential critical thinking task: asking important questions about ideas and information. This chapter will show you both the mind's basic actions and the thinking processes that use those actions. You will explore what it means to be an open-minded critical and creative thinker, able to ask and understand questions that promote your success in college, career, and life.

WHAT IS CRITICAL THINKING?

Critical thinking is thinking that goes beyond the basic recall of information. If the word *critical* sounds negative to you, consider that the dictionary defines its meaning as "indispensable" and "important." Critical thinking is important thinking that involves asking questions. Using critical thinking, you question established ideas, create new ideas, turn information into tools to solve problems and make decisions, and take the long-term view as well as the day-to-day view.

A critical thinker asks as many kinds of questions as possible. The following are examples of possible questions about a given piece of information: *Where did it come from? What could explain it? In what ways is it true or false, and what examples could prove or disprove it? How do I feel about it, and why? How is this information similar to or different from what I already know? Is it good or bad? What causes led to it, and what effects does it have?* Critical thinkers also try to transform information into something they can use. They ask themselves whether the information can+ help them solve a problem, make a decision, create something new, or anticipate the future. Such questions help the critical thinker learn, grow, and create.

Not thinking critically means not asking questions about information or ideas. A person who does not think critically tends to accept or reject information or ideas without examining them. Table 1-1 compares how a critical thinker and a noncritical thinker might respond to particular situations.

Asking questions (the focus of the table), considering without judgment as many responses as you can, and choosing responses that are as complete and accurate as possible are the ingredients that make up the skill of critical thinking.

CRITICAL THINKING IS A SKILL

Critical thinking has only recently begun to be taught as such in schools. It used to be assumed that students possessed various levels of thinking ability that would either stay the same or develop naturally in the course of studying particular subjects. Education used to focus primarily on teaching information rather than on how to question and process that information. Now, educators have begun to see critical thinking as a skill that can be taught to students at all different levels of thinking ability. Anyone can develop the ability to think critically.

Learning information is still an important part of education, and is in fact a crucial component of critical thinking. For instance, part of the skill of critical thinking is comparing new

		TABLE 1-1 NOT THINKING CRITICALLY VS. THINKING CRITICALLY	
YOUR ROLE	SITUATION	NON-QUESTIONING RESPONSE	QUESTIONING RESPONSE
STUDENT	Instructor is lecturing on the causes of the Vietnam War.	You assume that everything your instructor tells you is true.	You consider what the instructor says, write down questions about issues you want to clarify, initiate discussion with the professor or other classmates.
PARENT	Instructor discovers your child lying about something at school.	You're mad at your child and believe the instructor, or you think the instructor is lying.	You ask both instructor and child about what happened, and you compare their answers, evaluating who you think is telling the truth. You discuss the concepts of lying/honesty with your child.
SPOUSE/PARTNER	Your partner feels that he or she no longer has quality time with you.	You think he or she is wrong and defend yourself.	You ask how long he/she has felt this way, ask your partner and yourself why this is happening, and explore how you can improve the situation.
EMPLOYEE	Your supervisor is angry at you.	You ignore or avoid your supervisor, or you deny responsibility for what the supervisor is angry about.	You are willing to discuss the situation; you ask what you could have done better; you ask what changes you can make in the future.
NEIGHBOR	People different from you move in next door.	You ignore or avoid them; you think their way of living is weird.	You introduce yourself; you offer to help if they need it; you respectfully explore what's different about them.
CITIZEN	You encounter a homeless person.	You avoid the person and the issue.	You examine whether the community has a responsibility to the homeless and, if you find that it does, you explore how to fulfill that responsibility.
CONSUMER	You want to buy a car.	You decide on a brand-new car and don't think through how you will handle the payments.	You consider the different effects of buying a new car vs. buying a used car; you examine your money situation to see what kind of payment you can handle each month.

information with what you already know. Your prior knowledge provides a framework within which to ask questions about and evaluate a new piece of information. Without a solid base of knowledge, critical thinking is harder to achieve. For example, thinking critically about the statement "Shakespeare's character King Richard III is like an early version of Adolf Hitler" is impossible without basic knowledge of World War II and Shakespeare's play *Richard III*.

The skill of critical thinking focuses on generating questions about statements and information. To examine potential critical-thinking responses in more depth, explore the different questions that a critical thinker may have about one particular statement.

A CRITICAL-THINKING RESPONSE TO A STATEMENT

Consider the following statement of opinion: *"My obstacles are keeping me from succeeding in school. Other people make it through school because they don't have to deal with the obstacles that I have."*

Non-questioning thinkers may accept an opinion such as this as an absolute truth, believing that their obstacles will hinder their success. As a result, on the road to achieving their goals, they may lose motivation to overcome those obstacles. In contrast, critical thinkers would take the opportunity to examine the opinion through a series of questions. Here are some examples of questions one student might ask (the type of each question is indicated in parentheses):

"**What exactly are my obstacles?** I define my obstacles as a heavy work schedule, single parenting, being in debt, and returning to school after ten years out." *(recall)*

"**Are there other cases different from mine?** I do have one friend who is going through problems worse than mine, and she's getting by. I also know another guy who doesn't have too much to deal with that I can tell, and he's struggling just like I am." *(difference)*

"**What is an example of someone who has had success despite having to overcome obstacles?** What about Oseola McCarty, the cleaning woman who saved money all her life and raised $150,000 to create a scholarship at the University of Southern Mississippi? She didn't have what anyone would call advantages—money, a college education, membership in the middle or upper class." *(idea to example)*

"What conclusion can I draw from my questions? From thinking about my friend and about Oseola McCarty, I would say that people can successfully overcome their obstacles by working hard and not giving up, focusing on their abilities, and concentrating on their goals." *(example to idea)*

"Who has problems similar to mine? Well, if I consider my obstacles specifically, I might be saying that single parents and returning adult students will all have trouble in school. That is not necessarily true. People in all kinds of situations may still become successful." *(similarity)*

"Why do I think this? Maybe I am scared of returning to school and adjusting to a new environment. Maybe I am afraid to challenge myself, which I haven't done in a long time. Whatever the cause, the effect is that I feel bad about myself and don't work to the best of my abilities, and that can hurt both me and my family who depends on me." *(cause and effect)*

"How do I evaluate the effects of this statement? I think it's harmful. When we say that obstacles equal difficulty, we can damage our desire to try to overcome those obstacles. When we say that successful people don't have obstacles, we might overlook that some very successful people have to deal with hidden disadvantages such as learning disabilities or abusive families." *(evaluation)*

Remember these types of questions. When you explore the seven mind actions later in the chapter, refer to these questions to see how they illustrate the different actions your mind performs.

THE VALUE OF CRITICAL THINKING

Critical thinking has many important advantages. Following are some ways you may benefit from putting energy into critical thinking.

You will increase your ability to perform thinking processes that help you reach any kind of school, career, or life goal. Critical thinking is a learned skill, just like shooting a basketball or making roses with frosting or using a word-processing program on the computer. As with any other skill, the more you use it, the better you become. The more you ask questions, the better you think. The better you think, the more effective you will be when completing schoolwork, managing your personal life, and performing on the job. You will learn more about different critical-thinking processes later in this chapter.

You can produce knowledge, rather than just reproduce it. When you think critically and ask questions, the interaction of new information with what you already know creates new knowledge. When you think critically about lectures or reading materials rather than just learn them for a test, you will retain knowledge that will serve you after you leave school. The usefulness of knowledge comes in how you apply it to new and different situations. It won't mean much for an early-childhood-education student to quote the stages of child development on an exam unless he or she can make judgments about children's needs when on the job.

You can be a valuable employee. You certainly won't be a failure in the workplace if you follow directions. However, you will be even more valuable if you think critically and ask strategic questions about how to make improvements, large or small. Questions could range from "Is there a better way to deliver phone messages?" to "How can we increase business to keep from going under?" An employee who shows the initiative to think critically will be more likely to earn responsibility and promotions.

You can increase your creativity. You cannot be a successful critical thinker without being able to come up with new and different

"We do not live to think but, on the contrary, we think in order that we may succeed in surviving."

JOSÉ ORTEGA Y GASSETT

289

questions to ask, possibilities to explore, and ideas to try. Creativity is essential in producing what is new. Being creative generally improves your outlook, your sense of humor, and your perspective as you cope with problems. Later in this chapter, you will look at ways to awaken and increase your natural creativity.

In the next section, you will read about the seven basic actions your mind performs when asking important questions. These actions are the basic blocks you will use to build the critical-thinking processes you will explore later in the chapter.

HOW DOES YOUR MIND WORK?

Critical thinking depends on a thorough understanding of the workings of the mind. Your mind has some basic moves, or actions, some combination of which it uses each time you think. Sometimes it uses one action by itself, but most often it uses two or more.

MIND ACTIONS: THE THINKTRIX

You can identify your mind's actions using a system called the Thinktrix, developed by educators Frank Lyman, Arlene Mindus, and Charlene Lopez.[1] They studied how students think and named seven mind actions that are the basic building blocks of thought. These actions are not new to you, although some of their names may be. They represent the ways in which you think all the time.

Through exploring these actions, you can go beyond just thinking and learn *how* you think. This will help you take charge of your own thinking. The more you know about how your mind works, the more control you will have over thinking processes such as problem solving, decision making, creating, and strategic planning.

Following are explanations of each of the mind actions. Each explanation has the name of the action, words that define it, and examples that explain it. As you read, write your own examples in the blank spaces provided. Each action is also represented by a picture or *icon* that helps you visualize and remember it.

Recall: *Facts, sequence, and description.* This is the simplest action. When you **recall** you describe facts, objects, or events, or put them into sequence. *Examples:*

♦ Naming the steps of a geometry proof, in order
♦ Remembering your best friends' phone numbers

Your example: Recall some important events this month.

_____

_____

The icon: A string tied around a finger is a familiar image of recall or remembering.

Similarity: *Analogy, likeness.* This action examines what is ***similar*** about one or more things. You might compare situations, ideas, people, stories, events, or objects. *Examples:*

♦ Comparing notes with another student to see what facts and ideas you have both considered important
♦ Analyzing the arguments you've had with your partner this month and seeing how they all seem to be about the same problem

Your example: Tell what is similar about two of your best friends

_____

_____

The icon: Two alike objects, in this case triangles, indicate similarity.

Difference: *Distinction, contrast.* This action examines what is ***different*** about one or more situations, ideas, people, stories, events, or objects, contrasting them with one another. *Examples:*

♦ Seeing how two instructors differ in style—one divides the class into small groups and encourages discussion;

291

the other keeps desks in straight lines and lectures for most of the class

♦ Contrasting a weekday where you work half day and go to school half day with a weekday when you attend class and then have the rest of the day to study

Your example: Explain how your response to a course you like differs from how you respond to a course you don't like as much.

_____

_____

The icon: Two differing objects, in this case a triangle and a square, indicate difference.

Cause and effect: *Reasons, consequences, prediction.* Using this action, you look at what has **caused** a fact, situation, or event, and/or what *effects,* or consequences, come from it. In other words, you examine both what led up to something and what will follow because of it. *Examples:*

♦ Staying up late at night causes you to oversleep, which has the effect of your being late to class. This causes you to miss some of the material, which has the further effect of your having problems on the test.

♦ By paying your phone and utility bills on time, you create effects such as a better credit rating, uninterrupted service, and a better relationship with your service providers.

Your example: Name what causes you to like your favorite class, and the effects that liking the class has on you.

_____

_____

The icon: The water droplets making ripples indicate causes and their resulting effects.

Example to Idea: *Generalization, classification, conceptualization.* From one or more **examples** (facts or events), you develop a

general *idea* or ideas. Grouping facts or events into patterns may allow you to make a general statement about several of them at once. Classifying a fact or event helps you build knowledge. This mind action moves from the specific to the general. *Examples:*

- You have had trouble finding a baby sitter who can match your schedule. A classmate even brought her child to class once. Your brother has had to drop off his daughter at your mom's and doesn't like being unable to see her all day. From these examples, you derive the idea that your school needs an on campus day-care program.
- You see a movie and you decide it is mostly about pride.

Your example: Name examples of activities you enjoy, and from them, come up with an idea of your choice of vacation.

———————————————————————————

———————————————————————————

The icon: The arrow and "Ex" pointing to a light bulb on their right indicate how an example or examples lead to the idea (the light bulb, lit up).

Idea to Example: *Categorization, substantiation, proof.* In a reverse of the previous action, you take an *idea* or ideas and think of **examples** (events or facts) that support or prove that idea. This mind action moves from the general to the specific. *Examples:*

- When you write a paper, you start with a thesis statement, which communicates the central idea: "Men are favored over women in the modern workplace." Then you gather examples to back up that idea: Men make more money on average than women in the same jobs; there are more men in upper management positions than there are women; women can be denied advancement when they make their families a priority.
- You talk to your instructor about changing your major, giving examples that support your idea: You have worked in the field you want to change to, you have fulfilled some of the requirements for that major already, and you are unhappy with your current course of study.

Your example: Name an admirable person. Give three examples of why that person is admirable.

_____

_____

The icon: In a reverse of the previous icon, this one starts with the light bulb and has an arrow pointing to "Ex". This indicates that you start with the idea, the lit bulb, and then branch into the example or examples that support the idea.

Evaluation: *Value, judgment, rating.* Here you *judge* whether something is useful or not useful, important or unimportant, good or bad, or right or wrong by identifying and weighing its positive and negative effects (pros and cons). Be sure to consider the specific situation at hand (a cold drink might be good on the beach in August, not so good in the snowdrifts in January). With the facts you have gathered, you determine the value of something in terms of both predicted effects and your own needs. Cause and effect analysis always accompanies evaluation. *Examples:*

- You decide to try taking later classes for a semester. You schedule classes in the afternoons and spend your nights on the job. You find that instead of getting up early to use the morning time, you tend to sleep in and then get up not too long before you have to be at school. From those harmful effects, you evaluate that it doesn't work for you. You decide to schedule earlier classes next time.
- Someone offers you a chance to cheat on a test. You evaluate the potential effects if you are caught. You also evaluate the long-term effects on you of not actually learning the material. You decide that it isn't worth your while to participate in the plan to cheat.

Your example: Evaluate your mode of transportation to school

_____

_____

The icon: A set of scales out of balance indicates how you weigh positive and negative effects to arrive at an evaluation.

294

You may want to use a *mnemonic device*—a memory tool—to remember the seven mind actions. Try recalling them using the word DECRIES—each letter is the first letter of a mind action. You can also make a sentence of words that each start with a mind action's first letter. Here's an example: "Really Smart Dogs Cook Eggs In Enchiladas" (the first letter of each word stands for one of the mind actions).

HOW MIND ACTIONS BUILD THINKING PROCESSES

The seven mind actions are the fundamental building blocks that your mind uses every day. Note that you will rarely use them one at a time in a step-by-step process, as they are presented here. You will usually combine them, overlap them, and repeat them more than once, using different actions for different situations. For example, when you want to say something nice at the end of a date, you might consider past comments that had an effect *similar* to what you want now. When a test question asks you to explain what prejudice is, you might name similar *examples* that show your *idea* of what prejudice means.

When you combine mind actions in working toward a specific goal, you are performing a thinking process. The next few sections will explore six of the most important critical-thinking processes: solving problems, making decisions, constructing effective arguments, establishing truth, shifting your perspective, and planning strategically. Each thinking process helps you succeed by directing your critical thinking toward the achievement of your goals. Figure 1-3, appearing later in the chapter, shows all of the mind actions and thinking processes together and reminds you that the mind actions form the core of the thinking processes.

HOW DOES CRITICAL THINKING HELP YOU SOLVE PROBLEMS AND MAKE DECISIONS?

Problem solving and decision making are probably the two most crucial and common thinking processes. Each one requires various mind actions. They overlap somewhat, because every problem that needs solving requires you to make a decision. However, not every decision requires that you solve a problem (for example, not many people would say that deciding what to order in a restaurant is a problem). Each process will be considered separately here. You will notice similarities in the steps involved in each.

Although both of these processes have multiple steps, you will not always have to work your way through each step. As you become more comfortable with solving problems and making decisions, your mind will automatically click through the steps you need whenever you encounter a problem or decision. Also, you will become more adept at evaluating which problems and decisions need serious consideration and which can be taken care of more quickly and simply.

PROBLEM SOLVING

Life constantly presents problems to be solved, ranging from average daily problems (how to manage study time or learn not to misplace your keys) to life-altering situations (how to care for a sick elderly relative or design a custody plan during a divorce). Choosing a solution without thinking critically may have negative effects. For example, if you decide to move a sick elderly relative into your home without considering the effects of your work schedule, the relative may be alone in the evenings with no one to help should a medical emergency arise. However, if you use the steps of the following problem-solving process to think critically, you have the best chance of coming up with a favorable solution.

You can apply this problem-solving plan to any situation or issue that you want to resolve. Using the following steps will maximize the number of possible solutions you generate and will allow you to explore each one as fully as possible.

1. *State the problem clearly.* What are the facts? *Recall* the details of the situation. Be sure to name the problem specifically, without focusing on causes or effects. For example, a student might state this as a problem: "I'm not understanding the class material." However, that may be a *cause* of the actual problem at hand: "I'm failing my economics quizzes."

2. *Analyze the problem.* What is happening that, in your opinion, needs to change? In other words, what *effects* does the situation have that cause a problem for you? What *causes* these effects? Look at the *causes* and *effects* that surround the problem. Continuing the example of the economics student, if some effects of failing quizzes include poor grades in the course and disinterest, some causes may include poor study habits, poor test-taking skills, lack of sleep, or not understanding the material.

3. *Brainstorm possible solutions.* **Brainstorming** will help you think of examples of other similar problems and how you solved them. Consider what is different about this problem, and see if the thoughts you generate might lead you to new possible solutions. You will find more about brainstorming later in this chapter. *It's very important to base your possible solutions upon causes rather than effects.* Getting to the heart of a problem requires addressing the cause rather than putting a bandage on the effect. If the economics student were to aim for better assignment grades to offset the low quiz grades, that might raise his GPA but wouldn't address the cause of not understanding the material. Looking at this cause, on the other hand, might lead him to work on study habits or seek help from his instructor, a study group, or a tutor.

4. *Explore each solution.* Why might your solution work? Why not? Might a solution work partially, or in a particular situation? *Evaluate* the pros and cons, or the positive and negative effects, of each idea. Create a chain of causes and effects in your head, as far into the future as you can, to see where you think this solution would lead. The economics student might consider the effects of improved study habits, more sleep, tutoring, or dropping the class.

5. *Choose and execute the solution you decide is best.* Decide how you will put your solution to work. Then, execute your solution. The economics student could decide on a combination of improved study habits and tutoring.

6. *Evaluate the solution that you acted upon,* looking at its *effects.* What are the positive and negative effects of what you

Brainstorming
The spontaneous, rapid generation of ideas or solutions, undertaken by a group or an individual, often as part of a problem-solving process.

297

FIGURE 1–1 Problem-Solving Plan

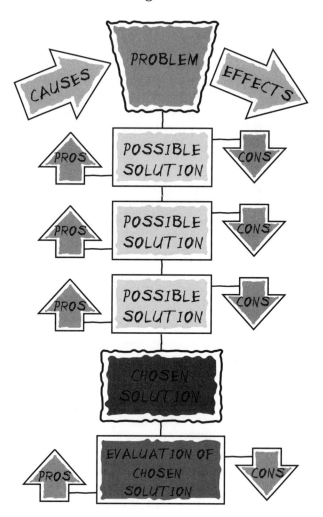

did? In terms of your needs, was it a useful solution or not? Could the solution use any adjustments or changes in order to be more useful? Would you do the same again or not? Evaluating his choice, the economics student may decide that the effects are good but that his fatigue still causes a problem.

7. *Continue to refine the solution.* Problem solving is always a process. You may have opportunities to apply the same

solution over and over again. Evaluate again and again, making changes that you decide make the solution better. The economics student may decide to continue to study more regularly but, after a few weeks of tutoring, could opt to trade in the tutoring time for some extra sleep. He may decide to take what he has learned from the tutor so far and apply it to his increased study efforts.

Using this process will enable you to solve personal, educational, and workplace problems in a thoughtful, comprehensive way. Figure 1–1 is a think link that demonstrates a way to visualize the flow of problem solving. Figure 1–2 contains a sample of how one person used this plan to solve a problem. Figure 1–2 represents the same plan as 1 but gives room to write so that it can be used in the problem-solving process.

DECISION MAKING

Although every problem-solving process involves making a decision (when you decide which solution to try), not all decisions involve solving problems. Decisions are choices. Making a choice, or decision, requires thinking critically through all of the possible choices and evaluating which will work best for you and for the situation. Decisions large and small come up daily, hourly, even every few minutes. Do you call your landlord when the heat isn't coming on? Do you drop a course? Should you stay in a relationship? Can you work part time without interfering with school?

Before you begin the decision-making process, evaluate the level of the decision you are making. Do you have to decide what to have for lunch (usually a minor issue), or whether to quit a good job (often a major life change)? Some decisions are little, day-to-day considerations that you can take care of quickly on your own. Others require thoughtful evaluation, time, and perhaps the input of others you trust. The following is a list of steps to take in order to think critically through a decision.

1. *Decide on a goal.* Why is this decision necessary? In other words, what result do you want from this decision? Considering the *effects* you want can help you formulate your goal. For example, say a student currently attends a

FIGURE 1–2 How One Student Worked Through A Problem

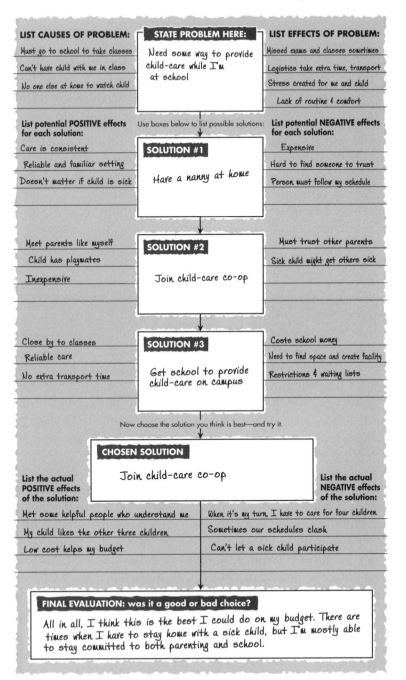

LIST CAUSES OF PROBLEM:
Must go to school to take classes
Can't have child with me in class
No one else at home to watch child

STATE PROBLEM HERE:
Need some way to provide child-care while I'm at school

LIST EFFECTS OF PROBLEM:
Missed exams and classes sometimes
Logistics take extra time, transport
Stress created for me and child
Lack of routine & comfort

List potential **POSITIVE** effects for each solution:
Care is consistent
Reliable and familiar setting
Doesn't matter if child is sick

Use boxes below to list possible solutions:

SOLUTION #1
Have a nanny at home

List potential **NEGATIVE** effects for each solution:
Expensive
Hard to find someone to trust
Person must follow my schedule

Meet parents like myself
Child has playmates
Inexpensive

SOLUTION #2
Join child-care co-op

Must trust other parents
Sick child might get others sick

Close by to classes
Reliable care
No extra transport time

SOLUTION #3
Get school to provide child-care on campus

Costs school money
Need to find space and create facility
Restrictions & waiting lists

Now choose the solution you think is best—and try it.

CHOSEN SOLUTION
Join child-care co-op

List the actual **POSITIVE** effects of the solution:
Met some helpful people who understand me
My child likes the other three children
Low cost helps my budget

List the actual **NEGATIVE** effects of the solution:
When it's my turn, I have to care for four children
Sometimes our schedules clash
Can't let a sick child participate

FINAL EVALUATION: was it a good or bad choice?
All in all, I think this is the best I could do on my budget. There are times when I have to stay home with a sick child, but I'm mostly able to stay committed to both parenting and school.

small private college. Her goal is to become a physical therapist. The school has a good program, but her financial situation has changed and has made this school too expensive for her.

2. *Establish needs. Recall* the needs of everyone (or everything) involved in the decision. The student needs a school with a full physical therapy program; she and her parents need to cut costs (her father changed jobs and her family cannot continue to afford the current school); she needs to be able to transfer credits.

3. *Name, investigate, and evaluate available options.* Brainstorm possible choices, and then look at the facts surrounding each. *Evaluate* the good and bad effects of each possibility. Weigh these effects and judge which is the best course of action. Here are some possibilities that the student in the college example might consider:
   - *Continue at the current college.* **Positive effects:** I wouldn't have to adjust to a new place or to new people. I could continue my course work as planned. **Negative effects:** I would have to find a way to finance most of my tuition and costs on my own, whether through loans, grants, or work. I'm not sure I could find time to work as much as I would need to, and I don't think I would qualify for as much aid as I now need.
   - *Transfer to the state college.* **Positive effects:** I could reconnect with people there that I know from high school. Tuition and room costs would be cheaper than at my current school. I could transfer credits. **Negative effects:** I would still have to work some or find minimal financial aid. The physical therapy program is small and not very strong.
   - *Transfer to the community college.* **Positive effects:** They have many of the courses I need to continue with the physical therapy curriculum. The school is twenty minutes from my parents' house, so I could live at home and avoid paying housing costs. Credits will transfer. The tuition is extremely reasonable. **Negative effects:** I don't know anyone there. I would be less independent. The school doesn't offer a bachelor's degree.

4. *Decide on a plan of action and pursue it.* Make a choice based on your evaluation, and act on your choice. In this case the student might decide to go to the community college for two years and then transfer back to a four-year school to earn a bachelor's degree in physical therapy. Although she might lose some independence and contact with friends, the positive effects are money saved, opportunity to spend time on studies rather than working to earn tuition money, and the availability of classes that match the physical therapy program requirements.

5. *Evaluate the result.* Was it useful? Not useful? Some of both? Weigh the positive and negative effects. The student may find with her transfer decision that it can be hard living at home, although her parents are adjusting to her independence and she is trying to respect their concerns as parents. Fewer social distractions result in her getting more work done. The financial situation is much more favorable. All things considered, she evaluates that this decision was a good one.

Making important decisions can take time. Think through your decision thoroughly, considering your own ideas as well as those of others you trust, but don't hesitate to act once you have your plan. You cannot benefit from your decision until you act upon it and follow through.

HOW DO YOU CONSTRUCT AN EFFECTIVE ARGUMENT?

Persuade

To convince someone through argument or reasoning to adopt a belief, position, or course of action.

In this case, "argument" does not refer to a fight you would have with someone; it is a persuasive case that you make to prove or disprove a point. In every aspect of your life you will encounter situations in which your success depends on your being able to *persuade* someone to agree with you on some idea. You may need to convince an instructor that you deserve a second chance on an assignment; you may need to persuade a parent that you're making the right choice in a relationship; you may need to persuade a prospective employer that you are the one for the job.

When you come to crossroads in your life, much is at stake—

a grade, a relationship, a job, and more. If you want your persuasive argument to help you achieve what's at stake, it requires the use of your critical thinking. Put the mind actions to work asking questions about the situation, using the following steps:

Establish the goal—what's at stake. No argument is an absolute guarantee of achieving a goal, but a persuasive argument will give you your best shot. Ask yourself what you want. As an example, imagine that you want a raise and promotion to a new position at work.

Gather examples that support your idea. What can you say that will support your request? In this case, your examples may be that you have worked at this company part time for a year and full time for half a year; you are almost always on time; you have gotten good reviews from your supervisor; and you have ideas for the position to which you want to be promoted.

Anticipate questions. What will the other person or people ask you to explain? In the promotion example, they could ask you about your prior track record, what you have achieved in your current position, what you know about the position you want to take, whether you know the people you would be working with, and what new and creative ideas you have.

Anticipate points against you. What might someone bring up that argues against your position? Whatever you think of, decide what you will say to oppose it. If your supervisor says that you can't handle the longer hours the new position would require, you may have looked into adjusting your school schedule. If the supervisor says that you don't have the necessary experience, you may have studied the job or talked with people who do that type of work.

Be flexible. You never know what will happen as you present your argument. You might not even need to push; on the other hand, it may turn out to be much tougher than you thought. By rehearsing your response to questions beforehand, you will be as prepared as possible to handle any twists and turns the conversation may take.

HOW DO YOU ESTABLISH TRUTH?

Investigating the truth and accuracy of information, rather than automatically accepting it as true, is an important critical-thinking process. In order to seek truth through critical thinking, you question the validity of statements or information. Critical-thinking experts Sylvan Barnet and Hugo Bedau state that when you test for the truth of a statement, you "determine whether what it asserts corresponds with reality; if it does, then it is true, and if it doesn't, then it is false."[2] In order to determine to what degree a statement "corresponds with reality," ask questions based on the mind actions. The search for truth takes two primary forms: distinguishing fact from opinion and challenging assumptions.

DISTINGUISHING FACT FROM OPINION

Fact, according to the dictionary, is information presented as objectively real. *Opinion* is defined as a belief, conclusion, or judgment. Being able to evaluate what in a piece of reading material is fact and what is opinion is crucial to your understanding of the material. Fact and opinion generate different reactions in a reader. If you decide that a statement is opinion, you may focus on deciding whether you agree with that opinion based on how it is explained and supported. If you decide that a statement is fact, you have agreed to accept it as true, and your focus moves to evaluating how that tact is used to support other ideas or opinions.

There is a degree of overlap to fact and opinion. Opinions can be proved to be partially or completely factual after investigation. Statements that seem factual may emerge as opinions if any part of them is proven wrong through questioning. Qualifiers, such as *all, none, never, often, sometimes,* and *many,* will often mean the difference between fact and opinion. Absolute qualifiers such as *all* and *none* indicate an opinion more often than a fact, while indefinite qualifiers such as *some* and *many* may make a fact out of what seems to be an opinion. For example, "All college students need to take math" is an opinion, whereas "Some college students need to take math" is a fact.

Both facts and opinions require investigation through questioning. Even though opinions would seem to require more examination than facts, some opinions masquerade as facts and are revealed only through examination. For example, an article may state, "Twenty to thirty minutes of vigorous exercise three to five times a week is essential for good health." That may sound like a fact. When you examine it through questioning, however, you may reveal it as the opinion of the author. To be safe, consider all statements opinions until proven otherwise. Questions you may ask include the following:

- What facts or examples provide evidence of truth?
- How does the maker of the statement know this to be true?
- Is there another fact that disproves this statement or information, or shows it to be an opinion?
- How reliable are the sources of information?
- What about this statement is similar to or different from other information I consider to be fact?
- How could I test the validity of this statement or information?

Even though you may find a truth in and agree with the statement after examining how the author supports it, the statement remains an opinion. The observation that some healthy people exist who do not exercise in this way proves that the statement is not completely factual.

Take a different statement as another example. It has been stated as a fact that the economically poor take unfair advantage of the welfare system. A critical thinker who questions this statement may find that the statement is actually an opinion with some degree of truth. Some citizens may try to cheat the welfare system, while others may have an honest claim to their welfare checks and may try hard to find work. See Table 2 for some more examples of factual statements vs. statements of opinion.

Another crucial step in determining the truth is to question the assumptions that you and others hold, and which are the underlying force in shaping opinions.

TABLE 1-2 EXAMPLES OF FACTS AND OPINIONS

SUBJECT	FACTUAL STATEMENT	STATEMENT OF OPINION
Animal speed	The cheetah has been clocked at speeds that prove it to be the world's fastest animal.	No animal can ever escape the speed of the cheetah.
Weather	It's raining outside.	This is the worst rainstorm in recent history.
Fats in foods	Two slices of stuffed-crust pizza have more fat than a Big Mac.™	Diners will have more luck avoiding fat at a pizza place than at a burger joint.

CHALLENGING ASSUMPTIONS

Assumption

An idea or statement accepted as true without examination or proof.

"If it's more expensive, it's better." "It's best to start your day before 8 A.M." "Famous people have easy lives." These statements reveal **assumptions**—often evaluations, or generalizations, based on observing cause and effect—that can often hide within seemingly truthful assertions. Important life choices can come from your assumptions—you may assume that you should get married and have children, own a car, or eat three meals a day. Many people live without questioning what their assumptions are or whether they make sense, nor do they challenge the assumptions of others.

Assumptions come from sources such as parents or relatives, TV and other media, friends, and your personal experiences. As much as you think such assumptions work for you, it's just as possible that they don't. Assumptions can close your mind to opportunities and even harm people. For example, the old false assumption that people who speak with a regional or foreign accent are somehow less intelligent or less qualified has caused a great deal of harm through the years.

Think critically to uncover and investigate assumptions. Ask these questions:

1. Is the truth of this statement supported with fact, or does it hide an assumption?

306

2. In what cases is this assumption true or not true? What examples prove or disprove it?

3. Has making this assumption benefited me or others? Has it hurt me or others? In what ways?

4. If someone taught me this assumption, why? Did that person think it over or just accept it?

5. What harm could be done by always taking this assumption as fact?

For example, here's how you might use these questions to investigate the following statement: "The most productive schedule involves getting started early in the day."

1. This statement hides an assumption that the morning is when all people feel most energetic and are able to get lots of things done.

2. The assumption may be generally true for people who enjoy early morning hours and have good energy during that part of the day. But the assumption may be not true for people who work best in the afternoon or evening hours.

3. Society's basic standard of daytime classes and 8 A.M. to 5 P.M. working hours supports this assumption. Therefore, the assumption may work for people who have early jobs and classes or children who get up early. It may not work, however, for people who work late or overnight shifts or who take classes in the evening.

4. Maybe people who believe this assumption were raised in a household where people started their days early. Or, perhaps they just say this because it goes along with what seems to be society's standard. Still, there are plenty of people who operate on a different schedule and yet enjoy successful, productive lives.

5. Taking this assumption as fact could hurt people who don't operate at their peak in the earlier hours. For example, if a "night owl" tries to conform to an early schedule of classes, he or she may experience concentration and focus problems that would not necessarily occur during later classes. In situations that favor their particular characteristics—later classes; jobs that start in the late

morning, afternoon, or evening; or career areas that don't require early morning work—such people have just as much potential to succeed as anyone else.

Be careful to look for and question all assumptions, not just the ones that seem problematic right from the start. It's a rare assumption that is ***completely*** "good" or "bad." Because assumptions may work differently in different situations, a generally good assumption may even cause problems under particular circumstances. Every new situation is worth a critical look. Here are two examples of assumptions that may have both good and bad sides:

"We should keep finding new uses for computers." Computers have improved industry and communication. However, many have lost their jobs because what they used to do by hand is now being performed by a computer. Some people may become addicted to computers and neglect other important activities. You also may miss talking to a real person when you get a computer answering system on the phone—"Press '7' if you want . . ."

"Never argue in front of a child." It can be extremely damaging for children to witness angry or even violent arguments in the home. However, it can be helpful for them to see parents or guardians work through problems reasonably and try to find solutions. In this way the child sees that people can work through conflict in a positive way and bring about a useful result.

WHY SHIFT YOUR PERSPECTIVE?

Perspective

A mental point of view or outlook, based on a cluster of related assumptions, incorporating values, interests, and knowledge.

Seeing the world only from your ***perspective,*** or point of view, is inflexible, limiting, and frustrating to both you and others. You probably know how hard it can be to relate to someone who cannot understand where you are coming from—a co-worker who's annoyed that you leave early on Thursdays for physical therapy, a parent who doesn't see why you can't take a study break to visit, a friend who can't understand why you would date someone of a different race. Seeing beyond one's own perspective can be difficult, especially when life problems and fatigue take their toll.

On the other hand, when you shift your own perspective to consider someone else's, you open the lines of communication. Trying to understand what other people feel, need, and want makes you more responsive to them. They then may feel respected by you and respond to you in turn. For example, if you want to add or drop a course and your advisor says it's impossible, not waiting to hear you out, the last thing you may feel like doing is pouring your heart out. On the other hand, if your advisor asks to hear your point of view, you may sense that your needs are respected. Because the advisor wants to hear from you, you feel valued; that may encourage you to respond, or even to change your mind.

Every time you shift your perspective, you can also learn something new. There are worlds of knowledge and possibilities outside your individual existence. You may learn that what you eat daily may be against someone else's religious beliefs. You may discover people who don't fit a stereotype. You may find different and equally valid ways of getting an education, living as a family, relating to one another, having a spiritual life, or spending free time. Above all else, you may see that each person is entitled to his or her own perspective, no matter how foreign it may be to you.

Asking questions like these will help you maintain flexibility and openness in your perspective.

- What is similar and different about this person/belief/ method and me/my beliefs/my methods?
- What positive and negative effects come from this different way of being/acting/believing? Even if this perspective seems to have negative effects for me, how might it have positive effects for others, and therefore have value?
- What can I learn from this different perspective? Is there anything I could adopt for my own life—something that would help me improve who I am or what I do? Is there anything I wouldn't do myself but that I can still respect and learn from?

Shifting your perspective is at the heart of all successful communication. Each person is unique. Even within a group of people similar to yourself, there will be a great variety of perspectives. Whether you decide that each world community has different customs or you understand that a friend can't go out on weekends because he spends that time with his mother, you have increased your wealth of knowledge and shown respect to others. Being able to shift perspective and communicate more effectively may mean the difference between success and failure in today's diverse working world.

WHY PLAN STRATEGICALLY?

Strategy

A plan of action designed to accomplish a specific goal.

If you've ever played a game of chess or checkers, participated in a wrestling or martial arts match, or had a drawn-out argument, you have had experience with *strategy*. In those situations and many others, you continually have to think through and anticipate the moves the other person is about to make. Often you have to think about several possible options that person could put into play, and you consider what you would counter with should any of those options occur. In competitive situations, you try to outguess the other person with your choices. The extent of your strategic skills can determine whether you will win or lose.

Strategy is the plan of action, the method, the "how" behind any goal you want to achieve. Specifically, strategic planning means having a plan for the future, whether you are looking at the next week, month, year, ten years, or fifty years. It means exploring the future positive and negative effects of the choices you make and actions you take today. You are planning strategically right now just by being in school. You made a decision that the requirements of attending college are a legitimate price to pay for the skills, contacts, and opportunities that will help you in the future.

You don't have to compete against someone else in order to be strategic. You can be strategic on your own or even in a cooperative situation. For example, as a student, you are challenging yourself to achieve. You are learning to set goals for the future, analyze what you want in the long term, and prepare for the job market to increase your career options. Being strategic with yourself means challenging yourself as you would challenge a competitor, urging you to demand that you work to achieve your goals with conviction and determination.

What are the benefits, or positive effects, of strategic planning?

Strategy is an essential skill in the workplace. A food company that wants to develop a successful health-food product needs to examine the anticipated trends in health consciousness. A lawyer needs to think through every aspect of the client's case, anticipating how to respond to any allegation the opposing side will bring up in court. Strategic planning creates a vision into the future that allows the planner to anticipate all kinds of possibilities and, most importantly, to be prepared for them.

Strategic planning powers your short-term and long-term goal setting. Once you have set goals, you need to plan the steps that will help you achieve those goals over time. For example, a strategic thinker who wants to own a home in five years' time might drive a used car and cut out luxuries, put a small amount of money every month into a mutual fund, and keep an eye on current mortgage percentages. In class, a strategic planner will think critically about the material presented, knowing that information is most useful later on if it is clearly understood.

Strategic planning helps you keep up with technology. As technology develops more and more quickly, jobs become obsolete. It's possible to spend years in school training for a career area that will be drying up when you are ready to enter the work force. When you plan strategically, you can take a broader range of courses or choose a major and career that are expanding. This will make it more likely that your skills will be in demand when you graduate.

Effective critical thinking is essential to strategic planning. If you aim for a certain goal, what steps will move you toward that goal? What positive effects do you anticipate these steps will have? How do you evaluate your past experiences with planning and goal setting? What can you learn from similar or different previous experiences in order to take different steps today? Critical thinking runs like a thread through all of your strategic planning.

Here are some tips for becoming a strategic planner:

Develop an appropriate plan. What approach will best achieve your goal? What steps toward your goal will you need to take one year, five years, ten years or twenty years from now?

FIGURE 1–3   The Wheel of Thinking

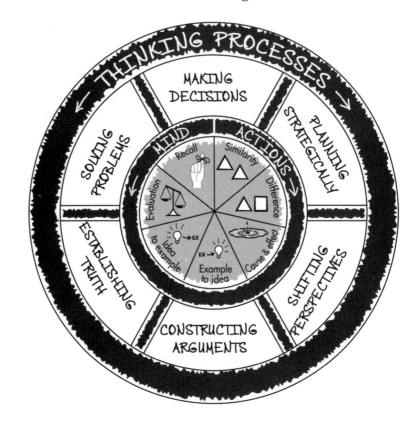

Anticipate all possible outcomes of your actions. What are the positive and negative effects that may occur?

Ask the question "how?" How do you achieve your goals? How do you learn effectively and remember what you learn? How do you develop a productive idea on the job? How do you distinguish yourself at school and at work?

Use human resources. Talk to people who are where you want to be, whether professionally or personally. What caused them to get there? Ask them what they believe are the important steps to take, degrees to have, training to experience, knowledge to gain.

In each thinking process, you use your creativity to come up with ideas, examples, causes, effects, and solutions. You have a capacity to be creative, whether you are aware of it or not. Open up your mind and awaken your creativity. It will enhance your critical thinking and make life more enjoyable.

HOW CAN YOU DEVELOP YOUR CREATIVITY?

Everyone is creative. Although the word "creative" may seem to refer primarily to artists, writers, musicians, and others who work in fields whose creative aspects are in the forefront, *creativity* comes in many other forms. It is the power to create anything, whether it is a solution, idea, approach, tangible product, work of art, system, program—anything at all. To help you expand your concept of creativity, here are some examples of day-to-day creative thinking:

Creativity
The ability to produce something new through imaginative skill.

- Figuring out an alternative plan when your baby-sitter unexpectedly cancels on you
- Planning how to coordinate your work and class schedules
- Talking through a problem with an instructor, and finding a way to understand each other
- Working to improve a relationship with a partner, child, parent, or friend
- Planning a budget so that you can pay your bills on time each month

Creative innovations introduced by all kinds of people continually expand and change the world. Here are some that have had an impact:

- Susan B. Anthony and other women fought for and won the right for women to vote.
- Art Fry and Spencer Silver invented the Post-It™ note in 1980, enabling people to save paper and protect documents by using removable notes.

- Henry Ford introduced the assembly-line method of automobile construction, making cars cheap enough to be available to the average citizen.
- Rosa Parks refused to give up her seat on the bus to a white person, thus setting off a chain of events that gave rise to the civil rights movement.
- Alicia Diaz, director of the Center of Hispanic Policy, Research, and Development, developed corporate partnerships and internship programs that have become models for small, efficient government.

Even though these particular innovations had wide-ranging effects, characteristics of these influential innovators can be found in all people who exercise their creative capabilities.

CHARACTERISTICS OF CREATIVE PEOPLE

Creative people think in fresh new ways that improve the world and increase productivity, consistently responding to change with new ideas. Roger van Oech, an expert on creativity, highlights this kind of flexibility.[3] "I've found that the hallmark of creative people is their mental flexibility," he says. "Like race-car drivers who shift in and out of different gears depending on where they are on the course, creative people are able to shift in and out of different types of thinking depending on the needs of the situation at hand. . . . they're doggedly persistent in striving to reach their goals."

T. Z. Tardif and F. J. Sternberg[4] say that creative people are perceived as having particular characteristics. See Table 1–3 for these characteristics and examples.

Creative people combine ideas and information in ways that form completely new solutions, ideas, processes, uses, or products. Children often can tap into this creative freedom more easily than adults. Whether they make up a new game, wear a bowl as a hat, or create forts from chairs and blankets, they create naturally without worrying that their ideas might not be "right." See if you can retrieve some of that creative freedom from your childhood, using the suggestions you are about to read.

314

TABLE 1-3	CHARACTERISTICS OF CREATIVE PEOPLE
CHARACTERISTIC	**EXAMPLE**
Willingness to take risks	Taking a difficult, high-level course
Tendency to break away from customary limitations	Entering a marathon race, particularly when physically disabled
Tendency to seek challenges and new experiences	Taking on an internship in an unfamiliar and high-pressure workplace
Broad range of interests in which he or she becomes absorbed	Inventing new moves on the basketball court and playing guitar at an open-mike night
Ability to make unique things out of available materials and objects	Making curtains out of bedsheets or writing a poem
Tendency to question social norms and assumptions	Adopting a child of a different ethnic background than the family's
Willingness to deviate from popular opinion	Working for a small, relatively unknown political party
Curiosity and inquisitiveness	Wanting to know how a computer program works; asking about the secret to a cooking trick

Source: Adapted from "What do we know about creativity?" In R. J. Sternberg (Ed.), *The nature of creativity.* London: Cambridge University Press, 1988.

ENHANCING YOUR CREATIVITY

You are naturally creative. One way to spur your creative ability is to allow yourself to explore new territory and adjust to change. Although it may feel risky and uncomfortable to try out new ideas or behavior, it can open you to new and exciting possibilities. Your creative spirit may thrive in a state of change. When you feel yourself resisting change, remember that exploring new ideas doesn't mean that what you were doing before was wrong. You are just responding to change with flexibility and creativity.

Following are some ways to enhance your creativity, adapted from material by J. R. Hayes.[5]

Take the broadest possible perspective. At first, a problem may look like "My child won't stay quiet when I study." If you take a

315

wider look, you may discover hidden causes or effects of the problem, such as "I haven't chosen the best time of day to study," or "We haven't had time together, so he feels lonely," or "I need to plan activities for him in advance."

Choose the best atmosphere. T. M. Amabile says that people are more creative and imaginative when they spend time around other creative folk.[6] Spend time around innovative people whose thinking inspires you.

Give yourself time. Rushing can stifle your creative ability. When you allow time for thought to percolate, or you focus on a problem and then return to it after taking a break, you may increase your creative output. In addition, when you derive ideas and choose solutions, avoid evaluating them right away. If you criticize your creative ideas too soon, you tend to derail them.

Gather varied input. The more information and ideas you gather as you think, the more material you have to build a creative idea or solution. Every new piece of input offers a new perspective that may enlighten you.

Here are a few additional creativity tips from van Oech.[7]

Don't get hooked on finding the one right answer. There can be lots of "right answers" to any question, depending on your point of view. Shift your perspective and come up with a few. The more you generate, the better your chance of finding the best one.

Don't always be logical. Following strict logic may cause you to miss analogies or ignore your hunches.

Break the rules sometimes. All kinds of creative breakthroughs have occurred because someone bypassed the rules. Women and minorities can vote and hold jobs because someone broke a rule—a law—many years ago. When necessary, challenge rules with creative ideas.

Be impractical. Ask yourself, "What if?" Use your imagination to consider what would happen if you didn't follow the accepted pattern. Too much emphasis on practicality can narrow the scope of your ideas.

Let yourself play. People often hit upon their most creative ideas when they aren't trying to think about anything at all—when they are exercising, socializing, playing around, or just relaxing. Often when your mind switches into play mode, it can more freely generate new thoughts.

Let yourself go a little crazy. It's easy to conform to peer pressure and to do what everyone else does. Although you may feel weird doing something completely different, that independence could lead to some incredibly unique ideas. The idea for Velcro™ came from examining how a burr sticks to clothing. What seems like a crazy idea might turn into a brilliant discovery.

Don't fear failure. Even Michael Jordan got cut from the basketball team as a high school sophomore in Wilmington, N.C., and John F. Kennedy, Jr., needed a couple of tries to pass the exam to be licensed to practice law. If you insist on getting it right all the time, you may miss out on the creative path—often paved with failures—leading to the best possible solution. Failure can open your mind to new possibilities and reveal to you the value of critical thinking.

Always consider yourself creative. Use your positive self-talk. Telling yourself you are a creative person can help you act like one.

Brainstorming is a creative process that may combine many of these creativity strategies. You can use brainstorming for problem solving, decision making, and preparing to write an essay or paper. Anytime you need to free your mind to consider new possibilities, you can brainstorm.

BRAINSTORMING TOWARD A CREATIVE ANSWER

You are brainstorming when you approach a problem by letting your mind free-associate and come up with as many possible ideas, examples, or solutions as you can, without immediately evaluating them as good or bad. Brainstorming is also referred

"The world of reality has its limits. The world of imagination is boundless."

JEAN JACQUES ROUSSEAU

317

to as divergent thinking—you start with the issue or problem and then let your mind diverge, or go in as many different directions as it wants, in search of ideas or solutions. Here are some rules for successful brainstorming:[8]

Don't evaluate or criticize an idea right away. Write down your ideas so that you remember them. Evaluate later, after you have had a chance to think about them. Try to avoid criticizing other people's ideas as well. Students often become stifled when their ideas are evaluated during brainstorming.

Focus on quantity; don't worry about quality until later. Try to generate as many ideas or examples as you can. The more thoughts you generate, the better the chance that one may be useful. Brainstorming works well in groups. Group members can become inspired by, and make creative use of, one another's ideas.

Let yourself consider wild and wacky ideas. Trust yourself to fall off the edge of tradition when you explore your creativity. Sometimes the craziest ideas end up being the most productive, positive, workable solutions around.

Remember, creativity can be developed if you have the desire and patience. Be gentle with yourself in the process. Most people are harsher with themselves and their ideas than is necessary. Your creative expression will become more free with practice.

CREATIVITY AND CRITICAL THINKING

Critical thinking and creativity work hand in hand. Critical thinking is inherently creative, because it requires you to take the information you are given and come up with original ideas or solutions to problems. For example, you can brainstorm to generate possible causes of a certain effect. If the effect you were examining was fatigue in afternoon classes, you might come up with possible causes such as lack of sleep, too much morning caffeine, a diet heavy in carbohydrates, a natural tendency toward low energy at that time, or an instructor who doesn't inspire you.

Through your consideration of causes and solutions, you have been thinking both creatively and critically.

Creative thinkers and critical thinkers have similar characteristics—both consider new perspectives, ask questions, don't hesitate to question accepted assumptions and traditions, and persist in the search for answers. Only through thinking critically and creatively can you freely question, brainstorm, and evaluate in order to come up with the most fitting ideas, solutions, decisions, arguments, and plans.

You use critical-thinking mind actions throughout everything you do school and in your daily life. In this chapter, you will notice mind-action icons placed where they can help you to label your thinking.

Κρινειν

The word "critical'" is derived from the Greek word *krinein,* which means to separate in order to choose or select. To be a mindful, aware critical thinker, you need to be able to separate, evaluate, and select ideas, facts, and thoughts.

Think of this concept as you apply critical thinking to your reading, writing, and interaction with others. Be aware of the information you take in and of your thoughts, and be selective as you process them. Critical thinking gives you the power to make sense of life by deliberately selecting how to respond to the information, people, and events that you encounter.

Chapter 1: Applications

Name _____ Date _____

Key into Your Life
Opportunities to Apply What You Learn

Exercise 1: The Seven Mind Actions

One way to explore the seven mind actions is to apply them to a vocabulary word. Choose a vocabulary word from a course you are taking now.

Write your word here: _____

Recall. Write the definition here. Include two sentences—from the dictionary or from your class materials—that contain the word.

_____

_____

_____

Similarity. What synonyms—words with similar meanings—can you name?

_____

_____

_____

Difference. What antonyms—words with opposite meanings—can you name?

_____

_____

_____

Cause and effect. What effect is caused by using this word—what tone or connotation does it have?

_____

_____

_____

Example to idea. From looking at the synonyms and sentences, create a definition in your own words.

_____

_____

_____

Idea to example. From the idea or the definition, show an example of the use of the word by placing it in a sentence that you create.

_____

_____

_____

Evaluation. How well does the word fit in the sentence you have written? Explain.

_____

_____

_____

Using mnemonic devices will also help you remember mind actions. Try inventing your own mnemonic device for the actions. Write it here or, if it is a mental picture, describe it:

_____

_____

_____

_____

Endnotes

Chapter 1

[1]Frank T. Lyman, Jr., Ph.D., "Think-Pair-Share, Thinktrix, Think-links, and Weird Facts: An Interactive System for Cooperative Thinking." In *Enhancing Thinking Through Cooperative Learning,* ed. Neil Davidson and Toni Worsham (New York: Teachers College Press, 1992), 169–181.

[2]Sylvan Barnet and Hugo Bedau, *Critical Thinking, Reading, and Writing: A Brief Guide to Argument,* 2nd ed. (Boston: Bedford Books of St. Martin's Press, 1996), 43.

[3]Roger von Oech, *A Kick in the Seat of the Pants* (New York: Harper & Row Publishers, 1986) 5–21.

[4]T. Z. Tardif and R. J. Sternberg, "What do we know about creativity?" In *The Nature of Creativity,* ed. R. J. Sternberg (Cambridge, MA: Cambridge University Press, 1988).

[5]J. R. Hayes, *Cognitive Psychology: Thinking and Creating* (Homewood, IL: Dorsey, 1978).

[6]T. M. Amabile, *The Social Psychology of Creativity* (New York: Springer-Verlag, 1983).

[7]Roger von Oech, *A Whack on the Side of the Head* (New York: Warner Books, 1990), 11–168.

[8]Dennis Coon, *Introduction to Psychology: Exploration and Application,* 6th ed. (St. Paul: West Publishing Company, 1992), 295.

11

Goal Setting and Time Management

Mapping Your Course

In this chapter, you will explore answers to the following questions:

- What defines your values?
- How do you set and achieve goals?
- What are your priorities?
- How can you manage your time?
- Why is procrastination a problem?

Thinking It Through

Check those statements that apply to you right now:

- ❑ I haven't thought much about the sources of my values.
- ❑ I set goals but don't always feel that I achieve them.
- ❑ I feel that my priorities have changed since entering college.
- ❑ I have a date book but don't use it all that much.
- ❑ I know it doesn't help me, but I procrastinate.
- ❑ I don't think about the future; I just let things happen to me.

Taken from: *Keys to Success: How to Achieve Your Goals*, Second Edition, by Carol Carter, Joyce Bishop, and Sarah Lyman Kravits

People dream of what they want out of life, but not everyone knows how to turn dreams into reality. Often dreams and goals seem far off in time, too difficult, or even completely unreachable. It may seem that there is a vast desert between where you are now and where you aspire to be. You can build paths through the desert by identifying the steps you need to take, one by one, to arrive at your destination. The steps are goals. When you set goals, prioritize, and manage your time effectively, you increase your ability to take those steps to achieve your long-term goals.

The pursuit of personal and professional goals gives your life meaning. This chapter explains how taking specific steps toward goals can help you turn your dreams into reality. You will explore how your values relate to your goals. You will see how to create a framework for your life's goals—a personal mission statement—and how to set long-term and short-term goals. You will discover how setting priorities can help you work toward your goals more efficiently. The section on time management will discuss how to translate those goals into daily, weekly, monthly, and yearly steps to give shape and purpose to their achievement. Finally, you will explore the topic of procrastination, how it affects your life, and what you can do to minimize the problems it may cause.

WHAT DEFINES YOUR VALUES?

Values

Principles or qualities that one considers important, right, or good.

Your personal **values** are the beliefs that guide your choices. Examples of values include family togetherness, a good education, caring for others, worthwhile employment. The sum total of all your values is your *value system.* You demonstrate your particular value system in the priorities you set, how you communicate with others, your family life, your education and career choices, and even the material things with which you surround yourself.

Looking at sources is a good first step in the exploration of your values.

SOURCES OF VALUES

Values are choices. You are in control of choosing what you value. However, it may not always seem that way, because people often choose values based on what others value or what society or the media seem to value. A value system is constructed over time, using information from many different sources.

Sources of values include the following:

- Parents, guardians, or relatives
- Friends and peers
- Religious belief and study
- Instructors, supervisors, mentors, and other authority figures
- Books, magazines, television, or other media
- Workplace and school

A particular value may come from one or more sources. For example, a student may value education (primary source: parents), music (primary sources: media and friends), and spiritual life (primary sources: religious leader and grandparents). Another student may have abandoned all of the values that he or she grew up with and adopted the values of a trusted mentor. Still another may find that adopting certain values became important in order to succeed in a particular career area. Being influenced by the values of others is natural, although you should take care to follow what feels right to you.

CHOOSING AND EVALUATING VALUES

Examining the sources of your values can help you define those values, trace their origin, and question the reasons why you have adopted them. Value sources, however, aren't as important as the process of considering each value carefully to see if it makes sense to you. Some of your current values may have come from television or other media but still ring true. Some may come from what others have taught you. Some you may have constructed from your own personal experience and opinion. You make the final decision about what to value, regardless of the source.

Each individual value system is unique, even if many values come from other sources. Your value system is yours alone. Your responsibility is to make sure that your values are your own choice, and not the choice of others. Make value choices for yourself based on what feels right for you, for your life, and for those who are touched by your life.

You can be more sure of making choices that are right for you if you try to always question and evaluate your values. Before you adopt a value, ask yourself: Does it feel right? What effects might it have on my life? Am I choosing it to please someone else, or is it truly my choice? Values are a design for life, and you are the one who has to live the life you design.

Because life change and new experiences may bring a change in values, try to continue to evaluate values as time goes by. Periodically evaluate the effects that having each value has on your life, and see if a shift in values might suit your changing circumstances. For example, losing your sight may cause you to value your hearing intensely. The difficulty of a divorce may have a positive result: a new value of independence and individuality. After growing up in a homogeneous community, a student who meets other students from unfamiliar backgrounds may learn a new value of living in a diverse community. Your values will grow and develop as you do if you continue to think them through.

HOW VALUES RELATE TO GOALS

Understanding your values will help you set career and personal goals, because the most ideal goals help you achieve what you value. If you value spending time with your family, related goals may include living near your parents or writing to your grandmother every week. A value of financial independence may generate goals, such as working while going to school and keeping credit-card debt low, that reflect the value. If you value helping others, try to make time for volunteer work.

Goals enable you to put values into practice. When you set and pursue goals that are based on values, you demonstrate and reinforce values through taking action. The strength of those values, in turn, reinforces your goals. You will experience a much stronger drive to achieve if you build goals around what is most important to you.

HOW DO YOU SET AND ACHIEVE GOALS?

A *goal* can be something as concrete as buying a health insurance plan or as abstract as working to control your temper. When you set goals and work to achieve them, you engage your intelligence, abilities, time, and energy in order to move ahead. From major life decisions to the tiniest day-to-day activities, setting goals will help you define how you want to live and what you want to achieve.

Paul Timm, a best-selling author and teacher who is an expert in self-management, feels that focus is a key ingredient in setting and achieving goals. "Focus adds power to our actions. If somebody threw a bucket of water on you, you'd get wet, and probably get mad. But if water was shot at you through a high-pressure nozzle, you might get injured. The only difference is focus."[1] Each part of this section will explain ways to focus your energy through goal-setting. You can set and achieve goals by defining a personal mission statement, placing your goals in long-term and short-term time frames, evaluating goals in terms of your values, and linking your goals to five life areas.

Goal
An end toward which effort is directed; an aim or intention.

IDENTIFYING YOUR "PERSONAL MISSION STATEMENT"

Some people go through their lives without ever really thinking about what they can do or what they want to achieve. When duties and demands fill your days, it's easy to lose your drive. If you choose not to set goals or explore what you want out of life, you may look back on your past with a sense of emptiness. You may not know what you've done or why you did it. However, you can avoid that emptiness by periodically taking a few steps back and thinking about where you've been and where you want to be.

One helpful way to determine your general direction is to write a *personal mission statement.* Dr. Stephen Covey, author of the best-seller *The Seven Habits of Highly Effective People,* defines a mission statement as a philosophy that outlines what you want to be (character), what you want to do (contributions and achievements), and the principles by which you live. Dr. Covey compares the personal mission statement to the Constitution of the United States, a statement of principles that gives this country guidance and standards in the face of constant change. "A personal mission statement based on correct principles becomes the same kind of standard for an individual," he says. "It becomes a personal constitution, the basis for making major, life-directing decisions, the basis for making daily decisions in the midst of the circumstances and emotions that affect our lives. It empowers individuals with the same timeless strength in the midst of change."[2]

Your personal mission isn't written in stone. It should change as you move from one phase of life to the next—from single person to spouse, from parent to single parent to caregiver of an older parent. Stay flexible and reevaluate your personal] mission from time to time.

Here is an example of author Carol Carter's personal mission statement:

> My mission is to use my talents and abilities to help people of all ages, stages, backgrounds, and economic levels achieve their human potential through fully developing their minds and their talents. I also aim to balance work with people in my life, understanding that my family and friends are a priority above all else.

A company, like a person, needs to establish standards and principles that guide its many activities. Companies often have mission statements so that each member of the organization, from the custodian to the president, clearly understands what to strive for. If a company fails to identify its mission, a million well-intentioned employees might focus their energies in just as many different directions, creating chaos and low productivity.

Here is a mission statement from Northwest Airlines. It is displayed inside their company buildings and on the back of every employee's business card. Notice how it reinforces the company's goals of teamwork, leadership, and excellence.

> To build together the world's most preferred airline with the best people; each committed to exceeding our customer's expectations every day.

Another example is from Prentice Hall, the company that publishes this text:

> To provide the most innovative resources—books, technology, programs—to help students of all ages and stages achieve their academic and professional goals inside the classroom and out.

You will have an opportunity to write your own personal mission statement at the end of this chapter. Writing a mission statement is much more than an in-school exercise. It is truly for you. Thinking through your personal mission can help you begin to take charge of your life. It helps to put you in control instead of allowing circumstances and events to control you. If you frame your mission statement carefully so that it truly reflects your goals, it can be your guide in everything you do.

PLACING GOALS IN TIME

Everyone has the same twenty-four hours in a day, but it often doesn't feel like enough. Have you ever had a busy day flash by so quickly that it seems you accomplished nothing? Have you ever felt that way about a longer period of time, like a month or even a year? Your commitments can overwhelm you unless you decide how to use time to plan your steps toward goal achievement.

If developing a personal mission statement establishes the big picture, placing your goals within particular time frames allows you to bring individual areas of that picture into the foreground. It's a rare goal that is reached overnight. Lay out the plan by breaking a long-term goal into stages of what you will accomplish in one day, one week, one month, six months, one year, five years, ten years, even twenty years. Planning your progress step by step will help you maintain your efforts over the extended time period often needed to accomplish a goal. Goals fall into two categories: long-term and short-term.

SETTING LONG-TERM GOALS

Establish first the goals that have the largest scope, the *long-term goals* that you aim to attain over a lengthy period of time, up to a few years or more. As a student, you know what long-term goals are all about. You have set yourself a goal to attend school and earn a degree or certificate. Becoming educated is an admirable goal that takes a good number of years to reach.

Some long-term goals are lifelong, such as a goal to continually learn more about yourself and the world around you. Others have a more definite end, such as a goal to complete a course successfully. To determine your long-term goals, think about what you want out of your professional, educational, and personal life. Here is Carol Carter's long-term goal statement.

<u>Carol's Goals:</u> To accomplish my mission through writing books, giving seminars, and developing programs that create opportunities for students to learn and develop. To create a personal, professional, and family environment that allows me to manifest my abilities and duly tend to each of my responsibilities.

For example, you may establish long-term goals such as these:

♦ I will graduate from school and know that I have learned all that I could, whether my grade point average shows it or not.
♦ I will use my current and future job experience to develop practical skills that will help me later in life.
♦ I will build my leadership and teamwork skills by forming positive, productive relationships with classmates, instructors, and co-workers.

Long-term goals don't have to be lifelong goals. Think about your long-term goals for the coming year. Considering what you want to accomplish in a year's time will give you clarity, focus, and a sense of what needs to take place right away. When Carol thought about her long-term goals for the coming year, she came up with the following list:

1. Develop programs to provide internships, scholarships, and other quality initiatives for students.
2. Write a book for students emphasizing an interactive, highly visual approach to learning.
3. Allow time in my personal life to eat well, run five days a week, and spend quality time with family and friends. Allow time daily for quiet reflection and spiritual devotion.

In the same way that Carol's goals are tailored to her personality and interests, your goals should reflect who you are. Personal missions and goals are as unique as each individual. Continuing the example above, you might adopt these goals for the coming year:

- I will earn passing grades in all my classes.
- I will look for a part-time job with a local newspaper or newsroom.
- I will join two clubs and make an effort to take leadership roles in each.

SETTING SHORT-TERM GOALS

When you divide your long-term goals into smaller, manageable goals that you hope to accomplish within a relatively short time, you are setting *short term goals.* Short-term goals narrow your focus, helping you to maintain your progress toward your long-term goals. They are the steps that take you where you want to go. Say you have set the three long-term goals you just read in the previous section. To stay on track toward those goals, you may want to accomplish these short-term goals in the next six months:

- I will pass Business Writing I so that I can move on to Business Writing II.
- I will make an effort to ask my co-workers for advice on how to get into the news business.
- I will attend four of the monthly meetings of the Journalism Club.

These same goals can be broken down into even smaller parts, such as one month.

- I will complete five of the ten essays for Business Writing.
- I will have lunch with my office mate at work so that I can talk with her about her work experience.
- I will write an article for next month's Journalism Club newsletter.

In addition to monthly goals, you may have short-term goals that extend for a week, a day, or even a couple of hours in a given day. Take as an example the article you have planned to write for the next month's Journalism Club newsletter. Such short-term goals may include the following:

- Three weeks from now: Have a final draft ready. Submit it to the editor of the newsletter.

"Even if you're on the right track, you'll get run over if you just sit there."

WILL ROGERS

- Two weeks from now: Have a second draft ready, and give it to one more person to review.
- One week from now: Have a first draft ready. Ask my writing instructor if he will review it.
- Today by the end of the day: Freewrite about the subject of the article, and narrow it down to a specific topic.
- By 3 P.M. today: Brainstorm ideas and subjects for the article.

As you consider your long-term and short-term goals, notice how all of your goals are linked to one another. As Figure 2-1 shows, your long-term goals establish a context for the short-term goals. In turn, your short-term goals make the long-term goals seem clearer and more reachable. The whole system works to keep you on track. (Figure 2-1 is below.)

LINKING GOALS WITH VALUES

If you are not sure how to start formulating your mission, look to your values to guide you. Define your mission and goals based on what is important to you.

FIGURE 2–1 **Linking Goals Together**

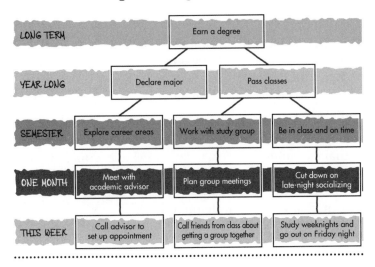

If you value physical fitness, your mission statement might emphasize your commitment to staying in shape throughout your life. Your long-term goal might be to run a marathon, while your short-term goals might involve your weekly exercise and eating plan. Similarly, if you value a close family, your personal mission might emphasize how you want to maintain family ties and stability. In this case, your long-term goals might involve finding a job that allows for family time or living in a town close to your parents. Your short-term goals may focus on helping your son learn a musical instrument or having dinner with your family at least twice a week.

CURRENT AND PERSONAL VALUES MEAN APPROPRIATE GOALS

When you use your values as a compass for your goals, make sure the compass is pointed in the direction of your real feelings. Watch out for the following two pitfalls that can occur.

Setting goals according to other peoples' values. Friends or family may encourage you to strive for what they think you should value, rather than what is right for you. If you follow their advice without believing in it, you may have a harder time sticking to your path. For example, someone who attends school primarily because a parent or spouse thought it was right may have less motivation and initiative than someone who made an independent decision to become a student. Look hard at what you really want, and why. Staying in tune with your own values will help you make decisions that are right for you.

Setting goals that reflect values you held in the past. What you felt yesterday may no longer apply, because life changes can alter your values. The best goals reflect what you believe today. For example, a person who has been through a near-fatal car accident may experience a dramatic increase in how he or she values time with friends and family, and a drop in how he or she values material possessions. Someone who survives a serious illness may value healthy living above all else. Keep in touch with your life's changes so your goals can reflect who you are.

GOALS IN FIVE LIFE AREAS

All goals are not the same, because they involve different parts of your life and different values. Approach goal-setting by establishing your long-term and short-term goals within five different areas: personal, family, school/career, financial, and lifestyle. As you set your goals in each area, remember that all your goals are interconnected. A financial goal, for example, will affect a career goal and a lifestyle goal.

Personal. This category includes your character, personality, physical appearance, and conduct. Do you want to gain confidence and knowledge? Develop a lean, athletic physique? Stop hanging out with people who bring you down? You can set your personal goals by taking a hard look at the difference between who you are and who you want to be.

Family. Do you want to stay single or marry? Do you want to have one or more children? If you have already started to build a family, do you want it to grow? Do you want to address problems with parents, improve your relationship with your spouse, or change the way you relate to your family? Do you want to live near relatives or far away? The goals you set can help you build a solid, satisfying family life.

School/Career. What kind of subjects or career field do you prefer? In school, consider the classes, instructors, class schedule, and available degrees or certificates. Think about your commitment to academic excellence and whether honors and awards are important goals. Then, think about the job you want after you graduate. Consider the requirements (degrees, certificates, or tests), job duties, hours, co-workers, salary, transportation, and company size and style that might be associated with your ideal job. Do you want to become a manager, a supervisor, an independent contractor, or a business owner? How much responsibility do you want? Identify goals that can point you toward your ideal education and career.

Financial. How much money do you need to pay your bills, maintain your chosen lifestyle, and save for the future? Do you need to borrow money for school or a major purchase such as a car? Do you already have heavy monthly bills that you want to reduce? Compare your current financial picture to how comfortable you eventually want to be, and set goals that will help you bridge the gap. These goals will also affect the career you choose.

Lifestyle. Where do you want to live (city, suburbs, country) and in what kind of space (apartment, condominium, town-house, single- or multi-family house, mobile home)? What kinds of values do you want to live by and encourage in others? How do you equip yourself with the skills necessary for dealing with diverse people? With whom do you want to live (extended/immediate family, roommates, friends, no one)? What do you want to give back to your community through service or volunteer work? What do you like to do in your leisure time? Consider goals that allow you to live the way you want to live.

Setting and working toward goals can be frightening and difficult at times. Like learning a new physical task, it takes a lot of practice and repeated efforts. As long as you do all that you can to achieve a goal, you haven't failed, even if you don't achieve it completely or in the time frame you had planned. Even one step in the right direction is an achievement. For example, if you wanted to raise your course grade to a B from a D, and you ended up with a C, you have still accomplished something important.

IDENTIFYING EDUCATIONAL GOALS

Education is a major part of your life right now. In order to define a context for your school goals, explore why you have decided to pursue an education. People have many reasons for attending college. You may identify with one or more of the following possible reasons.

- ♦ I want to earn a higher salary.
- ♦ I want to build marketable skills.
- ♦ My supervisor at work says that a degree will help me move ahead in my career.
- ♦ Most of my friends were going.

335

- I want to be a student and learn all that I can.
- It seems like the only option for me right now.
- I am recently divorced and need to find a way to earn money.
- Everybody in my family goes to college; it's expected.
- I don't feel ready to jump into the working world yet.
- I got a scholarship.
- My friend loves her job and encouraged me to take courses in the field.
- My parent (or a spouse or partner) pushed me to go to college.
- I am pregnant and need to increase my skills so I can provide for my baby.
- I am studying for a specific career.
- I don't really know.

All of these answers are legitimate, even the last one. Being honest with yourself is crucial if you want to discover who you are and what life paths make sense for you. Whatever your reasons are for being in school, you are at the gateway to a journey of discovery.

It isn't easy to enroll in college, pay tuition, decide what to study, sign up for classes, gather the necessary materials, and actually get yourself to the school and into the classroom. Many people drop out at different places along the way, but somehow your reasons have been compelling enough for you to have arrived at this point.

Don't worry if you go through periods of low motivation. Remember, asking important questions gives you power to make responsible decisions that are yours and yours alone. Recharge by asking yourself: What do I want out of my life? What would I like people to say about me? What is important to me? Now and again you may let a day get past you without making any progress, but don't let a whole life go by.

Achieving goals becomes easier when you are realistic about what is possible. Setting priorities will help you make that distinction.

WHAT ARE YOUR PRIORITIES?

When you set a *priority,* you identify what's important at any given moment. *Prioritizing* helps you focus on your most important goals, even when they are difficult to achieve. If you were to pursue your goals in no particular order, you might tackle the easy ones first and leave the tough ones for later. The risk is that you might never reach for goals that are important to your success. Setting priorities helps you focus your plans on accomplishing your most important goals.

To explore your priorities, think about your personal mission and look at your goals in the five life areas: personal, family, school/career, finances, and lifestyle. These five areas may not all be equally important to you right now. At this stage in your life, which two or three are most critical? Is one particular category more important than others? How would you prioritize your goals from most important to least important?

You are a unique individual, and your priorities are yours alone. What may be top priority to someone else may not mean that much to you, and vice versa. You can see this in Figure 2, which compares the priorities of two very different students. Each student's priorities are listed in order, with the first priority at the top and the lowest priority at the bottom.

First and foremost, your priorities should reflect your personal goals. In addition, they should reflect your relationships with others. For example, if you are a parent, your children's needs will probably be high on the priority list. You may decide to go back to school so you can get a better job, earn more money, and give them a better life. If you are in a committed relationship, you may consider the needs of your partner. You may schedule your classes so that you and your partner are home together as often as possible. Even as you consider the needs of others, though, never lose sight of your personal goals. Be true to your goals and priorities so that you can make the most of who you are.

Setting priorities moves you closer to accomplishing specific goals. It also helps you begin planning to achieve your goals within specific time frames. Being able to achieve your goals is directly linked to effective time management.

Priority
An action or intention that takes precedence in time, attention, or position.

337

FIGURE 2–2   Two Students Compare Priorities

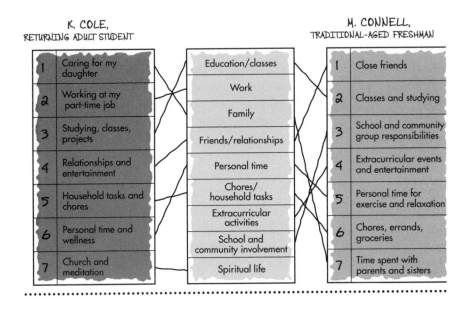

HOW CAN YOU MANAGE YOUR TIME?

Time is one of your most valuable and precious resources. Unlike money, or opportunity, or connections, time doesn't discriminate—everyone has the same twenty-four hours in a day, every day. Your responsibility, and your potential for success, lie in how you use yours. You cannot manipulate or change how time passes, but you can spend it taking steps to achieve your goals. Efficient time management helps you achieve your goals in a steady, step-by-step process.

People have a variety of different approaches to time management. Your learning style can help you identify the particular way you currently use your time. For example, factual and linear learners tend to organize activities within a framework of time. Because they stay aware of how long it takes them to do something or travel somewhere, they are usually prompt. Theoretical and holistic learners tend to miss the passing of time while they are busy thinking of something else. Because they focus on the big picture, they may neglect details such as structuring their activities within available time. They frequently lose track of time and can often be late without meaning to be.

Time management, like physical fitness, is a lifelong pursuit. No one can plan a perfect schedule or build a terrific physique and then be "done." You'll work at time management throughout your life, and it can be tiring. Your ability to manage your time will vary with your mood, your stress level, how busy you are, and other factors. You're human; don't expect perfection. Just do your best. Time management involves taking responsibility for how you spend your time, building a schedule, and making your schedule work through lists and other strategies.

TAKING RESPONSIBILITY FOR HOW YOU SPEND YOUR TIME

Being in control of how you manage your time is a key factor in taking responsibility for yourself and your choices. When you plan your activities with an eye toward achieving your most important goals, you are taking personal responsibility for how you live. Life changes and the judgments of others are among the factors that can affect your control.

LIFE CHANGES

Life's sudden changes and circumstances often make you feel out of control. One minute you seem to be on track, and the next minute chaos hits: Your car breaks down; your relationship falls apart; you fail a class; you or your child develops a medical problem; you get laid off at work. Coping with all of these changes can cause stress. As your stress level rises, your sense of control dwindles.

Although you cannot always choose your circumstances, you might be able to choose how to handle them. Dr. Covey says that language is important in trying to take action. Using language like "I have to" and "They made me" robs you of personal power. For example, saying that you "have to" go to school or move out of your parents' house can make you feel that others control your life. However, language like "I have decided to" and "I prefer" helps energize your power to choose. Then you can turn "I have to go to school" into "I prefer to go to school rather than working in a dead-end job."

JUDGMENTS OF OTHERS

Judgments
*Considered opinions,
assessments, or evaluations.*

The *judgments* of others can also intimidate you into not taking responsibility for your time. A student who feels no one will hire him because of his weight may not search for jobs. A student who feels her instructor is prejudiced against her might not study for that instructor's course. Try not to let these barriers rob you of your control of your time. Early in his life, Malcolm X was told that he had no business aspiring to be a lawyer in spite of his excellent record as a student. He was constantly demeaned because of his race. However, he did not let the ignorance of others stand in his way.

Instead of giving in to judgments, try to choose actions that improve your circumstances. If you lose a job, spending an hour a day investigating other job opportunities is a better use of your time than watching TV. If you have trouble with an instructor, you can address the problem with that instructor directly and try to make the most of your time in the course. If that doesn't work, you could drop the course, spend that time in other important pursuits, and retake the course in summer school while working part time. Try to find an option that will allow you to be in control of your time.

Time can be your ally if you make smart choices about how to use it. Building a schedule can help you decide when to accomplish the activities you choose.

BUILDING A SCHEDULE

Just as a road map helps you travel from place to place, a *schedule* is a time-and-activity map that helps you get from the beginning of the day (or week, or month) to the end as smoothly as possible. A written schedule helps you gain control of your life. Schedules have two major advantages: They allocate segments of time for the fulfillment of your daily, weekly, monthly, and longer-term goals, and they serve as a concrete reminder of tasks, events, due dates, responsibilities, and deadlines. Few moments are more stressful than suddenly realizing you have forgotten to pick up a prescription, take a test, or be on duty at work. Scheduling can help you avoid events like these.

KEEP A DATE BOOK

Gather the tools of the trade: a pen or pencil and a *date book* (sometimes called a planner). Some of you already have date books and may have used them for years. Others may have had no luck with them or have never tried. Even if you don't feel you are the type of person who would use one, give it a try. A date book is indispensable for keeping track of your time. Paul Timm says, "Most time management experts agree that rule number one in a thoughtful planning process is: Use some form of a planner where you can write things down."

There are two major types of date books. The *day-at-a-glance* version devotes a page to each day. While it gives you ample space to write the day's activities, this version makes it difficult to see what's ahead. The *week-at-a-glance* book gives you a view of the week's plans, but has less room to write per day. If you write out your daily plans in detail, you might like the day-at-a-glance version. If you prefer to remind yourself of plans ahead of time, try the book that shows a week's schedule all at once. Some date books contain additional sections that allow you to note plans and goals for the year as a whole and for each month. You can also create your own sheets for yearly and monthly notations in a notepad section, if your book has one, or on plain paper that you can then insert into the book.

Another option to consider is an *electronic planner*. These are compact mini-computers that can hold a large amount of information. You can use them to schedule your days and weeks, make to-do lists, and create and store an address book. Electronic planners are powerful, convenient, and often fun. On the other hand, they certainly cost more than the paper version, and you can lose a lot of important data if something goes wrong with the computer inside. Evaluate your options and decide what you like best.

SET WEEKLY AND DAILY GOALS

The most ideal time management starts with the smallest tasks and builds to bigger ones. Setting short-term goals that tie in to your long-term goals lends the following benefits:

"The right time is any time that one is still so lucky as to have. . . . live!"

HENRY JAMES

♦ Increased meaning for your daily activities
♦ Shaping your path toward the achievement of your long-term goals
♦ A sense of order and progress

For college students as well as working people, the week is often the easiest unit of time to consider at one shot. Weekly goal-setting and planning allows you to keep track of day-to-day activities while giving you the larger perspective of what is coming up during the week. Take some time before each week starts to remind yourself of your long-term goals. Keeping long-term goals in mind will help you determine related short-term goals you can accomplish during the week to come.

Figure 2–3 shows parts of a daily schedule and a weekly schedule.

LINK DAILY AND WEEKLY GOALS WITH LONG-TERM GOALS

After you evaluate what you need to accomplish in the coming year, semester, month, week, and day in order to reach your long-term goals, use your schedule to record those steps. Write down the short-term goals that will enable you to stay on track. Here is how a student might map out two different goals over a year's time.

This year:	Complete enough courses to graduate.
	Improve my physical fitness.
This semester:	Complete my accounting class with a B average or higher.
	Lose 10 pounds and exercise regularly.
This month:	Set up study-group schedule to coincide with quizzes.
	Begin walking and weight lifting.
This week:	Meet with study group; go over material for Friday's quiz.
	Go for a fitness walk three times; go to weight room twice.
Today:	Go over Chapter 3 in accounting text.
	Walk for 40 minutes.

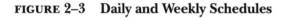
FIGURE 2–3 Daily and Weekly Schedules

MONDAY, MARCH 24		1997 PRIORITY
TIME	TASKS	
7:00 AM		
8:00	Up at 8am — finish homework	☆
9:00		
10:00	Business Administration	☆
11:00	Renew driver's license @ DMV	
12:00 PM		
1:00	Lunch	☆
2:00	Writing Seminar (peer editing today)	
3:00	↓	
4:00	check on Ms. Schwartz's office hrs.	
5:00	5:30 work out	
6:00	↳ 6:30	
7:00	Dinner	
8:00	Read two chapters for Business Admin	
9:00	↓	
10:00		
11:00		

Monday, March 24

8			
9	BIO 212	CALL: Maggie Blair	
10		Financial Aid Office	1
11	CHEM 203	EMS 262 ☆ Paramedic role-play ☆	2
12			3
Evening 6pm yoga class			4

Tuesday, March 25

			5
8	Finish reading assignment!		
9		Work @ library	
10	ENG 112		1
11	↓		2
12		(study for quiz)	3
Evening			4

Wednesday, March 26

			5
8		↓ until 7pm	
9	BIO 212	Meet w/advisor	
10			1
11	CHEM 203 ☆ QUIZ ☆	EMS 262	2
12			3
Evening 6pm Aerobics		☆ Pick up photos	4
			5

PRIORITIZE GOALS

Prioritizing enables you to use your date book with maximum efficiency. On any given day, your goals will have varying degrees of importance. Record your goals first, and then label them according to level of importance, using these categories: Priority 1, Priority 2, and Priority 3. Identify these categories using any code that makes sense to you. Some people use numbers, as above. Some use letters (A, B, C). Some write activities in different colors according to priority level. Some use symbols (*, +, -).

Priority 1 activities are the most important things in your life. They may include attending class, picking up a child from day care, putting gas in the car, and paying bills.

Priority 2 activities are part of your routine. Examples include grocery shopping, working out, participating in a school organization, or cleaning. Priority 2 tasks are important but more flexible than priority 1's.

Priority 3 activities are those you would like to do but can reschedule without much sacrifice. Examples might be a trip to the mall, a visit to a friend, a social phone call, a sports event, a movie, or a hair appointment. As much as you would like to accomplish them, you don't consider them urgent. Many people don't enter priority 3 tasks in their date books until they are sure they have time to get them done.

Prioritizing your activities is essential for two reasons. First, some activities are more important than others, and effective time management requires that you focus most of your energy on priority 1 items. Second, looking at all your priorities helps you plan when you can get things done. Often, it's not possible to get all your priority 1 activities done early in the day, especially if these activities involve scheduled classes or meetings. Prioritizing helps you set priority 1 items and then schedule priority 2 and 3 items around them as they fit.

KEEP TRACK OF EVENTS

Your date book also enables you to schedule *events*. Rather than thinking of events as separate from goals, tie them to your long-term goals just as you would your other tasks. For example, attending a wedding in a few months contributes to your commitment to spending time with your family. Being aware of quiz dates, due dates for assignments, and meeting dates will aid your goals to achieve in school and become involved.

Note events in your date book so that you can stay aware of them ahead of time. Write them in daily, weekly, monthly, or even yearly sections, where a quick look will remind you that they are approaching. Writing them down will also help you see where they fit in the context of all your other activities. For example, if you have three big tests and a presentation all in one week, you'll want to take time in the weeks before to prepare for them all.

Following are some kinds of events worth noting in your date book:

- Due dates for papers, projects, presentations, and tests
- Important meetings, medical appointments, or due dates for bill payments
- Birthdays, anniversaries, social events, holidays, and other special occasions
- Benchmarks for steps toward a goal, such as due dates for sections of a project or a deadline for losing five pounds on your way to twenty

LIST LOW-PRIORITY GOALS SEPARATELY

Priority 3 tasks can be hard to accomplish. As the least important tasks, they often get pushed off from one day to the next. You may spend valuable time rewriting these items day after day in your date book instead of getting them done. One solution is to keep a list of priority 3 tasks in a separate place in your date book. That way, when you have an unexpected pocket of free time, you can consult your list and see what you have time to accomplish—making a trip to the post office, writing a card, returning a borrowed tape, giving some clothes to charity, going to the hardware store. Keep this list current by crossing off items as you accomplish them and writing in new items as soon as you think of them. Rewrite the list when it gets too messy.

TIME MANAGEMENT STRATEGIES

Managing time takes thought and energy. Here are some additional strategies to try.

1. Plan your schedule each week. Before each week starts, note events, goals, and priorities. Look at the map of your week to decide where to fit activities like studying and priority 3 items. For example, if you have a test on Thursday, you can plan study sessions on the days up until then. If you have more free time on Tuesday and Friday than on other days, you can plan workouts or priority 3 activities at those times. Looking at the whole week will help you avoid being surprised by something you had forgotten was coming up.

2. Make and use to-do lists. Use a *to-do list* to record the things you want to accomplish. If you generate a daily or weekly to-do list on a separate piece of paper, you can look at all tasks and goals at once. This will help you consider time frames and priorities. You might want to prioritize your tasks and transfer them to appropriate places in your date book. Some people create daily to-do lists right on their date book pages. You can tailor a to-do list to an important event such as exam week or an especially busy day when you have a family gathering or a presentation to make. This kind of specific to-do list can help you prioritize and accomplish an unusually large task load.

3. Make thinking about time a priority. Mr. Timm recommends that you devote a minimum of 10 to 15 minutes a day to planning your schedule. Although making a schedule takes time, it can mean hours of saved time later. Say you have two errands to run, both on the other side of town; not planning ahead could result in your driving across town twice in one day. The extra driving time is far more than it would have taken to plan the day in advance.

4. Refer to your schedule. Many people make detailed schedules, only to forget to look at them. Carry your date book wherever you go and check it throughout the day. Find a date book size you like—there are books that fit into your briefcase, bag, or even your pocket.

5. Post monthly and yearly calendars at home. Keeping a calendar on the wall will help you stay aware of important

FIGURE 2–4   Monthly Calendar

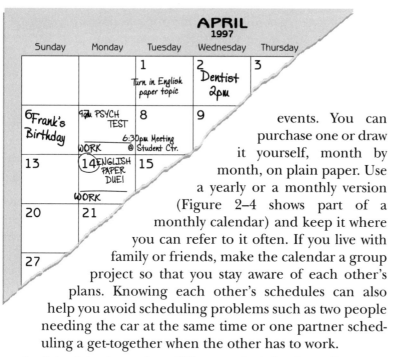

events. You can purchase one or draw it yourself, month by month, on plain paper. Use a yearly or a monthly version (Figure 2–4 shows part of a monthly calendar) and keep it where you can refer to it often. If you live with family or friends, make the calendar a group project so that you stay aware of each other's plans. Knowing each other's schedules can also help you avoid scheduling problems such as two people needing the car at the same time or one partner scheduling a get-together when the other has to work.

6. Schedule down time. When you're wiped out from too much activity, you don't have the energy to accomplish much with your time. A little *down time* will refresh you and improve your attitude. Even half an hour a day will help. Fill the time with whatever relaxes you—having a snack, reading, watching TV, playing a game or sport, walking, writing, or just doing nothing. Make down time a priority.

7. Be flexible. Since priorities determine the map of your day, week, month, or year, any priority shift can jumble your schedule. Be ready to reschedule your tasks as your priorities change. On Monday, a homework assignment due in a week might be priority 2. By Saturday, it has become priority 1. On some days a surprise priority such as a medical emergency or a family situation may pop up and force you to cancel everything else on your schedule. Other days a class may be canceled and you will

Down time
Quiet time set aside for relaxation and low-key activity.

347

have extra time on your hands. Adjust to whatever each day brings.

8. Leave unscheduled time in your schedule whenever possible. Just when you think you have control over your schedule, something inevitably comes along that will alter your plan. Try to keep some of your time unscheduled in case you have to shift tasks around. For example, if you get stuck working overtime, you may have to reschedule a meeting with a counselor for later in the day. If your baby-sitter doesn't show up, you can try to study while taking care of your child instead of using the study time you scheduled later.

No matter how well you schedule your time, you will have moments when it's hard to stay in control. Knowing how to identify and avoid procrastination and other time traps will help you get back on track.

WHY IS PROCRASTINATION A PROBLEM?

Procrastination

The act of putting off something that needs to be done.

Procrastination occurs when you postpone unpleasant or burdensome tasks. People procrastinate for different reasons. Having trouble with goal setting is one reason. People may project goals too far into the future, set unrealistic goals that are too frustrating to reach, or have no goals at all. People also procrastinate because they don't believe in their ability to complete a task or don't believe in themselves in general. As natural as these tendencies are, they can also be extremely harmful. If continued over a period of time, procrastination can develop into a habit that will dominate a person's behavior. Following are some ways to face your tendencies to procrastinate and *just do it!*

STRATEGIES TO FIGHT PROCRASTINATION

Weigh the benefits (to you and others) of completing the task versus the effects of procrastinating. What rewards lie ahead if you get it done? A burden off your shoulders? Some free time? Career advancement? What will be the effects if you continue to put it off? Which situation has better effects? Chances are you will benefit more in the long term from facing the task head-on.

Set reasonable goals. Plan your goals carefully, allowing enough time to complete them. Unreasonable goals can be so intimidating that you do nothing at all. "Pay off the credit-card bill next month" could throw you. However, "Pay off the credit-card bill in six months" might inspire you to take action.

Get started. Going from doing nothing to doing something is often the hardest part of avoiding procrastination. Once you start, you may find it easier to continue.

Break the task into smaller parts. If it seems overwhelming, look at the task in terms of its parts. How can you approach it step by step? If you can concentrate on achieving one small goal at a time, the task may become less of a burden.

Ask for help with tasks and projects at school, work, and home. You don't always have to go it alone. Instructors, supervisors, and family members can lend support, helping you to complete a dreaded task. For example, if you have put off an intimidating assignment, ask your instructor for guidance. If you avoid a project because you dislike the employee with whom you have to work, talk to your supervisor about adjusting the assignment of tasks or personnel. If you need accommodations due to a disability, don't assume that others know about it. Once you identify what's holding you up see who can help you face the task.

Don't expect perfection. No one is perfect. Being able to do something flawlessly is not a requirement for trying. Most people learn by starting at the beginning and wading through plenty of mistakes and confusion. It's better to try your best than to do nothing at all.

Consider how you would operate if you were looking forward to something you really wanted to do. You might not be late if you were headed to the airport for a flight to the Bahamas! See if you can transfer that behavior to a task that isn't quite as much fun.

Procrastination is natural, but it can cause you problems if you let it get the best of you. When it does happen, take some time to think about the causes. What is it about this situation that frightens you or puts you off? Answering that question can help you address what causes lie underneath the procrastination. These causes might indicate a deeper problem that needs to be solved.

OTHER "TIME TRAPS" TO AVOID

Procrastination isn't the only way to spend your time in less-than-productive ways. Keep an eye out for these situations too.

Saying "yes" when you really don't have the time. Many people, in their efforts to please others, agree to help with tasks they can't easily fit into their schedule. Being reliable is great, but not when it is at your own expense. Learn to say "no" when you need to. First, resist the desire to respond right away. Then ask yourself what effects a new responsibility will have on your schedule. Be honest with yourself about whether you have the time to make a new commitment. If it will cause you more trouble than it seems to be worth, say "no" graciously.

Studying at a bad time of day. At what point in the day do you have the most energy? Is that when you study? If not, you may be wasting time. When you are tired, you may need extra time to fully understand your material. If you study when you are most alert, you will be able to take in more information in less time.

Studying in a distracting location. Find an environment that helps you maximize study time. If you need to be alone to concentrate, for example, studying near family members or roommates might interfere with your focus. Conversely, people who require a busier environment to stay alert might need to choose a more active setting.

Not thinking ahead. Forgetting important things is a big time drain. One book left at home can cost you extra time going back and forth. One forgotten phone call can mean you have to do what you wanted to ask someone else to do. Five minutes of scheduling in the morning or the night before can save you hours.

Not curbing your social time. Time passes quickly when you're having fun. You plan to make a quick telephone call and the next thing you know you've been talking for an hour, losing time you could have used for studying or sleep. Don't cut out all socializing, but wear a watch and stay aware of the time. If friends invite you for dinner and you know you can't spend a whole evening out, consider joining them after dinner for coffee and dessert. Your friends will most likely respect your priorities and you will respect yourself when you see the rewards.

Not delegating. No one can take a test, read a chapter, or eat a meal for you, but you can delegate some tasks to other people. A relative might be able to shovel your walk or cut your grass. A friend going to the post office could pick up some stamps for you. Another day-care parent might be able to pick up your child on a day when your time runs short. Check into those possibilities, and don't forget to return the favor.

Pushing yourself too far. You've probably experienced one of those study sessions during which, at a certain point, you realize that you haven't absorbed anything for the last hour. Sometimes you just need a break. Stay aware of your energy level, and when you just can't seem to concentrate anymore, take a refresher—stretch, get a drink or a snack, go for a walk, take a nap. You're much better off using some of your time to revive yourself rather than trying in vain to focus.

חי

In Hebrew, the word *chai* means "life," representing all aspects of life—spiritual, emotional, family, educational, and career. Individual Hebrew characters have number values. Because the characters in the word *chai* add up to 18, the number 18 has come to be associated with good luck. The word *chai* is often worn as a good-luck charm. As you plan your goals, think about your view of luck. Many people feel that a person can create his or her own luck by pursuing goals persistently and staying open to possibilities and opportunities. Canadian, novelist Robertson Davies once said, "What we call luck is the inner man externalized. We make things happen to us."

Consider that your vision of life may largely determine how you live. You can prepare the way for luck by establishing a personal mission and forging ahead toward your goals. If you believe that the life you want awaits you, you will be able to recognize and make the most of luck when it comes around. *L'Chaim*—to life, and good luck.

Chapter 2: Applications

Name _____ Date _____

Key into Your Life
Opportunities to Apply What You Learn

Exercise 1: Your Values

Begin to explore your values by rating the following values on a scale from 1 to 4, 1 being least important to you, and 4 being most important. If you have values that you don't see in the chart, list them in the blank spaces and rate them.

Value	Rating	Value	Rating
Knowing yourself		Mental health	
Physical health		Fitness and exercise	
Spending time with your family		Close friendships	
Helping others		Education	
Being well-paid		Being employed	
Being liked by others		Free time/vacations	
Enjoying entertainment		Time to yourself	
Spiritual/religious life		Reading	
Keeping up with the news		Staying organized	
Being financially stable		Having an intimate relationship	
Creative/artistic pursuits		Self-improvement	
Lifelong learning		Facing your fears	

Considering your priorities, write your top five values here:

1. _____

2. _____

3. _____

4. _____

5. _____

Exercise 2: Your Personal Mission Statement

Using the personal mission statement examples in the chapter as a guide, consider what you want out of your life and create your own personal mission statement. You can write it in paragraph form, in a list of long-term goals, or in the form of a think link. Take as much time as you need in order to be as complete as possible. Write a draft on a separate sheet of paper and take time to revise it before you write the final version here. If you have created a think link rather than a verbal statement, attach it separately.

_____

_____

_____

_____

_____

_____

_____

_____

Exercise 3: Establishing and Tracking Long-Term Goals

The chapter described the importance of goal-setting in five different life areas. For each area, name an important long-term goal for your own life. Then imagine that you will begin working toward each goal. Indicate the steps you will take to achieve your goals on a short-term and long-term basis. Write what you hope to accomplish in the next year, the next six months, the next month, the next week, and the next day.

Your Goal	One Year	Six Months	Month	Week	Day
Example: I want to develop a better relationship with my father.	Instead of moving, I will complete my course of study at a school near my parents' home.	I will work to understand our relationship by talking with a counselor at school.	I will see my counselor every two weeks and make sure that I see my father at least once.	I will see if my father needs help with anything around the house this weekend.	I will call my dad after the basketball game because I know he'll be watching.
Personal					
Family					
School/Career					
Financial					
Lifestyle					

Exercise 4: Why Are You Here?

Why did you decide to enroll in school? Do any of the reasons listed in the chapter fit you? Do you have other reasons all your own? Many people have more than one answer. Write up to five here.

_____

_____

_____

_____

_____

Take a moment to think about your reasons. Which reasons are most important to you? Why? Prioritize your reasons above by writing 1 next to the most important, 2 next to the second most important, etc.

How do you feel about your reasons? You may be proud of some. On the other hand, you may not feel comfortable with others. Which do you like or dislike and why?

_____

_____

_____

_____

_____

III

Executive Communication

Improving Speaking Skills

In this chapter, you will explore answers to the following questions:

- How do I learn how to communicate more effectively?
- Why is communication so important in the business world?
- How will I know where to start when I have to write a speech?
- How should I edit my work after I've finished writing it?

Thinking It Through

Check those statements that apply to you right now:

- ❏ I never thought that communication was important in business.
- ❏ When I sit down to write a speech, I don't know where to start.

Taken from: *Keys to Success Reader,* by Joyce Bishop, Mary Jane Bradbury, and Julie Wheeler

> ❏ I have a difficult time speaking in front of people.
> ❏ When I am finished writing, whether speech or memo, I don't want to have to go back to it for editing.

Communication is an important part of professional life. Effective communication means effective management: Effective managers know their business and can communicate it. They create dynamic business associations with colleagues and employees, and build rapport, or harmony, with the people they relate to. Clearly, there is a relationship between being able to communicate and getting ahead. Used skillfully, communication can influence the behavior of others and produce enhanced results in all aspects of corporate life—from internal employee relations to a positive perspective of the company globally.

Yet communication skills are not always deemed important when designing degree plans for formal education. Communication courses fall into the category of "soft" skills, which often take a backseat to the "hard" information that leads to technical and scientific competence. However, with the emerging global economy and the technical ability to exchange information instantaneously, communication competence is becoming as essential as technical expertise. Author and communication expert Brent Filson interviewed dozens of CEOs about the importance of good communication skills in the workplace. Gerard R. Roche, chairman of Heidrick & Struggles, Inc. (an executive search firm) offers the following perspective:

> I address a number of business graduate schools a year, and I tell them that their courses are so overloaded with analytical studies and accounting and financial analysis and statistics and all these quantitative, measurable subjects that the students and the schools neglect one of the most important management skills of all: the ability to communicate.

Another CEO, John H. McConnell of Worthington Industries, adds, "Take all the speech courses and communication courses you can. Because the world turns on communication." There is a tremendous market today for communication improvement seminars, and most of the business is for companies training their employees to communicate better on the job. With this in mind, let's look at writing and speaking specifically as it applies to the workplace.

In order to communicate clearly, skilled executives must be able to transfer their thoughts into writing and speaking. Oral and written communication are accomplished through two different mediums—the spoken and the written word. The main difference is personal contact. Speaking involves face-to-face contact; when people hear and see you at the same time, everything about you is part of the communication experience.

While speaking gives you the advantage of using your entire being—vocal nuances, body language, and other nonverbal behaviors—to emphasize your message, you have only one opportunity to reach the audience. On the other hand, when you make a point in writing and the readers don't immediately understand, they can reread and investigate the material. Let's look at the ways in which executives communicate, beginning with speaking.

EXECUTIVE SPEAKING

IMPORTANCE OF SPEAKING IN A LEADERSHIP ROLE

Public speaking uses spoken language to influence human behavior. Beyond the words the speaker chooses, speaking involves seeing the similarities and differences in people, including yourself. Think about presentations that you have attended. What are the characteristics that made the experience a positive or negative one? How did you feel about the speaker, the message, the effectiveness of the talk? Did the speaker move you to take action or persuade you to take his position?

Many executives are not effective speakers, and that undermines their leadership positions because the audience perception is not favorable. Common critiques of poor presentations indicate that many speakers have low energy, read their speeches, fumble questions, have no sense of purpose or audience, and seem uncomfortable. You can avoid all of these by learning the basics of public speaking and adopting the attitude that a speaking engagement is an opportunity to assert a positive leadership presence. Let's look at the techniques for purposeful, powerful speech making.

COMPONENTS OF A GOOD SPEECH

A good speech builds on the flow of ideas that moves the listeners to action. Though it is important to write out your presentation as you develop it, it is not a written document and does not follow the rules of formal grammar. Delivery relies on informal, or conversational, style.

PURPOSE OF THE SPEECH

For executive communicators, all speaking is purposeful. Whether giving an impromptu talk or a formal presentation, your message—your commitment—should always be clear. This is what makes you the leader.

Speeches inform or persuade. What is your intention? If your intent is to inform, you must be clear, precise, and organized. If your intent is to persuade, you must go a step further and motivate your listeners to agree with you, change their behaviors or attitudes, or take action from your message. Use your speech to communicate change or a vision for the future, influence industry and investors, enhance sales and marketing, promote business growth, and build teamwork. The key to success in public speaking is knowing your intention and organizing your ideas around it—the audience expects you to know what you are talking about and to show it.

ORGANIZATION OF THE SPEECH

Preparation and organization are the keys to successfully presenting your message. Impromptu talks may appear to be off-the-cuff, but a successful manager has prepared in advance for any speaking opportunity. Many executives use everyday conversations to practice material and "test the waters." Impromptu talks are planned but flexible and immediate.

How do you prepare, regardless of the circumstances? The old sales adage applies here: Tell them what you are going to tell them, tell them, then tell them what you told them. A good speech has an engaging opening, a concise, informative body, and a powerful closing.

Beginning. A good beginning is essential. It captures the attention of the audience, states your purpose, and sets the tone. Openings can be dramatic or subtle. Use questions, statistics, quotations, and anecdotes to grab the attention of the audience. You want to engage your listeners and get them to think about your message—this is the time to challenge their assumptions. Always remember to focus on your message—you want to clash with issues, not your audience.

Body. The body of the speech is the place to make your points and carry your theme. Be dramatic and passionate. The more open you are about your position, the more your audience will trust you and be drawn into your position. Involve the audience in your enthusiasm. Use humor and visual aids to engage listeners and aid their retention. Build your background: Find stories and examples to support your position. Find something in common with the audience: People who have shared experience relate to each other, so relating to the audience brings them closer to you. Challenge them with questions. Show them what's in it for them. Organization is important—if you are focused and summarize as you go, the audience will stay with you.

Ending. The ending is your close. "Tell them what you told them". . . and why. Express your appreciation for their support, and call for action. What do you want them to do? The ending should be brief and optimistic. Highlight a positive aspect about your position and leave them inspired to follow your lead.

WRITING THE SPEECH

The task of organizing your ideas in written form can seem overwhelming. Where do you start? The important thing is to start. Get your ideas down on paper. The way in which you want to organize will become apparent as the process of writing down your ideas unfolds.

One technique is to write the body of the speech first. Write down the points, the theme, and the support details you want the audience to know. Next, write the conclusion. Restate your mission, call for action and ask for commitment. Then, write your introduction. Once you know where you will end, you can concentrate on the most effective way to begin. Finally, create a dynamic title. As you organize, remember the reason for your presentation.

The last, and most important step, is editing. Learning experts find that people will listen to you for 90 minutes, but they will retain only what is said in the first 20 minutes. Confine your message to this amount of time.

WHO IS THE AUDIENCE?

Leading communication theorist Kenneth Burke wrote, "You persuade a man only insofar as you talk his language by speech, gesture, tonality, order, image, attitude, ideas, identifying your ways with his." The arguments you use, the rapport you establish, and your approach to the issues are already impacted by what the audience believes before you begin. The more you understand your audience before you communicate with them, the more you can handle circumstances intelligently. Not all audiences are open-minded, especially in the business world. You must select what you say and how you say it based on your analysis of the audience. Audience analysis is an important part of your preparation.

Find out all you can about the people you are communicating with so that you consider their interests, needs, attitudes, knowledge, beliefs, values, and backgrounds in your speech. If your ideas are seeds you want to plant, it's a good idea to know the soil conditions in order to plan your approach!

With regard to your topic, where is your audience on this spectrum?

Knowledgeable . . . . Not Knowledgeable

Favorable . . . . Unfavorable

Willing . . . . Unwilling

Using this gauge to rate the receptivity of your audience will help you assess your approach and modify your message to win them over.

What are some of the other characteristics of the people who make up your audience? Consider cultural values, age, gender, occupation, education, group affiliation (for example, union or professional society), geography, and special areas such as disabilities. Again, the more you know about your audience, the more successful your presentation will be.

DELIVERY

The most organized and powerful collection of words in the world will fail to achieve results without a powerful delivery. Words make up less than 10 percent of the oral communication process. Vocal quality and body posture comprise the rest; body posture contributes over 50 percent. It's not only what you say, but how you say it!

Purpose. A good delivery is vital because it builds rapport and connects you and your message with the audience. You connect with the audience physically by how you look, sound, and make eye contact. You connect with them mentally by presenting ideas and challenging them to think about your presentation. You connect with them emotionally by identifying with them and their experiences.

Vocal quality. Vocal quality sets the tone of your presentation. A good speaking voice is pleasant and natural and conveys friendliness and sincerity. It balances volume, pitch, and rate. Varying these elements offers several options for creating the dynamics you want. For example, volume adds emphasis—the louder, the more assertive. Differences in pitch convey emotion and conviction—the higher, the more excitable. Changing your rate, or speed, of speech helps you change the mood, add emphasis, and avoid sounding boring.

Body posture. Body language brings the most important dimension to your speech. You show as well as tell, and the audience will believe your face and body as much or more than your words. Look people in the eye, keep your body open to the audience, and get out from behind the podium. Create a presence that your audience can trust. Use hand gestures to indicate size, shape, direction, and location. Use your hands and arms to show comparisons. Punctuate importance and urgency with a fist. Remember, body movement is not an outlet for nervous energy. It is a way to emphasize what you are saying.

Practice your speech. The best way to be prepared is to practice, practice, practice. There may be several unknowns about the actual presentation event, but if uncertainty of your material is one of them, you are at a disadvantage. Practice your material until you know it well and can concentrate on your delivery style and connecting with the audience. Videotape your practice; then watch yourself. Are you projecting the image, the intensity, and the message that you want? Would *you* believe, trust, and support this speaker if you were in the audience?

Remember that the audience is a mirror of the presenter. If you want to know how you are doing, observe the audience. How are they responding? If you are comfortable and at ease, they will be. If you wish you were somewhere else, so will they. Inspire them to share your passion by projecting that you know their business as well as you know your own. Be confident about the future. If you have done your homework and know your audience, the rapport you establish will help them see things your way.

Questions and answers. Questions and answers allow you to get feedback from your audience and provide additional information about your message. Listen attentively, be neutral, and answer with respect. Questions and answers at the end of your presentation provide the opportunity to interact personally with the audience, focus on the issues, and demonstrate further your sincerity and commitment to obtaining their support.

Remember, the only speech worth giving is one you believe in. Put your whole mind and body into it. Ask yourself, "What are you fighting for?" Believe in the cause because, if you don't, how will you convince your listeners?

CROSS-CULTURAL COMMUNICATION

At one time, international cross-cultural contact affected only a small portion of the world. New technology in transportation and information systems places us in instant and sometimes constant contact with people globally. Not long ago, only 5 percent of all American businesses faced international competition. Now, 75 percent of U.S. business is involved in international commerce. American executives communicate daily with people from other cultures. If cross-cultural communication is to enhance business relationships and increase productivity, it is imperative that the executive who anticipates speaking to another culture makes careful preparations.

TECHNIQUES FOR PRESENTING TO CROSS-CULTURAL AUDIENCES

Research the culture—know your audience. You don't need to know the culture as well as a native executive, but make a sincere effort to understand the people.

Common ground. Most North American and Northern European cultures focus on the bottom line—on doing business first and then becoming friends. However, many cultures value friendship first and then business. What is necessary to establish a relationship with each audience so that both sides are comfortable before proceeding to the issues?

Make the effort to establish common ground based on cultural values. If you are addressing an East Asian or American Indian culture, both of which believe in living harmoniously with nature, you want to be cautious about making recommendations that exploit the environment. Points of controversy and challenges are better met if you establish common ground.

Humor. Author Virginia Woolf wrote, "Humor is the first of the gifts to perish in a foreign tongue." Humor is certainly a powerful communication tool, but it does not translate well. Plays on words are rarely understood because they are taken literally. If you use humor, direct it toward yourself, never at the audience or their culture. For one culture, jokes about the elderly or religion may be fine, but for another, these subjects are sacred. Try out your humor in advance on people who understand the culture that you are trying to reach.

Body language. Body language is vital to communicating with cross-cultural audiences. The listeners may not understand the spoken language, so they will assess your message as much by what they see as what they hear. Every culture has taboos regarding gestures, and you can discover these by researching. The most important thing is to be natural and sincere. Your open, friendly manner will assure the audience that your verbal and nonverbal messages come from the heart and are meant with respect.

Speak slowly and in plain English. Some executives are fortunate to know the language of the people they are addressing. Others have the text of their speech translated phonetically and memorize it. Most use simultaneous translators. Whatever the circumstances, speak plainly. Idioms and sarcasm, like humor, may fall flat because the audience does not share your cultural context. Avoid jargon and puns unless you are sure the audience is familiar with them. Make your points with simple illustrations and anecdotes.

Audience reaction. Often, audiences from other cultures show little or no reaction to a presentation, and speakers wonder if their message is sinking in. If you do not get the reaction you expect, carry on. Continue to project respect and sincerity and don't be frustrated. Likewise, there may be no questions from the audience, even if you invite them. Many cultures are taught to respect authority, and it is unthinkable to question the authority of the speaker. To encourage discussion and questions, ask the audience to discuss your points in small groups and interact personally with the groups to address concerns directly.

SUMMARY FOR EXECUTIVE SPEAKING

Public-speaking skills are a valuable and indispensable tool for every successful executive. Seize every opportunity to speak; speak to inspire your employees and coworkers and to solidify your leadership. Uwe S. Wascher, head of General Electric Company's $5-billion-a-year plastics business, recommends: "If you want to be a business leader, you have to learn to speak in front of people. Speaking is one of the ways you carry out your management responsibilities. If you want to be the person who determines strategies, then you have no other choice but to be a good speaker. If you aren't, you lack something as a manager."

Learning to speak well is not a secret. With knowledge and practice, the most reluctant executive can become an effective speaker. Whether a student with little business experience or a seasoned veteran of the corporate world, you can use each opportunity to speak to enhance your personal and corporate success.

SUMMARY

Successful business leaders use communication skills to be effective managers. Good public-speaking skills are essential for successful communication in all aspects of education and business, especially in the corporate world. Whether you are in school or working, there are plenty of opportunities to practice and perfect these skills so that you can use them to enhance both personal and professional communication.

Brent Filson, author and president of Filson Communications, sums it up best when he says, "To be a successful executive, it's not enough to know your business. You must communicate your business. It's not enough to be a leader. You must communicate leadership. Communication isn't simply moving information. It's moving people by using information; it's transmitting a conviction from one person to another."

Web Site Resources

Note: These web sites are all authoritative and as permanent as any in this field.

Chapter I: Skills for Today and Tomorrow. The first web site to visit for information about the why and how of Peak Learning is my own home page at:

www.lifelong.com

Chapter II: Science Confirms It. The first web site to visit for information and references on current brain research is this one maintained by The Charles A. Dana Foundation:

www.danainfo@dana.org

Chapter III: Entering the Flow State. The first web site to visit for information and references on the topics covered in this chapter is the Flow Network devoted to exploring the concept developed by Mihaly Csikszentmihalyi (SIC):

www.flownetwork.com

Chapter IV: Building Your Learning Confidence. An inspiring web site to visit for information and references on the topics covered in this chapter is the following one devoted to self-education in the humanities and social sciences, developed by Charles Hayes, author of Self-University and founder of Self-University Week:

www.autodidactic.com

Chapter V: Discovering Your Personal Learning Profile. The first web site to visit for information and references on the topics covered in this chapter is the Project Zero site at the Harvard Graduate school of Education, developed around the work of Harold Gardner:

http://pzweb.harvard.edu

Chapter VI: Improving . . . Memory Skills etc. The first web site to visit for information and references on the topics covered in this chapter is the following one developed around the pioneering work on mind-mapping by Tony Buzan:

www.buzan.co.uk

Chapter VII: Critical and Creative. The first web site to visit for information and references on the topics covered in this chapter is the following one developed around the work of Edward de Bono, inventor of The Six Thinking Hats:

www.edwdebono.com

Chapters VIII–XII: Web sites, where needed and/or appropriate, are included in the texts of the chapters.

Bibliography

Adler, M. *How to Read a Book.* New York: Simon & Schuster, 1980.

Berkman, R. *Find It Fast.* New York: Harper and Row, 1986.

Bolles, R. *The Three Boxes of Life.* Berkeley: Ten Speed Press, 1981.

Bono, E. de. *Six Thinking Hats.* Boston: Little, Brown, 1985.

Buzan, T. *Make the Most of Your Mind.* New York: Simon & Schuster, 1984.

Cell, E. *Learning to Learn from Experience.* Albany: State University of New York Press, 1984.

Dixon, Pam. *Virtual College.* Princeton: Peterson's, 1996.

Dryden, G., and J. Vos. *The Learning Revolution.* Rolling Hills Estates, California: Jalmar Press, 1994

Dyson, E. *Release 2.0: A Design for Living in the Digital Age,* New York: Broadway Books (Bantam Doubleday Dell), 1997

Fenker, R. *Stop Studying, Start Learning.* Fort Worth: Tangram Press, 1981.

Gardner, H. *Frames of Mind.* New York: Basic Books, 1983.

Goldberg, P. *The Intuitive Edge*. Los Angeles: Jeremy P. Tarcher, 1983.

Goleman, D. *Emotional Intelligence*. New York: Bantam, 1995.

Guns, B. *The Faster Learning Organization*. San Francisco: Jossey-Bass, 1997.

Houle, C. *The Inquiring Mind*. Madison: University of Wisconsin Press, 1961.

Hutchison, M. *Megabrain*. New York: William Morrow, 1986.

Knowles, M. *Self-Directed Learning*. New York: Association Press, 1983.

Lewis, D., and J. Greene. *Thinking Better*. New York: Holt, Rinehart, and Winston, 1982.

McLagan, P. *Getting Results Through Learning*. St. Paul: McLagan Associates, 1982.

Oech, R. von. *A Kick in the Seat of the Pants*. New York: Warner Books, 1984.

Ostrander, S., and L. Schroeder. *Superlearning*. New York: Dell, 1979.

Perelman, L. *School's Out: Hyperlearning, the New Technology, and the End of Education*. New York: Morrow, 1992.

Rose, C. *Accelerated Learning*. New York: Dell, 1987.

Senge, P., and Associates. *The Fifth Discipline Fieldbook*. New York: Doubleday, 1994.

Shah, I. *Learning How to Learn*. New York: Harper and Row, 1981.

Smith, R. *Learning How to Learn*. Chicago: Follett, 1982.

Tough, A. *The Adult's Learning Projects*. Toronto: Ontario Institute for Studies in Education, 1975.

Wenger, Win. *How to Increase Your Intelligence*. East Aurora, New York: United Educational Services, 1986.

Willing, J. *The Lively Mind*. New York: Quill, 1982.

Wonder, J., and P. Donovan. *Whole-Brain Thinking*. New York: William Morrow, 1984.

Permissions

Index

This index only includes terms/pages from *Peak Learning*.